CAMBRIDGE STUDIES IN
CHINESE HISTORY, LITERATURE AND INSTITUTIONS

General Editors
PATRICK HANAN & DENIS TWITCHETT

The *Hsi-yu chi*

The *Hsi-yu chi*

A Study of Antecedents to the Sixteenth-Century Chinese Novel

by

GLEN DUDBRIDGE

*Lecturer in Modern Chinese in
the University of Oxford and
Fellow of Wolfson College*

CAMBRIDGE
AT THE UNIVERSITY PRESS
1970

Published by the Syndics of the Cambridge University Press
Bentley House, 200 Euston Road, London N.W.1
American Branch: 32 East 57th Street, New York, N.Y.10022

© Cambridge University Press 1970

Library of Congress Catalogue Card Number: 71–85718

Standard Book Number: 521 07632 3

Printed in Great Britain
at the University Printing House, Cambridge
(Brooke Crutchley, University Printer)

Contents

Illustrations

Between pages 48–9

1. Section of handscroll attributed to Li Kung-lin, depicting the story of Kuei-tzu-mu. Reproduced, by permission of the Trustees of the British Museum, from *La légende de Koei Tseu Mou Chen, Annales du Musée Guimet, Bibliothèque d'Art*, vol. I (Paris, 1905).

2. Kōzanji version, text A, p. 14a. Reproduced from *Chi-shih-an ts'ung-shu*.

3. Kōzanji version, text B, 3:10b. Reproduced from Lo Chen-yü's photographic reprint of 1916.

4. Shen-sha shen (*Jap.* Jinja-shin) as represented in a twelfth-century Japanese iconographical work, the *Shoson zuzō* 諸尊圖像. Reproduced, by permission of the Taishō Shinshū Daizōkyō Kankō Kai, from Taishō Tripitaka, Pictorial Section, vol. III, p. 743.

5. Monkey-headed figure carved in relief on the Western Pagoda of medieval Zayton (Story IV, NE). Reproduced, by permission, from Ecke and Demiéville, *The Twin Pagodas of Zayton*, (Harvard University Press, Cambridge, Massachusetts, 1935), plate 26. Copyright 1935 by the President and Fellows of Harvard College; 1963 by Paul Demiéville.

6. 'Dragon-prince' figure on the Western Pagoda at Zayton (Story IV, NE). Reproduced, by permission, from Ecke and Demiéville, *The Twin Pagodas of Zayton*, plate 24. Copyright 1935 by the President and Fellows of Harvard College; 1963 by Paul Demiéville.

Preface

A critical reader of the famous sixteenth-century Chinese novel *Hsi-yu chi* soon becomes aware that the book has two distinct aspects: on one hand the rich content of the story as such, with its echoes from the worlds of folklore, Buddhist tradition and popular mythology; on the other, what has been described as 'the organizing and transforming genius of single authorship',[1] making of this story a comic masterpiece whose characteristic ironies are hardly to be matched elsewhere in Chinese literature. Many scholarly and critical tasks are latent here. Among the first to suggest themselves are those which aim at defining the achievement and recognizing the art of the sixteenth-century author. They cannot be seriously attempted, however, until we have a clear idea of what materials lay at the author's disposal—in his study, in his memory, or in the society around him—as he sat down to prepare this hundred-chapter version of an already famous story. Moreover, the background in its own right, although diffuse and imperfectly accessible to us, presents a subject of independent interest and importance. It deserves study, not solely for the sake of forming value-judgements about the eventual, unique end-product, but also because in it we can examine the preoccupations of a great and vigorous society, over many centuries collectively moulding a legacy of historical tradition, pious legend and universal folklore into its own characteristic shapes.

This book undertakes such an independent examination. Because the appraisal of the hundred-chapter novel is seen as a fully distinct task, the evidence considered here is essentially that which is known to ante-date it (although the work at several points plays a necessary part in the argument). For practical reasons it has been necessary to impose a corresponding limit at the other extreme. The themes of mythology and world folklore have an important bearing on what is discussed here, and they are acknowledged wherever it has seemed necessary or useful to do so; but I have refrained from any detailed study of purely folkloristic questions, or questions of origins, that extend beyond present immediate

[1] C. T. Hsia, review of *A History of Chinese Literature* by Lai Ming (New York, 1964), in *Journal of the American Oriental Society* 85,3 (1965), 432.

concerns. My subject is, in short, the growth of the *Hsi-yu chi* story previous to the hundred-chapter novel.

Within this scope the book falls into two main parts. The first, which accounts for chapters 1–6, sets out to identify and characterize the sources which give some insight into the early development of the *Hsi-yu chi* story. The second concerns questions raised by Sun Wu-k'ung, the fantastic monkey-figure who came to usurp the leading role in this story of a Buddhist pilgrimage. The aims and materials of this part of the study are introduced at more length in chapter 7.

Few Western scholars have written on either topic. (The exceptions are acknowledged below in their due place.) In Chinese and Japanese, however, there exists a considerable, if uneven, scholarly literature on these and other aspects of the subject, gathering momentum in the early decades of the twentieth century and continuing uninterrupted down to the present. A study of this big secondary literature has impressed on me that the main lines of the subject are still far from being clearly defined. This is partly because some of the most responsible research was carried out unfortunately at times when the existence of certain important sources was not yet known, or under circumstances which made certain material inaccessible. But a more serious problem besetting the present-day student is that at every turn he is faced with numbers of conflicting theories, opinions and speculations, often also with apparent discrepancies in the stated facts. In such a situation the first need is to assemble all the relevant material from various quarters (some of it seriously acknowledged only in Japan), to evaluate it on the basis of first-hand observation, and, where relevant theories have been advanced, to test and if necessary modify or reject them. This book represents my own attempt at this preliminary task.

In fairness to the reader I should give notice here and now that several of the questions broached in the course of the book receive no final answer. To many readers it will also seem that the answers proposed in some other cases are obvious and unsurprising conclusions which need no elaborate justification. My own experience, however, is that in this subject the 'obvious' conclusions have in the past proved most difficult of access. Many misleading questions, many apparently unsupported theories and assumptions have sustained a hardy and stubborn existence in the pages of *Hsi-yu chi* criticism. They are not to be shrugged off lightly. The reason that they command so much attention here springs from a concern to draw a clear line between fact and speculation and to work towards the true implications of the material. The same concern has inhibited me from speculating in turn on aspects of the subject which still require detailed research, or on questions which by their nature will not submit to a clear-cut solution.

I shall be well content if this book can bring future researchers even only to the threshold of more positive solutions to the vast, but perpetually fascinating, problems raised by the *Hsi-yu chi*.

Certain assumptions about the authorship and early textual history of the hundred-chapter novel are built in to the argument of this book. They are described and defended in a separate article.[1]

As a rule Chinese characters for proper names and certain other expressions appear only at their first mention in the text, although in some cases it has been necessary to repeat them on subsequent occasions. The *General Index* offers a guide to the location of such characters. Bibliographical references in Chinese and Japanese are elaborated, with characters, in the *List of Works Cited* at the end of the volume: the reader is referred to it by a number of conventions: the sign (*q.v.*) in the text proper; in the case of primary sources—a simple romanized or abbreviated title; in the case of secondary sources—the author's surname, with the date of the work added where necessary.

I would acknowledge the great practical assistance derived during the earlier part of my studies from the bibliography of *Hsi-yu chi* scholarship published by Professor Torii Hisayasu (*q.v.*). I am also indebted to the directors and staff of a number of great libraries, in particular the British Museum and the Bodleian Library, for making available material without which this work would be incomplete. Most of the research presented here was done in the University Library, Cambridge, and I would especially thank Dr Scott for her kindness and assistance.

My personal thanks are above all due to Dr Chang Hsin-chang, who supervised my work throughout my years as a student in Cambridge: I owe much to his wisdom, guidance and encouragement. I am also most grateful to Mr Piet van der Loon who, apart from supplying information acknowledged in detail in the body of the text, has been constantly generous with expert advice and with his time. I would further thank Professor Denis Twitchett, an editor of this series, and Professor David

[1] Dudbridge (1969); cf. Dudbridge (1967), pp. 298–378.

Hawkes, both of whom helped me with much advice after reading this study in its original, unrevised form. From time to time I have received help in various ways from many other friends and colleagues in Cambridge, London, Hong Kong and Oxford, to all of whom I remain indebted. I wish to acknowledge in particular the trouble taken by my friend Professor James McMullen of Toronto University in obtaining for me, or helping me gain access to, much of the Japanese material used below. I am also most grateful to my wife for the many ways in which she has helped with the preparation of the book.

I would record my further indebtedness to Professor Patrick D. Hanan for valued advice on several points of detail, received after going to press but in most cases now incorporated in the text.

Finally, I would thank the Syndics of the Cambridge University Press for their generous cooperation in sponsoring and arranging the publication of this monograph.

G. DUDBRIDGE

April 1970

1

Introduction

ORAL TRADITION AND THE PROBLEM OF SOURCES

This book sets out to examine what remains of an old story-tradition. One central point of judgement dominates the examination: a balancing of the scattered and obviously incomplete remnants with what we know, or can gather, about the tradition as a whole. Bound up closely with it is a more general task: to consider, and if possible define, the notion of a tradition as we use it in this context. Our attempt at definition will not be complete until the point, later in the book, when the sources themselves have been discussed and their implications broadly assessed. These opening pages are concerned rather with the questions of historical and artistic context which bear most importantly on what follows.

The oral artist

For many years it has been recognised that, among the great vernacular novels of sixteenth-century China, at least some represent the final elaboration and realization of story-complexes transmitted from centuries back. The search for the earliest sources or antecedents has led scholars above all to the city-culture of the Sung dynasty, and specifically to the story-telling profession which, as the contemporary accounts assure us, flourished in the public pleasure-grounds of the northern and southern capital cities. Many pages of print have been devoted to the exposition and analysis of this subject in Chinese, Japanese and Western languages: one hesitates to add to the number. The aim here is not to rehearse or summarize the generally held theories, nor to attempt a whole new appraisal of the field. It is rather to offer grounds for some assumptions upon which the later argument is based, and to consider in particular one question which remains continually at issue: the authority of various literary sources and their relationship with the realities of oral narrative art in its true social environment.

Scholars live and work with books: written materials represent the overwhelming proportion of their daily stock-in-trade, and they are trained to respond to and work in terms of the written word above all else. Perhaps it is this simple fact which, in the field of early Chinese fiction studies, preserves one solitary bond of common interest between the Chinese commentators of the twelfth and thirteenth centuries, Lu Hsün, the author of the first full modern study of the subject,[1] and his successors through the subsequent decades. Sometimes perhaps scholars are the more ready to accept the testimony of their colleagues from another age because they share at least this basic preoccupation. But the subject of oral artists and their place in the old society is one over which we should take exceptional care. In studying them today we are dealing not with the artists' own testimony, but with what members of the fully literate educated class have written about them, and in considering this material we rarely make allowances for the total contrast in habits of mind which it may be hiding. A pertinent warning emerges for western readers from the findings of Professors Milman Parry and Alfred Lord among the folk epic singers of modern Yugoslavia,[2] for here was un-covered a living creative tradition totally at odds with the written word, and it reflects interestingly on us, his readers, that Professor Lord found it necessary to describe his conclusions persuasively, even challengingly, as if they represented something we could accept only with effort and adjustment.

If, prompted by such discoveries in Europe, we turn back to ask about the art and the creative methods of medieval Chinese story-tellers, we find that most current views are based either on bold inferences from a few story-texts of doubtful origin and date, surviving often in commer-cial popular editions, or on near-contemporary literary sources. The results do not come as a surprise. Lo Yeh, in his often cited early survey of narrative art,[3] describes the training and preparation of the oral artist entirely in terms of approved literary reading habits, listing among his reading matter such literary collections as *T'ai-p'ing kuang-chi* and *I-chien chih* (*qq.v.*), and such poets as Ou-yang Hsiu, Su Shih, Huang

---

[1] Lu Hsün (1923).

[2] For purposes of detailed comparison below, the monograph treatment of the subject by Lord, *The Singer of Tales*, will be used. For a valuable survey of the wider context of this investigation, cf. N. K. Chadwick and V. Zhirmunsky, *Oral Epics of Central Asia* (Cambridge, 1969), pp. 322 ff.

[3] *Tsui-weng t'an lu* (*q.v.*), in particular the section 'Hsiao-shuo k'ai-p'i'[a]. The work possibly reflects conditions in the thirteenth century (cf. Yen Tun-i (1957), pp. 57–8). Its true date has not, however, been finally established.

[a] 小說 開闢

T'ing-chien, Li Po, Tu Fu, Han Yü and Liu Tsung-yüan.[1] Throughout his comments, which at this point are framed as prescriptive criticism, we are left with the impression that an uneducated story-teller is a clear contradiction in terms. Another well-known passage, an address to a singing-girl, Miss Huang[a], by Hu Chih-yü[b] (1227–93), dwells in turn upon idealized qualities of performance.[2] But in reading it we should recognize, first that Hu wrote as a cultivated enthusiast of literary background, second that a distinct class of musical entertainers catered directly for such men.[3] His words, and those of similar authorities, tell us nothing of what other performances may have taken place before audiences drawn from the humbler classes in urban society—those who would be indifferent to the qualities of a Tu Fu or a Su Shih, but who would certainly have their own demands to make from entertainers. Such testimony as we have from these literate observers must therefore be critically used: it can help us with much information on such easily observed external features as names and themes, but it brings with it the dangers of a one-sided approach, a partial view of society and critical attitudes coloured by literary training.

For a truer insight something more like first-hand evidence is needed. But it is only in recent years that students have gained access to the real conditions of oral performance in China, and the results come to us in the form of scattered and sometimes inconspicuous publications. The more important facts and implications to emerge from these sources have been assembled and summarized by Mme Vena Hrdličková: I accept her contention that they are of great relevance to our study of the early popular fiction.[4]

We learn first that the public story-teller's art is acquired and cultivated in terms of hard experience. In the words of a maxim in use among the *p'ing-t'an*[c] artists of Soochow—'To listen to one recital is worth more than a thousand sessions of instruction; to recite yourself is worth more than listening to a thousand recitals'.[5] What this means is clarified by the Yang-chou story-teller Wang Shao-t'ang[e] (whose long prose saga

---

[1] *Tsui-weng t'an-lu, chia-chi* 1, p. 3.
[2] Quoted in summary form by Sun K'ai-ti (1956), p. 11, from *Tzu-shan ta-ch'üan-chi*[d], *chüan* 8.
[3] For material concerning these social divisions among entertainers, cf. Hu Chi, p. 29; Ch'en Ju-heng, p. 39; *Meng-liang lu*, 20:10*ab* (naming girl artists who entertained the well-to-do of the Southern Sung capital).
[4] Hrdličková (1965), pp. 226–7.
[5] P'an Po-ying and Chou Liang, pp. 56 and 57 (n.).

[a] 黃氏詩卷序   [b] 胡祗遹   [c] 評彈   [d] 紫山大全集   [e] 王少堂

on the *Shui-hu* hero Wu Sung, product of a local tradition known to extend back to the eighteenth century, has appeared in a rather heavily edited published version).[1] He explains:

Apart from your own personal efforts you have to hear and watch other people's things as well. Everyone has some strong point. Their reputation may not be as great as yours, but you ought to take pains to go and hear their things: they may perhaps have something good that you don't have yourself, and you can take it over and use it . . .[2]

Lord observed this same practice among the European artists.[3] Wang goes on to say:

If you want to make progress in the art, there's another important way. When you have finished a session and get down from the platform you should talk it over with the audience. . . There are some faults you don't notice even after a lifetime of telling stories. But the audience can tell, and they can point them out to you.[4]

This at once establishes the listeners' role in the oral tradition. Indeed it is obvious enough that in the competitive world of public performance the audience must always remain the final arbiter: every performer depends upon the approval of his listeners and will be prepared to make changes, sometimes radical ones, for their sake.[5]

The editors of *Wu Sung* note:

According to Mr (Wang) Shao-t'ang, the stories composed by narrative artists have for the most part not been taken down in writing. They are passed, purely by word of mouth, to apprentices or junior members of the family . . .[6]

The implication is that to artists of this branch of the Yang-chou *p'ing-hua* tradition the *Shui-hu chuan*, although for centuries widely circulated in a variety of editions, still does not represent an inviolable text, but rather provides a skeleton story upon which their own art is free to build in its characteristic ways. A distinct, but similar, example from a totally different part of the country is found in a verse epic, the *Life of Wu Sung*, in the 'fast story' genre of Shantung, which was

---

[1] *Wu Sung* (q.v.). For an account of the genre, see Ch'en Ju-heng, pp. 141 ff.

[2] *Wu Sung*, pp. 1–2.

[3] 'With years of experience the singer becomes an active listener to the songs of others. The really talented oral poet combines listening and learning in one process.' (Lord, p. 78.)

[4] *Wu Sung*, p. 2.

[5] Compare the singer cited by Lord (p. 19): 'when he was with Turks he sang Moslem songs, or his own songs in such a way that the Moslems won the battles . . .'

[6] *Wu Sung*, p. 1114.

taken down from the lips of three local singers.[1] Again the editors note that, while the broad lines of the story relate to the *Shui-hu chuan*, the epic is handed down from master to pupil without any resort to written texts, and in each generation the transmission results in clear divergences between their many individual performances.[2]

At this point it becomes relevant to note an observation by Lord:

> If the printed text is read to an already accomplished oral poet, its effect is the same as if the poet were listening to another singer. The song books spoil the oral character of the tradition only when the singer believes that they are *the* way in which the song *should* be presented.[3]

Here in a few words we face the central issue in the study of early popular story-traditions. Almost everyone who has written on the question in modern times has accepted in principle the 'prompt-book' theory bequeathed by Lu Hsün,[4] which claims that texts of stories were prepared for the use of performing artists, either by the performers themselves, or perhaps by relatively educated members of the semi-popular 'literary groups' (*shu-hui*[a]).[5] The theory's support was basically a retrospective gloss on the term *hua-pen*[b], which appears in some of the well-known thirteenth-century descriptions of the Southern Sung capital Hangchow,[6] and in a number of later vernacular sources. Its purpose was to account for the fact that stories of known oral background found their way into written versions. But Professor P. D. Hanan, writing about extant short-story texts, has made the present position quite clear:

> while we cannot doubt the connection of many stories with oral literature, the statement that any considerable number of them represent a story-teller's *script* is unproven. It is one of a number of widely accepted notions about fiction for which the bases of belief have not been investigated.[7]

The meaning of the term *hua-pen*, however, has been lucidly examined by Masuda Wataru (*q.v.*). After making the long overdue point that

---

[1] *Shantung k'uai-shu 'Wu Sung chuan'* (*q.v.*). For an account of the genre, see Ch'en Ju-heng, pp. 234–5.

[2] *Shantung k'uai-shu 'Wu Sung chuan'* pp. 339 ff.   [3] Lord, p. 79.

[4] Lu Hsün (1923), p. 251.

[5] Material on them is cited by Sun K'ai-ti (1941).

[6] *Meng-liang lu*, 20:13*a*; *Tu-ch'eng chi sheng*, 10*a*.

[7] P. D. Hanan, 'The early Chinese short story: a critical theory in outline', *Harvard Journal of Asiatic Studies* 27 (1967), 171. In note 5 on the same page there is a brief discussion, arriving at a negative verdict, on the story that is generally thought to represent oral literature most directly. For the question of how written versions of oral tales may have first come into being, see Hrdličková (1965), pp. 234–5.

[a] 書會   [b] 話本

Lu Hsün's original inference was unsoundly based, he goes on to show from numerous occurrences of the word in sources early and late that it need carry no more specific meaning than 'story', and that it is only one of a group of similar words with this connotation.

It has been claimed that the presence in some story-texts of conventional phrases and rhetorical devices characteristic of oral narrative demonstrates that they were intended first for professional use.[1] Once, however, it has been conceded that similar formal characteristics survived in stories aimed directly at a reading public,[2] the argument no longer carries much weight. If it was acceptable in fiction of the sixteenth or seventeenth centuries to evoke the narrator's presence with simple rhetorical mannerisms there is logically no reason why it should not have been also in the fourteenth or fifteenth. Nor does it seem probable that professional narrators of the day would need to be reminded by a written or a printed page of the phrases and gambits that were the most rudimentary tools of their trade.

If, as I believe, the factual basis for the traditional 'prompt-book' theory no longer stands, we should be prepared for more flexibility in reconstructing the development of some of the early oral cycles. It is possible that written material played a far less important part in the early stages than has been supposed. The role of the *shu-hui* remains obscure: among extant material only dramatic works are ascribed directly to them;[3] other references either involve some ambiguity between dramatic and narrative performance, or appear as consciously retrospective allusions in much later prose works.[4] What we know about the professional handbooks of some modern schools of narrators shows something very different from the familiar story-texts in old collections. Features of one secret manual (*mi-pen*[a]), as presented to a newly qualified artist, are summarised from the Chinese sources by Hrdličková in these terms:

> It contained valuable information about the guild to which his master, and along with him his pupils belonged, the names and nicknames of the heroes of the tales in which the storyteller specialized, and, finally, 'eulogies' on the hero—'*jen-wu-tsan*'[b]. Then there were also descriptions of weapons, various turns of speech characteristic of this or that hero . . .[5]

[1] See, for example, Průšek (1939), pp. 109–10.
[2] J. Průšek, 'Researches into the beginning of the Chinese popular novel . . .' (continuation), *Archiv Orientální* 23 (1955), 621.   [3] Cf. Sun K'ai-ti (1941), p. 349.
[4] Cf. Ch'en Ju-heng, pp. 91 ff.   [5] Hrdličková (1965), p. 233.
[a] 祕本   [b] 人物讚

Or again the 'scripts' (*chüeh-pen*[a]) seen and described by Szu Su:

> one kind was in the nature of an abstract, noting how many chapters there were in the story, what points of suspense there were in each chapter and where the comic interludes should come (*i.e.* the obligatory little songs and anecdotes, not including things brought in on the spur of the moment during performance)...This kind of script falls far short of what was actually spoken in performance.[1]

Even in these cases, where rudimentary written material is found in use, there is no ground for regarding the performers as subject to the discipline of stable source-texts. Lord's findings suggest how paralysing the internal use of written texts can be in an oral tradition. And the Yang-chou and Shantung performances, growing freely according to their own oral laws, demonstrate an independence from the written word which makes 'prompt-books' of a textual nature seem irrelevant: in such traditions they would serve only to hamper artists who had to adapt themselves moment by moment to a visible audience. We are not entitled to assume that such texts perverted the free growth of many oral traditions in the Sung, or in that uncertain earlier period during which the oral arts first took shape.

The many circumstantial similarities between Yugoslav epic poets and their counterparts in various parts of China until recent times might embolden us to seek the same creative processes at work in Chinese folk epic as were found in rural Yugoslavia. We are however held back by shortcomings in the material: it is published in limited quantities, and the publications which do lie at our disposal forfeit much of their value as material for study by consciously eliminating some of the most essential oral characteristics.[2] In the absence of responsibly collected original data, we are largely reduced to conjecture. This technical problem of course weighs all the more heavily in our study of medieval Chinese conditions. But the question of creative method does not become irrelevant because of it: we still need to be aware of the essential principles involved and ready to recognize them when, occasionally,

---

[1] Szu Su, p. 45.

[2] In the case of the Shantung *k'uai-shu*, the unfounded notion of a 'true version' passing through successive stages of corruption in transmission moved the editors to submerge differences between three distinct performances and construct a single text from them; they also frankly suppressed most of the repeated formulaic descriptive passages (pp. 346–7, 343–4). The editors of *Wu Sung* discarded much material as superfluous, distasteful or superstitious (pp. 1117 ff.), but with it went examples of recurrent motifs (*e.g.* the ominous appearances of a white-necked crow: cf. pp. 1118–19), which belong naturally to the story-teller's art.

[a] 脚本

clear signs emerge within the available material. Above all, it is necessary to allow for the complex activities of a now vanished world of oral entertainment, working in its own distinct and characteristic terms, around and beyond the printed texts and other forms of evidence which do survive to reach our bookshelves.

These are the concepts from the Parry/Lord analysis of most use here:

1. The fluidity of oral transmission.

The narrator constantly defers to his audience and learns from his colleagues. Such flexibility is possible because his tales are conceived not as immutable *texts*, but as stories which have each time to be re-created in performance.[1]

2. Its alienation from the written tradition.

It follows that the written text, with its inexorable implications of definitive form and wording, can present a serious menace to the freedom and hence to the life of an oral tradition. There are traditions alive in China now which are unfettered by writing. The earliest known written vernacular fiction was clearly related to established forms of oral narration—only the nature of the relationship is in question, and in the absence of plain evidence to the contrary we shall assume that such written fiction was originally a secondary product, not directly involved in the narrator's profession, and came to develop in its own ways.

3. Formula and theme.[2]

The nature of rapid spontaneous composition demands that the oral artist make constant use of tested formal units, whether verbal patterns, of particular use to performers in verse, longer 'set pieces'—to fulfil a recurrent descriptive function,[3] or conventional thematic units—in any given case appearing as simple episodes in a story, but formally related to corresponding episodes in other tales transmitted in the same environment.[4] Small independent motifs, while not always sharing this recognizable formal bond, are likely to be accessible to many stories by grace of the tradition's freedom and the performers' need for a fund of proven material.

---

1 These ideas are carefully documented and formulated in Lord's chapter 'Songs and the Song' (pp. 102–23).

2 For a full exposition of these structural units and their essential function in the Yugoslav oral tradition, I would refer the reader to Lord's chapter on each (pp. 30–98).

3 Such, presumably, are the *jen-wu-tsan* cited above, and the passages systematically eliminated by the editors of *Shantung k'uai-shu 'Wu Sung chuan'* (cf. above, p. 6 and p. 7, n. 2).

4 One likely example of this phenomenon is the episode associated with the monk Hung-fang, discussed below in ch. 2, pp. 33–5.

4. Regional characteristics.

Oral narration naturally relies upon circumstances of regular physical proximity and will therefore tend to have strong local characteristics. Ideally one should recognize the individuality of each performer, then of the local group to which he belongs. The most intimate relationships are likely to be found among stories from within such smaller groups. In China we must allow above all for the great north–south division of taste, and for infinite variation within the two divisions.

The broader context

One artificial restraint we incur when reading the familiar descriptions of entertainment in the Sung capitals is a rigid classification of genres. To the thirteenth-century authors and their readers the categories no doubt made good sense; to us, although the specialist jargon and textual complications of these passages put the full sense out of our reach, the categories can still be of use, given that we accept the broad formal divisions which underlie them, *e.g.* by treating story-telling as a fully exclusive class of expository performance. But in studying a story-tradition our concern is with content first, and it is important in this respect to realize that story-material belongs to a whole society: its accumulation and evolution may cut across whatever distinctions outside observers see fit to draw between kinds of performance. Here we are dealing with the whole popular milieu in its complexity of aspects, reaching beyond the bounds of purely narrative art to include many forms of dramatic and proto-dramatic entertainment, and beyond that again to include religious practices and other more general features of everyday life. While the full description of this aspect of medieval society has yet to be undertaken in the West, we can gain an impression of the formidable task from the profusion of material, much of it difficult or obscure, assembled by scholars like Jen Pan-t'ang[1] and Hu Chi (*q.v.*). It is a task which falls outside the scope of this study. The great complex still looms there in the background, and many facts discussed below gain meaning only when due account is taken of that wider context, but we must be content in each case to cite the particular, if limited, evidence that is of immediate concern.

A particularly important element in the imaginative life of medieval society was the popular publishing trade. From the surviving early

[1] Jen Pan-t'ang, *T'ang hsi-lung*[a], 2 vols (Peking, 1958).
[a] 任半塘, 唐戲弄

editions of fiction it is clear that publishers were exploiting the stories at large in society for a different, in some ways wider, distribution, and to them we owe virtually all our first-hand knowledge of popular fiction in the thirteenth and fourteenth centuries. In spite of certain stylistic distinctions, these old editions share several of the formal characteristics of later popular publications. The *Wu-tai shih p'ing-hua* (*q.v.*), a collection of historical narratives held by some to date from the thirteenth century,[1] prefaces the title of each *chüan* with a familiar popular commercial gambit—'Newly composed . . .'[a]; the group of five historical stories printed by the house of Yü[b] of Chien-an[c], Fukien, in the 1320s, uses the same kind of format, with illustrations running in strips along the top of each page, as we find in so many popular Fukien editions of fiction from the sixteenth century and later.[2] The earliest editions of a '*Hsi-yu chi*' cycle fit readily into this broad context.

From the thirteenth century on, above all in the great publishing boom of the late sixteenth century, the circulation of such story-books in ever increasing dimensions must have had its own influence on public taste (it naturally fostered the growth of a true written fiction), and hence, indirectly, on the public performers also. There seems thus to have been a complex, evolving situation in which commercial publishers played a dual role: to trap versions of a story at different times in a fixed text, and in doing so to exert an indirect stabilizing influence upon its tradition as a whole. Distinct from this again were the more recognizably literary concerns of creative writers later in the tradition, who faced the problem of how to compensate for the lively presence of a performer now absent from their written page. What remains now in writing must by and large be assigned to one or the other of these two groups.

The situation seems never to have been resolved conclusively in favour of one or another rival for the public's attention: the street entertainer, the actor, the hack publisher and the serious author all survived as parts of Chinese experience until recent times. Each of them deserves his due consideration. When we look back, however, to those more distant times when the stories first took shape, the men who wrote and printed easily gain an unfair advantage in our mind: they effec-

---

[1] The Sung dating was claimed first by Ts'ao Yüan-chung[d] in his postface of 1911. Cf. *Wu-tai shih p'ing-hua*, pp. 1–2, 249; Sun K'ai-ti (1957), p. 1. The Sung dating is rejected by Yeh Te-chün (p. 40).

[2] See *Ch'üan-hsiang p'ing-hua wu-chung*; cf. Sun K'ai-ti (1957), pp. 1–2.

[a] 新編   [b] 虞   [c] 建安   [d] 曹元忠

tively monopolize the material at our disposal. And this creates a tension in our argument: at every point there is a need to remain aware *in principle* of the many and widely differing forms in which the popular imagination found expression; yet for data one depends almost completely upon popular publication and creative writing. To speculate in cheerful independence of the material is both idle and dangerous: few of us are so well in tune with a remote society as to be able to recreate its lost subtleties with authority. So long as perfect understanding eludes us, we must accept the discipline of forming our ideas around written evidence, although part of that discipline consists in defining its limitations clearly, and part in resisting any too bold conclusions as to how these random and accidentally preserved specimens relate together.

It is on this basis that we shall proceed, here and in the following chapters, to study the growth of the *Hsi-yu chi* tradition.

EARLY TRADITIONS CONCERNING HSÜAN-TSANG AND HIS JOURNEY

The historical life of Hsüan-tsang[a] (d. 664), celebrated Buddhist traveller and translator of seventh-century China, is generously documented. There are three near-contemporary biographies,[1] apart from the *Ta-T'ang hsi-yü chi (q.v.)*, his own geographical and ethnical account of the lands to the west of the T'ang empire which he knew by personal experience or by report. Much of his career has been reconstructed from these sources.[2]

Hsüan-tsang had at an early age taken Buddhist vows and rapidly won a national reputation with his mastery of the Buddhist doctrines then known and accepted in China. He was still a young man when he resolved to leave for the far west, the source of Buddhism, in quest of instruction and of Sanskrit texts from the idealist Yogācāra school. His journey, undertaken alone and in defiance of imperial restriction, took sixteen years to complete (AD 629–45). Ever since the time of his return it has been counted among the great individual exploits in Chinese history. The remainder of his distinguished life was devoted to the

[1] *Ta-T'ang ku San-tsang Hsüan-tsang fa-shih hsing-chuang*[b] by the monk Ming-hsiang[c]: T. L, no. 2052; short life in *Hsü kao-seng chuan (q.v.)* pp. 446–58; *Ta Tz'u-en szu San-tsang fa-shih chuan* (hereafter abbreviated to '*Tz'u-en chuan*', *q.v.*) by the monks Hui-li and Yen-ts'ung. Waley (1952), pp. 280–1 comments on the authority of these various sources.

[2] A general account of his life is given in Waley (1952), pp. 9–130.

[a] 玄奘　　[b] 大唐故三藏玄奘法師行狀　　[c] 冥詳

systematic translation into Chinese of large numbers of Sanskrit
Buddhist texts, many of which he had himself brought to China for the
first time. He was dignified with the religious name Tripiṭaka (San-
tsang[a])—a title shared by other great Buddhist translators[1]—and it was
by this name that he was later best known to the public at large.[2]

The stories and legends which came to form the long popular tradition
to be discussed below bore hardly more than a nominal relationship to
this man as an historical figure. The Buddhist Master Tripitaka had in
a sense passed into legend almost in his own time. The early biographers
give some insight into how such a canonization could come about; and
indeed from the collected *Lives of Eminent Monks*[3] it is evident that this
was by no means the only great Buddhist of his age to become a legendary figure. Religious biographers tended to regard their subjects with
a pious awe close to pure superstition; for some, popular traditions
about the miraculous works of famous monks often served as legitimate
biographical material.[4] Elements of hyperbole and, on occasion, of
outright fable to be found in the early accounts of his life show that
even those historically closest to Hsüan-tsang were disposed to view
him fervently in the light of full sainthood.

Yet in the popular story-cycles of later centuries Tripitaka stood out
among the great names of his faith above all as a traveller of spectacular
achievement: it was his journey that held the imagination, a prolonged
excursion for readers and audiences into remote and semi-fabulous
territory.

Many have shared in the search through standard early sources for
the roots of this in its way unique popular celebration of the pilgrimage.
The results have been unspectacular. In the accounts dealing with
Hsüan-tsang's historical journey one finds a bare minimum of names and
themes which seem, in retrospect, to have provided some precedents for
later tradition. The value of such references may be judged from the
following examples, which represent the most important of their kind.

[1] E.g. Vajrabodhi[b] (663 ?–732 ?), see *Sung kao-seng chuan*, 1:712*a*; Śubhakarasiṃha[c]
(637–735), *ibid.* 2:714*c*; Amoghavajra[d] (705–74 ?), *ibid.* 1:711*b*.
[2] From this point on, except where translation or summary require otherwise, I shall
reserve the name Hsüan-tsang for the historical figure and refer to the hero of
popular legend as Tripitaka, for convenience omitting the diacritical mark.
[3] *Kao-seng chuan*[e] by *Hui-chiao*[f] (d. 554) (T. L, no. 2059); *Hsü kao-seng chuan, Sung
kao-seng chuan* (*qq.v.*).
[4] A good parallel example is the life of Hsüan-tsang's near-contemporary Saṅgha,
discussed below, p. 142.

[a] 三藏   [b] 金剛智   [c] 善無畏   [d] 不空金剛   [e] 高僧傳   [f] 慧皎

The Land of Women

Known to the mythology of Central Asia[1] and mentioned in several early Chinese sources,[2] the Land of Women is described by Hsüan-tsang (from report—he had not been there) in these terms:

To the south-west of the land Fu-lin[a], [3] on an island in the sea, is the Western Land of Women.[4] All are female: there is no male there at all. They have great quantities of precious jewels and merchandise.[5] They are subject to Fu-lin, and accordingly the King of Fu-lin each year sends over men to be their mates. Their custom is not to raise their male offspring . . .[6]

After some centuries of transmission this re-emerges in what below is termed the 'Kōzanji version' (thirteenth century?)[7] as an episode in

[1] Sylvain Lévi has shown that traces of the Romance of Alexander, with its Kingdom of Amazons, had reached India by the seventh century. See 'Alexandre et Alexandrie dans les documents indiens' (reprinted in *Mémorial Sylvain Lévi*, Paris, 1937), pp. 413–23, in particular pp. 421–3.

[2] The *Shan-hai ching* 2(*hsia*): 41*b* records a land of women[b] in which 'two women dwell, surrounded by water'. A note, one of those traditionally attributed to Kuo P'u[c] (276–324), adds: 'There is a Yellow Pool into which the women go to bathe, and when they emerge they are pregnant.' The *Liang-shu*, on the authority of a Buddhist monk Hui-shen[d], describes a land of women 'more than a thousand *li* east of the land of Fu-sang[e]' (itself held to be far to the east of China): cf. Lévi (1937), p. 422. Here too the women conceived by entering a stream, in the second or third month. 'They flee in alarm at the sight of other people and have a particular dread of men.' (*Liang-shu* 54:36*b*.) Precisely the same passage, attributed to the same authority, is found in the *Nan-shih* 79:8*ab*.

[3] The vexed question of the identity of Fu-lin is discussed at length by K. Shiratori in 'A New Attempt at the Solution of the Fu-lin Problem' (*Memoirs of the Research Department of the Toyo Bunko* 15 (Tokyo, 1956), pp. 165–329). From his pp. 210–47 it appears that at this period the name Fu-lin represented the Syrian section of the Roman Orient, or more generally the Byzantine Empire as a whole.

[4] Hsüan-tsang distinguishes this from the Eastern Land of Women, said to be ruled for generations by a line of queens, situated to the north of Brahmapura, to the south of Khotan and to the west of Tibetan[f] country (*Ta-T'ang hsi-yü chi*, 4:892c). A Land of Women in this region was known to Indian legend (Lévi (1937), p. 422). It also received mention in the *Sui-shu* (83:10*ab*). It would appear to correspond to the Land of Women cited by dignitaries of the Liang[g] court in protest against the mythological extravaganza of Wan-chieh kung[h]. (He was one of four 'unusual men'[i] who came to the court of Liang Wu-ti[j] in the early sixth century: *TPKC*, 81:517–22, quoting *Liang szu-kung chi*[k]). Wan-chieh, according to this account, proceeded to add six more exotic lands of women to the one he had already described.

[5] These riches were a legendary attribute of western regions throughout the mythology of Central Asia: cf. R. A. Stein, pp. 254–61.

[6] *Ta-T'ang hsi-yü chi*, 11:938*a*; cf. *Tz'u-en chuan*, 4:243*c*. Hsüan-tsang previously mentions the story of how this community came into being—begotten by the demon inhabitants of Persia upon a girl-refugee from southern India (*Ta-T'ang hsi-yü chi*, 11:933*a*, *Tz'u-en chuan*, 4:242*b*).

[7] See below, ch. 2.

[a] 拂懍   [b] 女子國   [c] 郭璞   [d] 慧深   [e] 扶桑   [f] 土蕃   [g] 梁
[h] 飄杰公   [i] 異人   [j] 武帝   [k] 梁四公記

which the pilgrim Tripitaka is entertained and tempted in opulent surroundings by the queen of the land. She eventually reveals her identity as compounded of two figures from popular Buddhism—the Bodhisattvas Mañjuśrī[a] and Samantabhadra[b]. In the still more highly coloured treatments of the episode found in later versions[1] the queen is a character in her own right, and the sixteenth-century novel assigns to another episode the device of Buddhist gods masquerading as tempters;[2] it also resurrects a motif originally alien even to Hsüan-tsang's account— the fertile stream from which women, in this case by drinking, can conceive.[3] Written versions of the 'Tripitaka' story from the thirteenth to the sixteenth centuries therefore suggest at least a continuity in the presence of this episode in the cycle, and it is no doubt reasonable to connect it in some way with Hsüan-tsang's reports in the *Ta-T'ang hsi-yü chi*. But it is as important to note that Hsüan-tsang was by no means alone among early geographers in recording a land of women; and equally that the subsequent popular versions freely incorporated motifs from other sources.

A river hazard

Hsüan-tsang's mishap in crossing the Indus River on the return journey, when numbers of canonical texts and rare seeds were washed away in a sudden squall,[4] was to reappear some nine hundred years later in the hundred-chapter *Hsi-yu chi*.[5] But after this lapse of time we find it transformed by the use of an old folk-motif long known to China in the parable literature of the Buddhist Canon—the turtle which bears men on its broad back, but is capable of plunging them abruptly into the waves.[6]

The 'Heart Sūtra'

Tripitaka's special association with the so-called *Heart Sūtra*[c] (the miniature text held to sum up the essence of the vast *Prajñāpāramitā sūtra*)[7] is a perennial theme which we may trace at least to the *Tz'u-en chuan*,

---

[1] The dramatic sequence *Hsi-yu chi* (for which see below, ch. 5), sc. 17, pp. 75–80; the hundred-chapter novel (*HYC*, chs. 53–4, pp. 610 ff.); see also below, p. 74.

[2] *HYC*, ch. 23, pp. 258–67. The deities are named as Li-shan Lao-mu[d] (for whom see below, pp. 145–6), Nan-hai p'u-sa[e] (i.e. Kuan-yin), Mañjuśrī and Samantabhadra (p. 266). The episode centres around the rich widow Chia[f] and her three daughters.

[3] *HYC*, ch. 53, pp. 610–11; cf. above, p. 13, n. 2.

[4] *Tz'u-en chuan*, 5:249b; cf. *Ta-T'ang hsi-yü chi*, 3:884b; Waley (1952), p. 71.

[5] *HYC*, ch. 99, p. 1118.

[6] Several ancient parables concerned with this theme of riding on turtle-back are translated by Chavannes (vol. 1, p. 121; vol. 3, pp. 29, 157 and 192–3); cf. Thompson, motif J1172.4.   [7] For the text, see T. VIII, no. 251, p. 848c.

[a] 文殊   [b] 普賢   [c] 心經   [d] 黎山老母   [e] 南海菩薩   [f] 賈

if not in this case to the historical Hsüan-tsang. In Szechuan he is said
to have met a sick man in rags . . .

In compassion he took him to the monastery and gave him the price of a meal
and some clothes. The sick man, out of gratitude, taught him this *sūtra*, and
he came to repeat it constantly. When he reached the River of Sands[a], encountered all the evil spirits, strange forms and monstrous beings that swirl
around men in front and behind, even invocations of the name of Kuan-yin
could not rid him of them completely, yet as soon as he recited this *sūtra* all
vanished at the sound of his voice.[1]

A similar tradition found its way into collections of apocryphal anecdotes
of the T'ang period. Two texts are quoted together in the late tenth
century *T'ai-p'ing kuang-chi*[2] as sources for a passage part of which includes the following. Tripitaka is threatened by tigers and leopards . . .

He did not know what to do: he sat behind locked doors, and when evening
came he opened them to see an old monk, his scalp and face covered with
sores, his body all pus and blood, sitting alone on a couch. There was no
knowing whence he had come. (Hsüan-)tsang saluted him ceremoniously and
earnestly begged his help. The monk taught him by word of mouth the *Heart
Sūtra* in one *chüan*[3] and made him repeat it. Upon this mountains and
streams were made level for him and the road laid upon . . .[4]

Thereafter, in the surviving prose works which represent the *Hsi-yu chi*
tradition, the *Heart Sūtra* stands apart in an independent episode. The
'Kōzanji' version withholds it from the sum of scriptures issued to
Tripitaka in the Western Paradise;[5] on the return journey he then sees
in the clouds a youthful monk of 'upright and earnest appearance'
who produces the *Heart Sūtra* from his sleeve and gives it to Tripitaka

---

[1] *Tz'u-en chuan*, 1:224b.

[2] *TPKC*, 92:606. The sources are named as *Tu-i chih*[b] (by Li K'ang[c]—variant Yin[d]
—of the early ninth century: cf. *SKCSTM*, 144:3a) and *(Ta-) T'ang hsin-yü*[e] (by
Liu Su[f], eighth century: cf. *SKCSTM*, 140:7b–8b). The passage in question here,
however, does not occur in the extant versions of these originals. Only the introductory words correspond to those in *Ta-T'ang hsin-yü* (*PCHSTK* ed.) 13:3a,
prefacing a more or less historical survey of Hsüan-tsang's life.

[3] The phrase *To^g-hsin-ching* is abbreviated from the full title *Prajñāpāramitā*, of which
to represents the final syllable. This was to become a most popular and familiar form
of the *sūtra*'s title.

[4] The passage, together with its continuation (cf. immediately below, p. 22), reappears
verbatim in the *Shen-seng chuan*[h] (T. L, no. 2064, 6:985b). This compendium of
pious biographies was produced in 1417. It appears to have drawn freely upon such
unofficial sources as the *TPKC*.

[5] A:8b (1955: p. 94); B 3:4a (1955: p. 57). (For these references, see below, ch. 2.)
Popular tradition identified India, the goal of Hsüan-tsang's journey, with the
Western Paradise, Mount Sumeru, where the Buddha and his saints dwelled.

[a] 沙河   [b] 獨異志   [c] 李亢   [d] 亢   [e] 大唐新語   [f] 劉肅
[g] 多   [h] 神僧傳

with many admonitions; he is the Dīpaṃkara Buddha[a] whose chief purpose is to summon Tripitaka to Paradise when his mission is completed.[1] The hundred-chapter novel has Tripitaka and his party of animal disciples meet a Buddhist master named Wu-ch'ao ch'an-shih[b] living in a nest on a tree;[2] it is he who offers the text of the *Heart Sūtra* as a protection from demons on the way, then adds prophecies and warnings of what dangers await them.

The three examples quoted above are not simple cases of elaboration in the course of time. Into each of the original themes later tradition has introduced radical features from other sources, some of long-established mythological origin: and in each case the 'story' content of the episode has undergone a fundamental change. The Land of Women now seeks to dazzle the pilgrim with secular temptations; the loss of scriptures in the Indus River becomes appended to a quite distinct episode far back in the story;[3] the *Heart Sūtra* is taught to Tripitaka incidentally by various important Buddhist figures who also have specific guidance to give him on his journey.

To these we should now add two more such sequences, each of some importance, and each involving a frankly mythological figure.

Kuei-tzu-mu

In Gandhāra Hsüan-tsang saw a *stūpa* marking the place where 'Śākya Tathāgata converted the Mother of Demons (Kuei-tzu-mu[c]), so that she should no longer do harm to men. That is why in this country the custom prevails of sacrificing to her in order to obtain children.'[4] In itself this passage is important as evidence of a widespread Indian popular fertility cult associated with the goddess Hārītī, whose Chinese name is Kuei-tzu-mu. The detailed circumstances of this cult, its sub-

---

[1] *Ibid.* A:9*ab* (1955: pp. 95–6); B 3:5*ab* (1955: pp. 59–60).

[2] *HYC*, ch. 19, pp. 220–1. This figure strongly recalls a monk of the eighth to ninth centuries whose story is told in the eleventh-century *Ching-te ch'uan-teng lu* (*q.v.*), 4:12*a*–13*a*, under the name Tao-lin ch'an-shih[d]. He retired to live in the boughs of a pine-tree near Hangchow, and magpies built their nests beside him. His contemporaries knew him as 'Ch'an Master of the Birds' Nests'[e]. The poet Po Chü-i[f] is said to have called on him when in office in the area. I am grateful to my friend Mr Tso Sze-bong of Hong Kong for drawing my attention to this reference.

[3] The ferrying of the pilgrims on turtle-back across T'ung-t'ien ho[g]: see *HYC*, ch. 49, pp. 571–3. The name of the river is historical, but it referred to the upper reaches of the Yangtze, not to the Indus.

[4] *Ta-T'ang hsi-yü chi*, 2:881*ab*.

[a] 定光佛   [b] 烏窠禪師   [c] 鬼子母   [d] 道林禪師   [e] 烏窠禪師
[f] 白居易   [g] 通天河

sequent modified forms in China and Japan, as well as the quite distinct monastic cult (in which Hārītī received daily offerings of food in all Buddhist monasteries), with its legendary justification in Buddhist scripture, all receive a full exposition in Noël Peri's learned monograph.[1] The legend of the *yakṣiṇī* Hārītī and her conversion is told in many Chinese Buddhist sources. A simple and relevant form suitable for quotation here reads, in part:

Kuei-tzu-mu bore a thousand sons. The youngest of those in Jambudvīpa, called Priyaṅkara[a], was the object of her special love and affection. She persistently ate the children of men, and the Buddha, with the aim of converting her, took Priyaṅkara and hid him under his almsbowl. The mother searched for him in Heaven and in the world of men, but fruitlessly. Then the Buddha converted her and commanded the community of monks to offer her food as alms . . .[2]

Hārītī's character as child-bringing or child-protecting goddess was held to derive from her undertaking, on conversion, to safeguard life in compensation for what she had taken: a sentiment prompted by the Buddha's appeal that her own maternal anguish awaken her to the suffering of her victims' mothers.[3]

In the early twelfth century the legend was represented on the walls of the Hsiang-kuo szu[b] in Pien-liang[c], capital of the Northern Sung.[4] A well-known painting of the subject originally by Li Kung-lin[d] (eleventh to early twelfth century)[5] has been handed down in the form of copies.[6] We know further that a similar story was known outside clerical and literary circles from the appearance of a title *Kuei-tzu-mu chieh po chi*[e] ('The story of Hārītī trying to lift the almsbowl clear') among plays attributed to the (late thirteenth century?) dramatist Wu Ch'ang-ling[f],[7] and some references to and fragments of an early southern play with the same title.[8]

[1] N. Peri, 'Hārītī la Mère-de-démons', *Bulletin de l'École Française d'Extrême-Orient* 17,3 (1917). See also Ōta Tatsuo (1966), pp. 145–6.
[2] An unidentified source named *Hsien-cheng lun*[g], cited in *Ch'ung-pien chu-t'ien chuan*[h] by Hsing-t'ing[i] (his preface dated 1173): see *Dai Nippon zokuzōkyō*, II, 2[j], *t'ao* 23, *ts'e* 2, p. 137*b*. Cf. Peri, p. 40.
[3] Cf. e.g. Peri, p. 11.   [4] *Tung-ching meng hua lu*, 3:4*a*.
[5] Cf. *Sung shih*, 444:15*b*–16*a*.   [6] See Pl. 1. Cf. Peri, p. 15, n. 3.
[7] *LKP*, p. 109. For this source, cf. below, p. 75. Peri wrote at a time when its existence, and that of the *Hsi-yu chi tsa-chü*, was not generally known, and therefore implied (p. 70) that the story of Hārītī was less well known in Chinese society at large than seems to have been the case. For Wu Ch'ang-ling, cf. below, p. 75, n. 2.
[8] Cf. Ch'ien Nan-yang, pp. 127–8.

[a] 愛奴   [b] 相國寺   [c] 汴梁   [d] 李公麟   [e] 揭鉢記   [f] 吳昌齡
[g] 顯正論 [h] 重編諸天傳 [i] 行霆   [j] 乙

Nevertheless, and in spite of the terms in which Hsüan-tsang himself had written about Kuei-tzu-mu, the name appears in the Kōzanji version in a disembodied, and even cryptic, form. In the version's ninth section, 'They enter the Land of Kuei-tzu-mu', the party of pilgrims find themselves among great numbers of three-year-old children, and receive a warm and devout welcome from the king of the land. He gives them rich gifts and finally reveals to them that this country, not far from the Western Paradise, is called Kuei-tzu-mu kuo[a]. The pilgrims then know that they have been addressing demons. The episode closes with a number of verses, some of which are put into the mouth of Kuei-tzu-mu.[1] If this is indeed a gesture in the direction of the historical Hsüan-tsang's experiences, it is no more than nominal. Only in one subsequent treatment of the 'Tripitaka' story does Kuei-tzu-mu reappear as a character:[2] the twelfth scene of the *tsa-chü* sequence introduces her as the mother of the demon Red Boy. This scene restores some of the themes from the original legend, but they seem chosen for their sensational value alone and distort the shape and sense of the story beyond recognition. Kuei-tzu-mu's child is again named Ai-nu-erh[b], but here is the Red Boy guilty of abducting Tripitaka. He is duly imprisoned beneath the Buddha's almsbowl, but now Kuei-tzu-mu, far from submitting to any appeal to her maternal sympathies, uses the pretext to mount an attack on the Buddha himself. She strives vainly to raise the bowl, and finally accepts conversion only, so to speak, at gunpoint.[3] Dramatically the scene is torn between the rival claims on our attention of the Red Boy and Kuei-tzu-mu. Its legendary force is totally lost.

Shen-sha shen

In the desert country to the west of Tun-huang, Hsüan-tsang had the appalling misfortune to upset his water-bottle in the sand. After several days of privation he had a dream in which, according to the *Tz'u-en chuan*, he saw

---

[1] Kōzanji version, B 2: 5 *a*–6*b* (1955: pp. 35–8).

[2] In the hundred-chapter version her name appears, but only incidentally: *HYC*, ch. 42, p. 485.

[3] The story takes precisely this turn as represented in the scroll-painting attributed to Li Kung-lin: while Kuei-tzu-mu sits in anguish, her subject demons attempt to force the almsbowl, with its prisoner, from the ground, and simultaneously hurl ineffective spears and arrows against the impassive figure of the Buddha: see *La légende de Koei Tseu Mou Chen, Annales du Musée Guimet, Bibliothèque d'Art*, vol. I (1905), pp. 16–17. Cf. Pl. I.

[a] 國   [b] 兒

a great spirit, many feet in height, wielding a halberd with which he directed him onwards, saying: 'Why are you lying about here, and not pressing forward?' The Master awoke with a start and moved on some ten *li*. Suddenly his horse took a different path and would not be reigned back. Then, after several *li*, he saw some acres of green grass...and eventually reached a pool of water.[1]

Perhaps there are elements of pious romance even here, but to later writers the episode came to suggest more extravagant possibilities. One version, from a source entitled *T'ang San-tsang chi*[a] which I have not succeeded in tracing, is quoted in the eleventh-century Japanese icono-graphical collection *Jōbodai shū*[b]:[2]

On his way to the Western Land to fetch the scriptures, he came to the Moving Sands[3] and there, in the midst of the desert with not a soul at hand, when the hour of each monastic meal came round there was a pool, freshly sprung up by the roadside, whose waters were as sweet as ambrosia[c], and a meal of the rarest and most fragrant food and drink. Only there was no man to be seen. Tripitaka marvelled at this and thought: 'What man is it that provides these pools of water and this food here in the vast desert, out beyond the last signs of human habitation? I want to know where they come from.' Then a voice in the air was heard addressing Tripitaka: 'I am a *deva*. Because you have come a great distance to fetch scriptures, I am your guardian spirit. Here there is no water and no man: I provide food and water especially for you.' When Tripitaka finished his meals the water would vanish, and only the desolate, uninhabited expanse of the Moving Sands was to be seen.

A comment follows—'This is the reason for the name Spirit of the Deep Sands (Shen-sha shen[d])'—which may not derive necessarily from the same source, but certainly reveals that in the mind of the eleventh-century compiler the voice of this desert guardian was that of Shen-sha shen. It was, however, by no means a late or purely local branch of the legend. The Japanese pilgrim Jōgyō[e], who visited China in the years 838–9, included in his report of the sacred books and objects brought back from the visit some items connected with Shen-sha shen: a short 'account' of the god (*Shen-sha shen chi*[f]), together with a liturgy of invocations,[4] and a statue, to which he adds a note explaining that when

---

[1] *Tz'u-en chuan*, 1:224 bc.
[2] T. Pictorial Section, vol. 8, no. 3189, p. 732 b. The work was compiled by Eiban[g] in 1094: cf. *Shōwa hōbō sōmokuroku*, vol. 3, p. 514 a.
[3] Liu-sha[h]: an ancient generalized term for the desert lands of the north-west.
[4] *Jōgyō wajō shōrai mokuroku*, T. LV, no. 2163, p. 1070 a. The work is dated 839. Cf. Ōta Tatsuo (1966), pp. 144–5.

[a] 唐三藏記　　[b] 成菩提集　　[c] 甘露　　[d] 深沙神　　[e] 常曉　　[f] 記
[g] 永範　　　　[h] 流沙

Tripitaka journeyed to India 'he received a vision of this god, who is a manifestation of Vaiśravaṇa, the King of the North. At present among the people of China it is the general practice to honour this god, in order to seek benefits and protection from calamities...'.[1]

There is not space here to describe in full the background of this minor Buddhist deity and the extent and nature of his cult, but one aspect is relevant here. His name appears in the title of a Tantric text translated in the eighth century by Amoghavajra,[2] and, in the several Japanese iconographical texts of the eleventh and succeeding centuries which deal with him, he is attended by much of the apparatus of Tantric magical practices.[3] His appearance in particular masks a benevolent nature behind the characteristically ferocious attributes of certain Tantric divinities. In a manifestation said to have taken place before the monk Fa-ch'uan[a] on 10 February 566 he described himself in these terms:

I am manifested in an aspect of great fury[b]. My head is like a crimson bowl. My two hands are like the nets of heaven and earth. From my neck hang the heads of seven demons. About my limbs are eight serpents, and two demons' heads seem to engulf my (nether-) limbs...[4]

Such is indeed the figure we see several times represented in the later iconographical manuals (one example of which is reproduced in plate 4).

Once again it was this sensational and horrific aspect which asserted itself in the popular 'Tripitaka' tradition. The fragmentary eighth section of the Kōzanji version opens with the words:

'...thing?' He replied, 'I don't know.' Shen-sha[c] said, 'Slung here from my neck are the dry bones from when I twice before devoured you, monk!'[5]

Shen-sha shen is presented in this story frankly as a demon of the sands.[6] He submits to Tripitaka's threatening rebuke and, amid spec-

[1] *Ibid.* pp. 1070c–1071a. Cf. Ōta (1966), pp. 144–5.
[2] Cf. T. xxi, no. 1291.
[3] E.g. T. Pictorial Section, vol. 3, no. 3006, p. 54; no. 3007, pp. 613–14; vol. 5, no. 3022, pp. 560–2 (p. 561b identifying the skulls in his necklace as those of seven past incarnations of Hsüan-tsang); vol. 9, no. 3190, pp. 522–4 etc.
[4] *Jōbodai shū*, p. 733b. The closing phrase seems corrupt, like so many others in these Japanese MSS. A descriptive word may be absent before *jan*. My translation attempts to reconcile the phrase with the most usual pictorial forms.
[5] Kōzanji version, B 2:4a (1955: p. 33).
[6] The reference in the twelfth-century *Kakuzen shō*[d] noted above (p. 20, n. 3) obviously reflects this kind of tradition, which may still be no more than a thoroughly popular version.

[a] 法傳   [b] 分心＝忿   [c] 深沙   [d] 覺禪鈔

tacular natural phenomena, holds out a golden bridge with silver rails for the pilgrims to pass over the hazard of the Deep Sands. As they leave him they add to their thanks a promise of intercession on his behalf.

Losing his benevolent, protective function, the god is now degraded to the status (in addition to the appearance) of a man-eating *yakṣa* at large in the wilds, who has to be subdued by the holy traveller.[1] This remained his lot throughout all subsequent versions of the story known to us.[2] Although his name changed to Sha Ho-shang[a], and he was recruited as a disciple to join the party of pilgrims, his introduction in the story, always with the characteristic Tantric necklace of skulls, remained the same and in effect represented his only high moment in the cycle. In this astonishing transition, from the thirsting Hsüan-tsang's dream to the skull-necklace of Sha Ho-shang, with the god Shen-sha shen as its pivotal figure, the episode loses all but a crudely pictorial significance. The author of the sixteenth-century novel could not be blamed if he regarded Sha Ho-shang, securely established in the story after centuries of transmission, as a liability. It is hardly surprising that, 'though in some inexplicable way essential to the story, he remains throughout singularly ill-defined and colourless'.[3]

These latter two illustrations, aside from their intrinsic interest in reflecting the development of two independent legends, demonstrate unambiguously just what kind of relationship prevailed between stories which would have been recognizable to Hsüan-tsang and his contemporaries, and, on the other hand, the same stories seen through the eyes of popular tradition. It is as though the moulders of popular tradition were not concerned merely with infusing colour into basically laconic references, or with allowing an accretion of folklore to form about them. They seem to go further in rudely brushing aside the pietistic nature of the myths in their quoted form. In short, they seem to imply that no story, however adventurous or colourful it might seem, was acceptable for their purpose unless refashioned entirely according to their own terms.

---

[1] There are of course clear precedents for this theme in Buddhist mythology: cf. the story of the *yakṣa* Āṭavaka[b], who may have been associated with Hārītī (A. Getty, *The Gods of Northern Buddhism*, second ed. (Oxford, 1928), p. 158).

[2] *PTS*, p. 294 (N vi); *tsa-chü Hsi-yu chi*, sc. 11, pp. 47–8; *Hsiao-shih Chen-k'ung pao-chüan* (see below, ch. 6), l. 34; *HYC*, ch. 8, pp. 82–4, ch. 22, pp. 245 ff.

[3] Arthur Waley, preface to *Monkey* (London, 1942).

[a] 沙和尚   [b] 曠野神

Such parallels as we find between what may be called the historical sources on Hsüan-tsang's journey and the cycle of stories attached to the legendary Tripitaka therefore tell us little: the distance between them seems overwhelming. And the parallels are in any case few. Those described above represent the most important known material of their kind. From all the circumstance and detail preserved in the seventh-century accounts there remain few major themes which were echoed in popular tradition.

Through an ensuing span of almost six hundred years, from the seventh to the thirteenth centuries, there is a virtual silence in written sources on the early formation of a popular 'Tripitaka' cycle. Occasional fragments of literary testimony appear, but they offer little useful insight.

Preserved in the ninth-century *Tu-i chih*[1] is an apocryphal tradition concerning a pine-twig planted by Tripitaka at the time of his departure: he ordained that it should point westward for as long as he travelled towards the Western Paradise and reverse towards the east only when he returned. This little story, of which there is no prior trace, survived more or less unchanged as a detail in two known versions of the popular cycle, but both comparatively late and sophisticated productions.[2] In the earliest popular sources it does not appear. The mode of its transmission is obscure: we may even suspect some straightforward literary affiliation, particularly as the passage is quoted in the *T'ai-p'ing kuang-chi*. Coming down to us in this form, such passages represent in the first instance the gleanings of literary men. Whether truly popular traditions were reflected in them remains a matter of guesswork, and we can conclude nothing about the conditions in which such traditions may have circulated.[3]

In 1036 Ou-yang Hsiu[a] (1007–72) recorded a visit to a Yang-chou monastery (Shou-ning szu[b]), founded in the early years of the Southern T'ang dynasty (937–); he was told that, of all the mural paintings which had suffered neglect and dilapidation during the occupancy of a Later Chou Emperor (Shih-tsung[c], r. 954–8), only that representing Hsüan-

---

[1] Cf. above, p. 15. For the passage, see *TPKC*, 92:606 and *Tu-i chih*[d] (*Ts'ung-shu chi-ch'eng*[e], based on *Pai-hai*[f] ed.) 1 (*shang*): 11–12.

[2] *Tsa-chü Hsi-yu chi*, sc. 5, p. 27 and sc. 22, p. 100 (cf. App. C); and *HYC*, ch. 12, p. 141 and ch. 100, p. 1124.

[3] The same reservations apply to two anecdotes included by Ch'ien I[g] (early eleventh century) in his *Nan-pu hsin-shu*[h] (*HCTY*) 2:12b and 7:4a. They concern Tripitaka's visit to Vimalakīrti's dwelling in the west and to the monastery at Nālandā.

[a] 歐陽修   [b] 壽寧寺   [c] 世宗   [d] 獨異志   [e] 叢書集成   [f] 稗海
[g] 錢易   [h] 南部新書

tsang fetching the scriptures survived.[1] Yet he left no hint as to what scenes this painting portrayed, and here too we are unable to gather what sources inspired it. We can only guess at whether this tenth-century representation of the pilgrimage may have shown some fruits of a tradition now more than two centuries old.

An attempt has been made, by Torii Ryūzō (*q.v.*), to trace actual pictorial evidence in a group of tombs excavated in the neighbourhood of An-shan[a], in Liao-ning. Torii's suggested dating places these tombs and their carved stone walls late in the Liao dynasty (ending *circa* 1125). The claimed reflection of early 'Tripitaka' legends comes in the form of three among the many scenes carved on the tomb walls. Readers of Torii's article must depend on the accompanying reproductions of his rubbings as their sole authority in judging the claim. On this basis it is difficult to accept his interpretations as more than tentative. The most important of the three scenes—in which Torii sees Tripitaka standing respectfully before a huge and imposing monkey-featured figure seated upon a cloud-throne[2]—is precisely the one which prompts the most doubt. If a 'Tripitaka' story is indeed represented here, it still seems far from clear that the enthroned figure is in fact a monkey; it might be equally possible to discern there Shen-sha shen, whose meeting with Tripitaka is attested at this period, and whose appearance, particularly hair, could arguably be reconciled with what appears on the rubbing.

A second scene features three figures, one of whom is holding a leafy branch, while another salutes the third, seated and capped figure who is taken to be Tripitaka. Torii identifies this with the legend of the pine-twig quoted above.[3] The remaining scene centres upon a figure, again capped, presumed to be riding a lion (whose head is however missing): this in turn Torii relates to a brief episode in the 'Kōzanji' text.[4] If the interpretations are correct, we have some confirmation of features in the story known to us from literary sources of slightly different periods. But so laconic, and even cryptic, is the pictorial evidence that it depends for its present meaning entirely on what we are prepared to read into it on the strength of those literary sources, and in practice this comes to seem very much a matter of hopeful conjecture.

[1] *Ou-yang Wen-chung kung wen-chi*, 125:4b–5a.
[2] Torii Ryūzō, p. 15.
[3] *Ibid.* p. 20.
[4] *Ibid.* pp. 19–20. The encounter with lions in Section 5: cf. App. C, p. 189.
[a] 鞍山

Such glimpses and guesses are of interest because, from this intervening period of centuries, they are all we have; yet they reach us mostly only through the condensing and no doubt selective medium of literary note-books, some non-committal, some of doubtful date. Even where points of comparison are possible, the main questions raised by later 'Tripi-taka' traditions remain unanswered. We are still ignorant of when and how Tripitaka first came to the attention of popular audiences as a legendary hero. Almost without exception, we have yet to bridge the gulf which divides these relatively sober literary anecdotes from the seemingly irresponsible fantasy of later popular cycles.

The 'Kōzanji' version, dating (at a reasonably cautious estimate) from the thirteenth century, appears almost without warning. Yet it represents already a story-cycle with certain characteristic figures and episodes. The text is by later standards brief (even allowing for the fragmentary condition of the two remaining editions), but the work exhibits an unexpected wealth and versatility of content. Its service to our under-standing of this long interval of near silence lies in the particular nature of these contents: they will be found to imply a background quite dis-tinct from the pious biography and literary apocrypha of the T'ang and Sung periods. It is to this source that we must look for confirmation of what will be sketchily apparent from this chapter—that the origins and formation of such a cycle are not to be pinned down in terms of episodes which the historical Hsüan-tsang was known, or devoutly supposed, to have experienced. There is here already a freer range of reference, which extends at times into the province of universal folklore, bound by its own patterns and laws. This material must now be de-scribed and discussed more closely.

2

The First Reflections of a Popular Cycle

THE KŌZANJI VERSION

Two famous texts in Japanese collections represent the earliest known written version of a *Hsi-yu chi* story and are in fact among the earliest known examples of printed popular fiction in China. They are:

A. *Hsin-tiao Ta-T'ang San-tsang Fa-shih ch'ü ching chi*[a], in the collection of the late Tokutomi Sohō[b],[1] now housed in the Ochanomizu[c] Library in Tokyo.

B. *Ta-T'ang San-tsang ch'ü ching shih-hua*[d], in the Ōkura Museum[e].[2]

Originally both belonged to a Kyoto monastery, the Kōzanji[f] on Mount Toganoo[g].[3] A catalogue of sacred literature in the monastery, dated 21 December 1633, has an entry: '*Hsüan-tsang ch'ü ching chi*— two sets'[h].[4] Copy A bears the stamp of the monastery on one of its pages (the first of the third *chüan*). B was discovered in the eighteenth century, according to a Japanese preface of the time, among the monastery's collection of Chinese books.[5] Copy A eventually passed into the hands of Tokutomi Sohō, and it was while in his possession that public attention was first drawn to it in 1916 by Lo Chen-yü[i]. He published a photographic facsimile in his *Chi-shih-an ts'ung-shu*[j], adding a postface[k]. B was examined in 1911, while in the possession of General Miura[l], by

---

[1] It appears among the rare books listed in his *Seikidō zempon shomoku*[m] (Tokyo, 1932), pp. 298–9.
[2] Cf. Nagasawa Kikuya and others, *Isson shomoku*[n] (Tokyo, 1933), p. 47.
[3] The monastery was founded under this title in 1206: cf. Mochizuki Shinkō, p. 1045*c*.
[4] *Kōzanji seikyō mokuroku*, 1[o]:917*b*. Cf. Ogawa Kanichi, p. 58.
[5] Ogawa Kanichi, p. 56. I have not been able to verify this evidence from the original.

[a] 新雕大唐三藏法師取經記   [b] 德富蘇峰   [c] お茶の水
[d] 大唐三藏取經詩話   [e] 大倉集古館   [f] 高山寺   [g] 栂尾山
[h] 玄奘取經記二部   [i] 羅振玉   [j] 吉石盦叢書   [k] 跋
[l] 三浦將軍   [m] 成簣堂善本書目   [n] 佚存書目   [o] 上

Lo Chen-yü and Wang Kuo-wei[a]. Lo published a separate photographic facsimile of B in 1916, appending postfaces by Wang Kuo-wei (dated 1915) and himself (1916). The Commercial Press, Shanghai, brought out an edition of B in moveable type in 1925. A further modern reprint, again based principally upon B but making some use also of A, appeared in 1954,[1] and the facsimiles have been reissued together, in a rather inferior reproduction and with B photographically enlarged, in 1955.[2]

The two represent essentially a single text, with a number of minor discrepancies in the printing. Both are in fragmentary condition: of the three *chüan* into which each is divided, A lacks the opening pages of the first and the whole of the second; B lacks the first folio of the first *chüan* and the second and third folios of the second. B is a specimen of the 'pocket editions'[b] of early Chinese printing. At the close of its third *chüan* is the mark—'Printed by the Chang house of the Central Pleasure-ground[c].'[3]

Dating and sequence

Beginning with Wang Kuo-wei and Lo Chen-yü, these texts have been studied in turn by many of the most celebrated scholars in the field of popular literature, but the question of their dating has still not been finally settled. These are the central points of evidence:

(i) The printer's mark in B.

Wang Kuo-wei was the first to suggest that the Central Pleasure-ground may correspond to a site in the Southern Sung capital Lin-an[d] (modern Hangchow) recorded in the contemporary work *Meng-liang lu*.[4] The same work also records the existence of a bookseller named Chang, at a slightly different address.[5] The Northern Sung capital at K'ai-feng also had a Central Pleasure-ground.[6]

[1] Published by Chung-kuo ku-tien wen-hsüeh ch'u-pan-she, Shanghai.

[2] By Wen-hsüeh ku-chi k'an-hsing-she, Peking and Shanghai. References below are to the original facsimiles, but for further convenience references to the 1955 reprint are added in each case. The original pagination of A can no longer be discerned. My numbers refer simply to the fifteen leaves of Lo's facsimile.

[3] *Wa-tzu*: for a note on this term, see Průšek (1939), p. 112, n. 4.

[4] *Meng-liang lu*, 19:6b (*Wa-she*[e]). The date of the preface to this detailed description of the Southern Sung capital has been variously interpreted, but is not earlier than 1274 (Sun K'ai-ti, *K'uei-lei hsi k'ao yüan* (Shanghai, 1953), p. 43). The Lin-an Gazetteer of the Hsien-ch'un reign (1265–74) records similar details of the Central Pleasure-ground (*Hsien-ch'un Lin-an chih*, 19:18b; cf. Hu Chi p. 58).

[5] *Meng-liang lu*, 13 (*P'u-hsi*[f]):3b–4a.

[6] *Tung-ching meng-hua lu* 2:5b–6a. The preface by the author Meng Yüan-lao is dated 1147; the work records the features and life of the northern capital so recently lost by the Sung to the Chin Tartars.

[a] 王國維   [b] 巾箱本   [c] 中瓦子張家印   [d] 臨安   [e] 瓦舍   [f] 舖席

(ii) The taboo on the character *ching*[a].

This was the personal name of the grandfather of Chao K'uang-yin[b], founder of the Sung dynasty. During the Sung period it was customary for writers and printers to omit the final stroke of the character, whether used in its simple form or in phonetic derivatives. In what remains of A this taboo is observed without fail whenever such occasions arise;[1] B observes it in three clear cases,[2] but in all others appears to print the character in its original form.[3]

(iii) Paper and printing.

Those who have seen the texts in the originals are unanimous in accepting them both, on the grounds of paper-quality and form of characters, as Sung prints. The cautious suggestion once advanced and subsequently defended by Lu Hsün, that copy B may have been produced by a printing house which survived into the Yüan period,[4] has been keenly resisted, most convincingly by Nagasawa Kikuya, who found his own judgement of the text reversed when he saw the original. He claims B to be a finer print than the more popular A.[5]

(iv) It may be noted that the two texts share the mention of a place-name—Ching-tung lu[c]—used only in the Northern Sung.[6]

By comparing the minor discrepancies between the two[7] it will be found that B has a greater proportion of inferior readings than A. By this token A would seem to be closer to the original text.[8] A more positive indication is to be found by examining a discrepancy between corresponding passages in A:13b and B 3:10a.[9] The former reads:[10]

京東路遊奕
便探聞法師取經回程已次京界上表奏聞口
宗明皇時當炎暑遂排大駕出百里之間迎接
法師七人相見謝恩

[1] To judge at least from the facsimile: A:1a, l. 1 (twice); 9a, l. 8; 11b, l. 5; 13a, l. 8.
[2] B 1(shang):6b, l. 2 (twice) (1955: p. 18); and B 2 (chung):7b, l. 3 (1955: p. 40).
[3] B 2:4a, l. 5; 5b, l. 3; 6b, l. 4; 11a, ll. 4 and 5; 11b, l. 6; 3:4b, l. 10; 7b, l. 6; 9b, l. 5—in each case the simple character[d].
[4] Lu Hsün (1923), ch. 13, p. 260; (1927), pp. 372 ff.; (1931), pp. 262 ff.
[5] Nagasawa Kikuya (1939), p. 166.
[6] A:13b (1955: p. 104); B 3:10a (1955: p. 69). Cf. *Sung shih* 85:13a; Ōta Tatsuo (1960), p. 409.   [7] They are tabulated in Nagasawa Kikuya (1939), pp. 166–8.
[8] This is Nagasawa's conclusion (1939, p. 169). The 1954 edition was based principally upon B and unfortunately accepts many of the poor readings.
[9] 1955: p. 104 and p. 69. Cf. Pls. 2 and 3.
[10] The lineation of this and the following passage as printed here corresponds exactly to that in the originals.

[a] 敬   [b] 趙匡胤   [c] 京東路   [d] 敬

At the corresponding point B reads:

京東路

遊変探聞法師取經回程已次京界上來奏

聞迎接明皇時當炎暑遂排大駕出百里

之間迎接法師七人相見謝恩

It will be seen that the two differ most seriously at the division of the
second and third lines: where A has '— *tsung*'[a], B has '*ying-chieh*'[b]. In
the B version the phrase *ying-chieh*, 'meet, receive', thus occurs twice:
here, and in the following line.

The better reading seems to emerge when we punctuate and translate
the two versions. In A the natural punctuation would seem to fall after
ch'eng[c], *chieh*[d], *huang*[e], *shu*[f], *chia*[g], *chieh*[h] etc. It would then mean:

A patrol[1] in Ching-tung lu found out that the Master had fetched the scriptures, was returning, and had already reached the bounds of the capital.
They submitted a memorial to — tsung Ming-huang reporting it. At the time
it was hot summer. (But) the state coach was brought out and (the Emperor)
went out a hundred *li* to meet him. The Master in his party of seven met (the
Emperor) and thanked him for such goodness . . .

Although the missing title of the Emperor leaves us with a puzzle,[2] the
passage remains a plausible one. The version in B however is more difficult to punctuate and elucidate. If the punctuation fell after *huang*[e],
Ming-huang would then become the object of the verb 'receive' (*ying-
chieh*), which is impossible in the context of the story; if the punctuation
were moved forward to before *Ming*[i], the preceding phrase would have
to mean 'presented a memorial for him to be received', and *Ming-huang*
would stand awkwardly at the head of the sentence 'At the time it was
hot summer.' B seems therefore less satisfactory than A. It is surely
significant that B enters *ying-chieh* at a point which in A falls at the end
of a line and follows the word *wen*[j], written cursively; while in version
A, *ying-chieh* appears in precisely this position *at the foot of the following
line*, again immediately after the similar character *chien*[k], also in cursive

---

[1] Literally 'roving troop': a term in use under the Sung to indicate that a military unit
had no fixed station, but enjoyed full mobility.

[2] Historically, the Emperor to receive the returning Hsüan-tsang was T'ai[l]-tsung;
and indeed T'ai-tsung is mentioned by name in the last line of each of the two texts.
But the name Ming-huang has always been associated with Hsüan[m]-tsung, some of
whose legendary adventures are alluded to in these texts. From what remains of the
top part of the missing character in A, I would regard *T'ai* as the more likely reconstruction, and allow for popular confusion over the names of the two most famous
T'ang emperors.

[a] 口宗   [b] 迎接   [c] 程   [d] 界   [e] 皇   [f] 暑   [g] 駕   [h] 接   [i] 明
[j] 聞   [k] 間   [l] 太   [m] 玄

form. The coincidence suggests strongly that the problematical first *ying-chieh* in B found its way into the text through the careless copying, by scribe or printer, of the legitimate phrase at the foot of the following line in A; and hence that the B-type text was printed on the basis of a text similar in format and contents to A.

Here, then, is support for Nagasawa's conclusion that the A text lies closer to the original.[1] Its scrupulous observance of the *ching* taboo helps us to assign it more confidently to the Sung period (ending *circa* 1280), or at least to the thirteenth century. The material of the story preserved in this text is no doubt considerably older (as the place-name Ching-tung lu readily suggests), and there may have been several printed versions before that which survives now. Again, more than one reprint may lie between this and B, with its deteriorated text. The dating of B is a matter which students of the original have claimed as their own prerogative. But since it appears to yield precedence to A we should be wise not to stress unduly the title *shih-hua* which is found only in the later text and therefore need not belong essentially to the work represented here. For this reason I have preferred the general designation 'Kōzanji version'. The two texts reposed in the monastery possibly since the time of their importation, which may have taken place during the brisk traffic between Sung China and Japan of the Kamakura period.[2]

The book's contents

Scholars have been anxious to see in this work an early example of '*hua-pen*', conceived even as a prompt-book. But there are few formal features in the text itself to support the idea. The '*chi*' of the title in A is characteristic of many older tales in the literary language; '*shih-hua*' in B has no equivalent in any other comparable text and is usually taken as a simple descriptive indication that here is a tale incorporating verse in *shih*[a] metres. The verses themselves—usually pious comments on the action, crudely written—are put into the mouths of characters in the

[1] It has been claimed (by Ōta Tatsuo (1966), p. 137) that some of the textual faults in A are such that nothing in their context would give a clue to the more correct expressions that are in fact found in B. This is taken to imply that B was after all the earlier text. On examination, one of the three examples cited by Ōta is easily disqualified: the character *lo*[b], misprinted as *wei*[c] in A:6a, l. 3, is given correctly twice on the same page (ll. 2 and 5). If Ōta's basic point still stands, it suggests rather that A and B each derived independently from an original version, or series of versions. The arguments set out above would nevertheless still indicate that the A version lies closer, in text and format, to that original.

[2] Cf. Ogawa Kanichi, p. 61.

[a] 詩   [b] 羅   [c] 維

story and introduced rather deliberately at the conclusion of each episode. It has often been pointed out that verse used thus resembles the
gāthā verses in certain Buddhist scriptural texts. It plays no integral
part in the narration or embellishment of the action.

The language of the Kōzanji version is predominantly literary in
idiom, and although certain features of colloquial usage slip into the more
detailed passages, particularly dialogue,[1] the work lacks any of the conventional devices which in other so-called '*hua-pen*' texts recall the
professional story-teller—(*ch'üeh shuo*[a]...'But now we tell...' etc.).[2]
There is a curious disproportion in length between the seventeen main
episodes into which the story is formally divided: certain of them run to
only a few lines, with the verses taking up much of the bulk. The scraps
of prose narrative in such cases do not often furnish any wealth of incident suitable for extempore expansion. Few of these characteristics
suggest a clear link with actual performance.[3]

For our purpose a more modest assessment is enough. It will not
court danger to regard the work simply as a collection of related traditions, current perhaps both in oral and written form, strung together
by a writer for an audience of humble readers. It is in this capacity that
it presents its outstanding interest for the present study. Here is an
early and extremely rich fund of the material which had become associated with the 'Tripitaka' story. Although the work's medium is the
printed page, its contents give clues as to what kind of sources were
feeding the *Hsi-yu chi* tradition, and indeed the world of popular
fiction, at the time.

---

[1] I refrain here from a more detailed consideration of linguistic features because anything short of an intense and comprehensive study of all available colloquial sources
from the thirteenth century and before would be unlikely to yield criteria precise
enough to judge this version's background. It is however worth remarking that
Ōta Tatsuo (1960, p. 410) notes a number of expressions which he associates with
the tenth and eleventh centuries, and elsewhere (1957, p. 87) relates certain rhyme-
sounds to those of the Southern poetic tradition in the twelfth and thirteenth
centuries.

[2] This is one of the points made by Hirano Kensho (p. 46), whose general conclusion
supports the idea that the text is unlikely to have served professional narrators as a
prompt-book.

[3] One formal characteristic should be noted here. It is the term *ch'u*[b], which designates
the episodes themselves, appearing as the last word in each title and followed by
an ordinal number. Ch'eng I-chung (pp. 93–4) compares this with similar features
found in several of the popular literary texts recovered from Tun-huang, seeking to
explain them in terms of oral expositions associated with paintings. Although some
excellent studies of this general question have appeared in Japanese, it remains too
speculative to be of real assistance here.

[a] 却說   [b] 處

A summary of the story will be found in Appendix C.

The implications of this material are broad enough to deserve mono-graph treatment in their own right. To account in full for every detail would however go well beyond the bounds of our present concern. A certain amount of explanation and commentary on the contents of the story has been presented by Japanese scholars, notably Shimura Ryōji (*q.v.*), Ogawa Kanichi (*q.v.*), Ōta Tatsuo (1960). What follows here is added with a view to studying the nature of the *Hsi-yu chi* tradition in its early stages. But it is at the same time intended to develop points which are not fully covered in the Japanese accounts.

Section 2: 'On their journey they meet the Monkey Novice-Monk'

Attributes of the monkey-hero

Appearing from due east in the guise of a *hsiu-ts'ai*[a] in plain clothes the monkey introduces himself:

> I am none other than the king of eighty-four thousand bronze-headed, iron-browed monkeys of Tzu-yün-tung[b] (Purple-cloud cave) on Hua-kuo shan[c] (Mountain of Flowers and Fruit). I come now to help you to fetch the scriptures...[1]

His name is changed to Hou Hsing-che[d]—the Monkey Novice-Monk—implying his admission to a religious status. Throughout the story the monkey serves as Tripitaka's guide. The whole question of his back-ground and role in the *Hsi-yu chi* tradition will be taken up in detail later in this book,[2] but here we can first comment briefly on the smaller attributes of the monkey-king and his tribe.

Both the characteristic figure 'eighty-four thousand' and the term *mi-hou*[e] ('macaque'), which is the word rendered here as 'monkey', take us back directly to Buddhist scripture, and specifically to the parable literature of the Buddhist canon.[3] This clear echo is certainly of some interest, but it is important not to prejudge the question of the monkey-hero's origin as such on the strength of it, and in chapter 11 below the broader issue is reconsidered more fully.

The *hsiu-ts'ai* in plain clothes has proved in subsequent Chinese fiction to be a common disguise-motif associated with both humans and

[1] B 1:2*ab* (1955: pp. 9–10).   [2] Chs. 7 to 11.
[3] For random examples, see *Po-yü ching*[f] (T. IV, no. 209, p. 555*c*), *Liu-tu chi-ching*[g] (T. III, no. 152, p. 27*b*), *Fo pen-hsing chi-ching*[h] (T. III, no. 190, p. 798*bc*); cf. Shi-mura Ryōji (1959), p. 77; also the passages cited below in ch. 11, pp. 155–7.

[a] 秀才   [b] 紫雲洞   [c] 花果山   [d] 猴行者   [e] 獼猴
[f] 百喻經   [g] 六度集經   [h] 佛本行集經

supernatural beings.[1] Throughout the Chinese tradition the term 'white (*or* 'plain') clothing' has been a mark of non-official, or sometimes menial, status, and in the context of Indian Buddhism white robes were proper to the laity.[2] Its use as a disguise, in conjunction with the *hsiu-ts'ai* title (implying a junior academic qualification with no automatic official status), may invoke this 'commoner' or 'non-clerical' connotation as conferring anonymity on the wearer. We meet white clothing later in the text as the guise of a white tiger demon.[3]

Section 3: 'They enter the Palace of the Mahābrahmā Devarāja'

Tripitaka's sermon in Heaven

Asked about his age, the monkey replies:

'Nine times I have seen the Yellow River run clear.'. . .The Master said: 'If you have seen the Yellow River run clear nine times, do you know all about Heaven and Hell?' Hsing-che said: 'How could I fail to know?' The Master asked: 'What is going on in Heaven today?' Hsing-che said: 'Today Vaiśravaṇa of the North, the Mahābrahmā Devarāja[a], is giving a feast for religious in the Crystal Palace.'. . .[4]

The monkey then takes them all by magical means to the Crystal Palace, where, before the Devarāja and a company of arhats and saints, Tripitaka is invited to expound the *Lotus Sūtra*. Later the Devarāja provides the party with magical aids—a cap of invisibility,[5] a gold-banded monk's staff, an almsbowl.[6] He is Tripitaka's protector for the rest of the journey, always at hand when danger threatens the party.

[1] Cf. the dragon of the *Hsi-yu chi* fragment in the *Yung-lo ta-tien* (discussed below in ch. 3 and translated in App. B); the corresponding character in the hundred-chapter novel (*HYC*, ch. 10, p. 104), and the White-patterned Snake-demon[b] (*HYC*, ch. 17, p. 190). In the *Shui-hu chuan* the same disguise is used by the Emperor Hui-tsung[c] (*SHC*, ch. 81, p. 1339) and Ch'ai Chin[d] (*SHC*, ch. 114, p. 1709); it also provides a nickname for Wang Lun[e] (substituting *shih*[f] for *ts'ai*) (*SHC*, ch. 11, p. 163).

[2] Hsüan-tsang himself observed this: cf. *Ta-T'ang hsi-yü chi*, 2:876*b*.

[3] A:4*a* (1955: p. 85); B 1:10*a* (1955: p. 25). For further references to female demons wearing white, and to studies of this question from the folklorist's point of view, see Ting Nai-t'ung, 'The Holy Man and the Snake-Woman', in *Fabula* 8,3 (1966), 172–3.   [4] B 1:3*ab* (1955: pp. 11–12).

[5] A universally familiar folklore motif: cf. Thompson, motif D1361.15. For its use in the Tibetan epic context, see R. A. Stein, pp. 306 (n. 63), 465, 542, 565–6 (n. 14).

[6] This motif of staff and almsbowl is found in the famous Chinese Buddhist legend of Mu-lien[g] (Maudgalyāyana). In popular versions they became magic attributes bestowed by the Buddha to aid Mu-lien in the quest for his mother's soul: cf. *Tun-huang pien-wen chi*, pp. 704 and 717, where the almsbowl is revealed as a vehicle of

[a] 北方毗沙門大梵天王   [b] 白花蛇怪   [c] 徽宗   [d] 柴進   [e] 王倫
[f] 士   [g] 目連

Several strands are there to be unravelled in this interesting episode, and in the composition of the important figure of the Devarāja. A striking parallel to the episode as a whole appears as one of a series of legends involving the monk Hung-fang Ch'an-shih[a], preserved in the *T'ai-p'ing kuang-chi*.[1] The several distinct stories treated there share as their common theme the summoning of this mortal monk to perform religious duties in supernatural and heavenly places. At one stage[2] Hung-fang is approached by a *yakṣa*, 'bearing on his left shoulder a many-coloured rug', who invites him to come before the Heavenly King Indra[b] [3] and expound the *Mahāparinirvāṇa sūtra*. He tells the monk to close his eyes and transports him with the help of a folding chair[c].[4] In his new surroundings heavenly light dazzles his eyes, and his mortal body is found to be diminutive. These hindrances are resolved by calling on the name of Maitreya. Hung-fang is showing some reluctance to begin his sermon when a Great Deva[d], 'his body several times the size of Indra', enters to recall him, on behalf of the Mahābrahmā Devarāja, to his earthly duties. Hung-fang is prevailed on to accept Indra's hospitality at a heavenly feast and deliver his sermon to the multitude of saints before being hastily returned to earth.

The 'magic carpet' transportation recalls Tripitaka's adventure in the Kōzanji text: he also is made to close his eyes and reopen them in celestial surroundings;[5] he, like Hung-fang, is hampered by mortal

---

magic travel transporting him likewise to the 'Brahmaloka Palace'[e]. The motif reappears in a later treatment of the story in the *pao-chüan* genre (for which see below, ch. 6), quoted by Cheng Chen-to (1954), vol. 2, p. 321; also in the sixteenth-century *ch'uan-ch'i*[f] drama by Cheng Chih-chen: *Mu-lien chiu mu ch'üan-shan hsi-wen*, vol. 3 (*hsia*):11b and 66b.

[1] *TPKC*, 95:631–5. The source is named as *Chi-wen*[g], a title attributed to Niu Su[h] in *Hsin T'ang-shu*, 59:20a and *Sung shih*, 206:3b. All except the closing lines of this long excerpt reappear in the *Shen-seng chuan*, 6:989–90, but I have found no notice on this monk in any more reliable early source.   [2] *TPKC*, 95:633–4.
[3] A variant here gives the name as Śakra[i] (*TPKC*, p. 633).
[4] For an historical study of this chair in China, also known as *hu-ch'uang*[j], see C. P. Fitzgerald, *Barbarian Beds* (London, 1965), on p. 16 describing the *hu-ch'uang* as 'a kind of large folding camp stool'; also Eberhard (1942), Part 1, pp. 22–3.
[5] B 1:3b (1955: p. 12). Chavannes (vol. 1, p. 359) translates a story from the third-century collection of parables *Chiu tsa p'i-yü ching*[k] in which a Buddhist is borne on his couch through the air to a dragon palace. (Cf. T. IV, no. 206, p. 512a.) 'Magic air journey' is a recognized universal folk motif (Thompson, no. D2135). A Chinese folk-tale in one version of which the journey is contrived by a monkey is discussed by Eberhard ((1941), pp. 203–4 and (1937), pp. 234–5). R. A. Stein (p. 362) finds the same motif in the *Gesar* epic, in which monkeys use a magic tiger-skin carpet to transport a duped king to heaven; cf. also his pp. 305 (n. 62), 413 (n. 108), 542.

[a] 洪昉禪師   [b] 帝釋天王   [c] 繩牀   [d] 大天人   [e] 梵天宮   [f] 傳奇
[g] 紀聞   [h] 牛肅   [i] 釋迦   [j] 胡牀   [k] 舊雜譬喩經

limitations in attempting to ascend the Crystal Throne to deliver his sermon;[1] again, he earns warm praise for his eloquence and partakes of the heavenly feast.[2] Above all, the scene is dominated, directly in Tripitaka's story, indirectly in that of Hung-fang, by a deity bearing the name Mahābrahmā.

In orthodox Buddhist cosmology Mahābrahmā, whose origins like those of Indra lay at the head of the Hindu pantheon, was the king of a group of gods dwelling in the Brahmaloka, within the region of Form (Rūpadhātu[a]).[3] In the Kōzanji version he is to all appearances artlessly identified with Vaiśravaṇa, one of the Buddhist Lokapāla, or Guardians of the Four Quarters. It is of some consequence that Vaiśravaṇa appears here as Tripitaka's protector. In his capacity as patron saint of the north he had long won a significance in the mythology of Central Asia out of proportion to his formal position in the Buddhist pantheon. To the people of Khotan in particular he appeared as the patron and founder of their country and its royal house,[4] but the extensions of this cult stretched eastwards through Tibet to China. A series of Tantric sūtras translated into Chinese allegedly by Amoghavajra celebrated Vaiśravaṇa as both military and personal protector-figure. His identification with Kuvēra, the ancient Hindu god of wealth, is well known.[5] It was this which accounted for his association with the Crystal Palace, the dwelling of *nāgas*.[6] As god of the northern regions, renowned for their fine horses and warriors, Vaiśravaṇa came also to assume the role of supreme Warrior-king. In Tibet this role served to relate him to the epic hero Gesar;[7] in China he eventually became associated in the popular mind with the famous general Li Ching[b], who assisted Li Shih-min[c] in the establishment of the T'ang dynasty.

It is a Vaiśravaṇa coloured with these heroic traditions whom the Kōzanji version now invokes to safeguard Tripitaka's party through the fabulous dangers of Tibet and Central Asia. And this seems to have been

---

[1] B 1:4*a* (1955: p. 13).　　　　　　　[2] B 1:4*b* (1955: p. 14).

[3] For a general exposition of the place of this deity in Chinese Buddhism, see *Hōbō-girin* pp. 113–21.

[4] See *Hōbōgirin*, p. 79*b*; R. A. Stein, pp. 282 ff.

[5] *Hōbōgirin*, p. 81.

[6] The visit to the Dragon Palace to possess its riches was originally the exploit of Kuvēra. As a symbolic assertion of supremacy it became attached, among others, to Vaiśravaṇa. He is represented crossing the ocean on this mission in at least two silk paintings from Tun-huang: cf. Waley (1931), pp. 79–80; M. A. Stein, *Serindia* (Oxford, 1921), vol. 4, Pls. LXXII and LXXIII.

[7] R. A. Stein, pp. 284 ff.

[a] 色界　　[b] 李靖　　[c] 李世民

not without precedent in the popular 'Tripitaka' tradition: we have noted above (p. 20) that Shen-sha shen, a figure inextricably tangled with the legend of Tripitaka's desert journey, and whose initial function was to be his guardian spirit, was by some identified precisely with Vaiśravaṇa. Although in later Chinese fiction of the supernatural Vaiśravaṇa was to become familiar as the warrior king Devarāja Li and the centre of an independent group of domestic legends featuring his sons Naṭa[a] and Moksha[b],[1] the Kōzanji text is unique in showing how he became involved in popular fiction, and how the flavour of the cult still remained with him in his role of supreme power and protective good-will.

If we catch here the echoes of a great mythological complex originating in the Buddhist countries of Central Asia, we have in the same episode identified another, distinct theme: the monk-hero's flight to the splen-dours of Mahābrahmā's Heaven, clearly duplicated in both the Hung-fang legends and, more briefly, in at least one early 'Mu-lien' cycle.[2] The 'Tripitaka' narrator weaves into his performance a theme from a repertoire associated in his mind, no doubt unconsciously, under some such heading as 'journeys of a saintly folk-hero'. In this theme the personality of Mahābrahmā would seem to be a necessary ingredient. So it comes about that the two figures, each with a claim to appear per-sonally in the story, are here fused into one. Once again popular tradition bends its orthodox religious material into bizarre shapes.

Section 6: 'They pass the Long Pit and the Great Serpent Range'

A *yakṣa*—the battle with the white tiger

The party encounters a woman in white who, when challenged, turns into a tiger . . .

Hou Hsing-che transformed his gold-ringed staff into a *yakṣa*, its head touch-ing the sky and its feet the earth, and brandishing in its hands a demon-felling club. Its body was blue as indigo, its hair red as vermilion...The tiger spirit said: 'I'm not surrendering!' Hou Hsing-che said: 'If you don't

---

[1] Something of the distribution of these legends and many incidental details can be gathered from Liu Ts'un-yan (1962), pp. 217 ff.

[2] Cf. above, p. 32, n. 6. It is of interest to note also that Mahābrahmā appears to correspond to the Rūpadhātu Devarāja[c] of the Far West, endowed with fabulous riches, of whom we read in the story *Liang szu-kung chi* (*TPKC*, 81:520-1: cf. above, p. 13, n. 4).

[a] 哪吒   [b] 木叉   [c] 色界天王

surrender, look out for a monkey in your belly!' The tiger spirit heard this
but did not go on to surrender. When called, the monkey in the white tiger's
stomach responded...[1]

The tiger is forced to disgorge this monkey, and many others like it.
Finally Hou Hsing-che himself becomes a stone in the tiger's stomach
and swells until the monster bursts.

The particulars in this description of the *yakṣa* conform to a style of
demon representation which we find in the iconography of Northern
Buddhism, including, more specifically, a number of silk-paintings from
Tun-huang.[2] It provides a clear early example of what later becomes a
cliché in Chinese fiction of the supernatural: the 'blue face, protruding
fangs and red hair' are too familiar to require further illustration.

The attack from within the enemy's belly is a motif even more
widely distributed. It will be found in a source as remote and ancient as
the classical *Rāmāyaṇa* of Vālmīki;[3] closer to our own time, in the
Tibetan epic of Gesar;[4] eventually, in Chinese fiction of the sixteenth
century, it emerges as one of the most dependably recurrent motifs in
the repertoire.[5]

This brief episode, in its two main features, serves both to illustrate
the forms which the popular imagination, under the influence of
Buddhist cults and folklore from the west, impressed upon early popular
fiction in China, and to anticipate some of the standard themes of much
later fiction. In this it resembles, but more modestly, the episode concerning Vaiśravaṇa. The Kōzanji version as a whole, however, has a
wider variety of content to offer.

Section 11: 'They enter the Pool of the Queen (of the West)'

The stolen peaches

The Master said: 'Have you been here?' Hsing-che said: 'When I was eight
hundred years old I came here and stole some peaches to eat. Twenty-seven
thousand years have passed since then, and I have not returned until now.'

[1] A:4*b*–5*a* (1955: pp. 86–7); B 1:11*a* (1955: p. 27).
[2] Getty, *The Gods of Northern Buddhism*, pp. 142 ff., affords many examples of the
blue-painted bodies of *yakṣa* and Guardian deities. Cf. Waddell, p. 334; Waley
(1931), pp. 55, 147 etc.; M. A. Stein, *Serindia* (1921), Pls. LXIII and LXXII.
[3] *Ramayana*, vol. 2, pp. 25, 337.
[4] Cf. the modern performance adapted by Mme David-Neel: *The Superhuman Life of
Gesar of Ling* (revised English ed. London, 1959), pp. 222–3.
[5] For random examples, see *HYC*, ch. 17, p. 201, ch. 59, p. 683, ch. 66, p. 758, ch. 67,
p. 768, ch. 75, pp. 863–5, ch. 82, p. 941; *Feng-shen yen-i*, ch. 40, p. 375, ch. 60,
pp. 580–1, ch. 63, p. 603, ch. 92, p. 918; *Pei-yu chi*, ch. 11, p. 194, ch. 14, p. 199,
ch. 15, p. 203; *Nan-yu chi*, ch. 2, p. 60, ch. 6, p. 70, ch. 11, p. 84.

The Master said: 'I wish that today the peaches could bear fruit, and then we could steal a few to eat.' Hsing-che said: 'It was because I stole ten peaches when I was eight hundred years old that I was seized by the Queen and sentenced to eight hundred strokes from an iron cudgel[a] on my left side and three thousand on the right, then banished to Tzu-yün tung on Hua-kuo shan. It still hurts down my side even now.'[1]

This is the clearest example in the text of a story with long attested native Chinese precedents. The old legend of Tung-fang Shuo[b], who stole divine peaches intended by the Queen of the West[c] for the Emperor Han Wu-ti[d], is found in its earliest form in the context of the *Han-Wu ku-shih*[e], a fictional work of the pre-T'ang era.[2] The relevant passage runs:

From Tung-chün[f] a dwarf was offered up...The Emperor suspected that it was a mountain spirit...and summoned Tung-fang Shuo to ask him... The dwarf pointed at Shuo and said to the Emperor: 'The Queen[g] grows peaches which bear seed only once in three thousand years. This child has been wicked enough to steal them on three occasions. So he fell from the Queen's favour and accordingly was banished to come here'...[3]

From about the thirteenth century onwards (and probably from a much earlier period too) a secondary legend on these lines re-emerges as the centre of a whole series of stage works. The Queen and her peaches became a standard subject for dramatic entertainments at birthday celebrations. In the many extant dramatic compositions on this theme produced in recent centuries it is clear that the centre-piece of the entertainment was the Queen's anniversary feast, to which she invited various auspicious deities and offered them the famous peaches. Much of the text would be given to congratulatory verses. But in one of the earliest surviving plays, by Chu Yu-tun[h] (1374–1437), there is a subsidiary episode in which Tung-fang Shuo steals a crop of peaches.[4] The peaches flower and mature at intervals of three thousand years;

---

[1] B 2:9*b*–10*a* (1955: pp. 44–5).

[2] Yü Chia-hsi (*tzu*, 7:37*b*–38*b*) argues, but on scanty evidence, that two works with this name may originally have existed, one by Ko Hung[i] (third–fourth centuries), one by Wang Chien[j] (452–89), extracts from both of which may come down to us in the form of numerous quotations in T'ang and Sung sources.

[3] Text as reconstructed by Lu Hsün (1912, pp. 462–3). A version of the same traditional story appears among the popular literature recovered from Tun-huang: cf. *Tun-huang pien-wen chi*, p. 162.

[4] *Ch'ün-hsien ch'ing-shou p'an-t'ao-hui*[k] (in the collection *Ch'eng-chai yüeh-fu*[l]), preface dated 1429.

[a] 鐵棒   [b] 東方朔   [c] 西王母   [d] 漢武帝   [e] 漢武故事
[f] 東郡   [g] 王母   [h] 朱有燉   [i] 葛洪   [j] 王儉
[k] 群仙慶壽蟠桃會   [l] 誠齋樂府

Tung-fang Shuo steals and eats them after eluding the vigilance of the maidens set to guard them; like Hou Hsing-che in the above quotation, he is reappearing after a cycle of 27,000 years; on discovery, he is punished. This later and rather more developed legend of Tung-fang Shuo, dispensing with the figure of Han Wu-ti and presented in a new setting, has much in common with the famous episode in the monkey-hero's celestial career as told in later versions of the *Hsi-yu chi*.[1] The resemblance is strong enough to make us look with added interest at the Kōzanji episode and its implication. We are left with a situation to which there is no clear answer: did the Tung-fang Shuo legend first evolve into its very explicit later form, which then became grafted on to the 'Tripitaka' tradition—vaguely referred to in the Kōzanji version, more minutely reproduced in later narrative works? Or did the 'Tripitaka' cycle first receive the legend in its simple ancient form and evolve from it a circumstantial adventure in the orchard, with the monkey as central figure, which Chu Yu-tun and his like later borrowed back for their plays on the Tung-fang Shuo theme? The actual situation may well have been more complicated still, and there is little advantage to be gained from guesswork. What is of interest here is above all the fact of the story's presence in the 'Tripitaka' cycle at this early stage.

The iron cudgel was later to become famous as Sun Wu-k'ung's own versatile weapon, bound by rings of gold, carried off from the Dragon Palace, and worn behind his ear.[2] Here it is used by the Queen of the West to punish him; elsewhere he uses the same weapon, together with the monk's staff and other attributes received from Vaiśravaṇa, to defeat nine dragons.[3] The staff was in fact itself ringed with gold,[4] just as that bestowed on Mu-lien was described as having twelve rings.[5] This motif seems in time to have become associated with Sun Wu-k'ung's iron cudgel. It is above all in Buddhist literature that the iron cudgel is familiar as a weapon of punishment or, in the hands of demons, aggression.[6] Later, when the same weapon appears in the *Hsi-hsiang chi* of

---

[1] *HYC*, ch. 5, pp. 48 ff. The author of the hundred-chapter version contrives an ironical situation in which Sun Wu-k'ung meets Tung-fang Shuo and jokes about this very story (*HYC*, ch. 26, p. 298).

[2] Cf. *HYC*, ch. 3, pp. 28 ff.

[3] B 2:1*b* (1955: p. 32).

[4] B 1:4*b* (1955: p. 14).

[5] *Tun-huang pien-wen chi*, p. 704.

[6] Particularly in accounts of sufferings in Hell: e.g. T. x, no. 299, p. 893*b*; XII, no. 333, p. 75*c* and no. 347, p. 185*c*; XVII, no. 721, pp. 62*c* and 87*a*; XX, no. 1050, p. 49*b*; XXV, no. 1509, p. 175*c*. Cf. *Tun-huang pien-wen chi*, pp. 347, 761–2.

Tung chieh-yüan, it is wielded by the redoubtable monk Fa-ts'ung[a] repulsing the rebels who threaten his monastery.[1] It evidently retained its Buddhist association. Tung Chieh-yüan, traditionally, lived under the Chin[b] dynasty.[2] If this is a correct attribution and dating of the work, which is famous both as a precursor of China's best known and loved romantic drama and as one of the rare survivals of the proto-dramatic form now known as *Chu-kung-tiao*[c],[3] then we have an illustration of the cudgel-motif appearing before Northern audiences of the twelfth or the thirteenth century.

Section 17: 'They reach Shensi, where the wife of a householder,[4] Wang, kills his son'

The 'boy in a fish' story

This, the final section of the work, is largely given to an incongruous episode only thinly related to Tripitaka's return journey to China. It is the story of Ch'ih-na[d], elder son of the merchant Wang, who during his father's absence suffers repeated attempts on his life by a jealous step-mother, assisted by her resourceful maid Ch'un-liu[e]. In turn he is im-prisoned and roasted beneath an 'iron lid'; has his tongue ripped out with an 'iron talon'[f]; is locked without food for a month in a storehouse; is pushed from a bridge into a flooding river. He survives each hazard with miraculous help, and it is only in the water that he is finally lost. The returning father, grief-stricken, arranges Buddhist memorial ser-vices. Tripitaka arrives at this point and demands, as his share of Wang's pious hospitality, a large fish. When the fish is produced Tripitaka announces that the lost son is inside it—and the miraculous reunion indeed takes place.[5]

Průšek[6] has drawn attention to the distinctive character of this par-ticular episode: the miracle here recounted and the form of its pre-sentation seem closer to the world of religious homily than the more

---

[1] *Tung chieh-yüan Hsi-hsiang chi* (q.v.), p. 38.

[2] Cheng Chen-to (1954, vol. 2, pp. 106–8) cites the various sources which associate him with the reign of Chang-tsung[g] (1190–1208).

[3] A mixture of narrative and song, which owes its current name to the free ranging through many different operatic musical modes that is its essential characteristic: see Cheng Chen-to's long article on the subject, reprinted in *Chung-kuo wen-hsüeh yen-chiu*, pp. 843–970.

[4] This renders the term *chang-che*[h], which is the Chinese equivalent of the Sanskrit *gṛhapati* as used in Jātaka literature.

[5] A:10*b*–13*b* (1955: pp. 98–104); B 3:6*a*–10*a* (1955: pp. 61–9).

[6] Průšek (1938), pp. 383 ff.

[a] 法聰　[b] 金　[c] 諸宮調　[d] 癡那　[e] 春柳　[f] 鐵甲
[g] 章宗　[h] 長者

simply spectacular marvels and legends that come before. Průšek sought to identify it with a form of oral story described in the thirteenth-century *Tu-ch'eng chi sheng* as '*ts'an-ch'ing*'[a]

which designates subjects such as 'guests and hosts'[b], meditation[c] and enlightenment[d].[1]

Tripitaka's presence in this story is made possible through the conventional relationship between devout patron and travelling monk. Possibly many other stories made use of the same framework and could be placed in this 'guest–host' category.[2] But the final intervention of a monk with second sight was by no means fundamental to this fable of the boy in a fish. The story-motif as such can be traced ultimately to an ancient legend associated with the Arhat Bakkula (or Vakkula)[e], an early disciple of the Śākyamuni Buddha distinguished for a life of untroubled good health and for his great age. The primitive story is summarized from early Pāli sources by Malalasekera in these words:

while being bathed by his nurse in the waters of the Yamunā, he slipped into the river and was swallowed by a fish. The fish was caught by an angler and sold to the wife of a Benares councillor. When the fish was split open the child was discovered unhurt, and cherished by the councillor's wife as her own son...[3]

Introducing the central 'fish' motif we find no more than a simple domestic accident, with no jealous step-mother and no series of ordeals. The point of the story is to give a miraculous demonstration of Bakkula's pre-ordained physical security.

This old and simple version of the story was available to Chinese Buddhists as one of the parables collected in the *Hsien-yü ching*[f].[4] In the story's more developed forms, to be found in other early Chinese Buddhist sources, it retains the same emphasis, although many added details bring it closer to the 'Kōzanji' episode: the step-mother now appears, as yet unsupported by her maid, and the young Bakkula suffers

---

[1] *Tu-ch'eng chi sheng* (1 *chüan*): p. 10*a*. This work is a description of the Southern Sung capital. The author's preface is dated 1235. The term *ts'an-ch'ing* is introduced, in a section dealing with the entertainers of the public pleasure-grounds, as representing one group of specialists among the professional story-tellers. It is preceded by the 'sūtra-narratives'[g] 'which recount and elaborate on Buddhist scriptures'.
[2] Cf. Průšek (1938), pp. 379 ff.
[3] See G. P. Malalasekera, *Dictionary of Pāli Proper Names* (London, 1960 reprint), vol. II, p. 261.
[4] Translated *circa* fifth century. See T. IV, no. 202, p. 385*bc*. Cf. Ōta Tatsuo (1966), p. 152.

[a] 參請   [b] 賓主   [c] 參禪   [d] 悟道   [e] 薄拘羅   [f] 賢愚經   [g] 說經

preliminary ordeals in the kitchen before being cast into the river. One version still lacks the summoning of monks to conduct memorial services: Bakkula's father chances to buy the fish himself, and directly hears his son's voice from inside it.[1] But in the sixth-century compendium *Ching-lü i-hsiang*[a] the monks appear, and the story as a whole takes on a close resemblance to that of Ch'ih-na in the Kōzanji version:

Once there was a man whose only son, named Bakkula, was just seven years old. His wife died and he married again. The second wife detested the previous wife's son. She was steaming cakes in a cauldron when the boy asked his (step-)mother for one. She took hold of him and put him into the cauldron, sealing off the top with a dish in the hope of killing the boy. The boy in the cauldron ate the cakes but did not die. Later she again took him and put him on a hot iron cooking-plate—but on the plate he ate cakes and made no hardship of it. Later, they went to the river-bank to wash clothes. She threw him into deep water, and he was swallowed by a fish. After seven days the father invited monks to conduct a grand ceremony on (the lost child's) behalf. He bought a fish and bore it home on a cart. Just when the belly of the fish was to be split open the boy said: 'Steady! Don't hurt my head!'

This child had previously respected the precept on the taking of life. Hence he was now five times delivered from death.[2]

There is still no doubt that, for Buddhist purposes, the point of this miracle story is not to lead up to a completely dispensable demonstration by a monk at the end, but rather to dramatize the boy's unassailable destiny of survival.

Průšek, without knowing of a specific antecedent, nevertheless argued as follows:

This episode which seems to be taken from some other source and incorporated into the narration about *Hsüan Tsang* is probably the oldest and best specimen of narrations about religious feasts, about patrons and guests. This narrative itself proves that the whole story about *Hsüan Tsang* must have been created in the circle of religious story-tellers. To the same conclusion points also the strong religious tendency pervading the whole work...[3]

I quote these remarks in full because they touch upon a number of questions basic to our interpretation of the Kōzanji version and its testimony.

---

[1] See *Fu-fa-tsang yin-yüan chuan*[b] (trans. fifth century): T. L, no. 2058, p. 308*b*. Cf. Ōta Tatsuo (1966), pp. 152–3.

[2] T. LIII, no. 2121, p. 201*c*. Cf. Chavannes, vol. 3, pp. 229–30. The passage is attributed to a *P'i-yü ching*[c], but has not been traced further. The 'boy-in-fish' theme appears in other passages quoted in *Ching-lü i-hsiang*: cf. *ibid.* pp. 94*c* and 229*c*; Chavannes, vol. 3, p. 244. For details of a story reflecting some of the other motifs found in the above, see Ōta Tatsuo (1966), p. 153.   [3] Průšek (1938), p. 384.

[a] 經律異相   [b] 付法藏因緣傳   [c] 譬喩經

Knowing more about the origins of the 'Ch'ih-na' episode we are in a position to verify the suggestion that this was a story originally alien to the 'Tripitaka' legends and, it may be, alien even to the 'patrons and guests' of Nai-te-weng's category. Its rather forced incorporation into the cycle here is the result of adaptation, either of the parable story preserved in something like its ancient form, or of a story already so developed as to centre around a famous monk. Whether or not we wish to force these stories into the categories named in the *Tu-ch'eng chi sheng* and its companion works, it remains in any case useful to know that material of recognizably scriptural origin was finding its way, at some removes, into metropolitan Chinese fiction at this period.

It is with Průšek's more general conclusion that we must take issue. If the series of episodes discussed above shows anything at all, it is the surprisingly wide range of mythological reference contained in the Kōzanji cycle; and if there is a religious element common to many of them, it belongs less to Buddhist orthodoxy than to a vague system of popular cults and superstitions spread throughout Central Asia. In speaking of a 'strong religious tendency pervading the whole work' Průšek evidently refers to the Buddhist sentiments served up in many of the verses which conclude each episode. Aside from wishful thinking, there is, however, nothing to guarantee that the verses were not inserted, clumsily enough, by the men who compiled these various secular traditions into their present written form. In terms of the episodes themselves, it is by no means obvious that all developed within a circle of specialized religious story-tellers; and certainly the 'Ch'ih-na' episode, shorn of its main religious point and in any case quite distinct from the rest, cannot prove anything about the cycle as a whole.

General considerations

In spite of the variety of episodes discussed here and in the previous chapter, one thing remains clear. The story is unquestionably conceived as a cycle, in which a simple framework allows the narrator ample scope to include whatever suitable episodes he is likely to meet in whatever quarter. This sets it apart from the bulk of popular stories to which we attribute origins in the Sung period or before.

It is of questionable usefulness to allow our thinking about the 'Tripitaka' cycle to be too closely circumscribed by the incompletely understood categories we inherit from the thirteenth-century city-descriptions. Of the themes and stories discussed above, a good propor-

tion relate to what Arthur Waley describes, in connection with the
'Mu-lien' story, as 'monkish folklore'.[1] (I take this to imply an assimilation, not peculiar to China alone, of popular and heroic tradition with
personalities and stories of Buddhist origin.)

Waley points out—

In later times popular Mu-lien plays, lasting several days, were performed at
the Avalambana season.[2] They were enlivened by boisterous and often scurri-
lous *intermezzi*.[3]

The nature of these *intermezzi* is illustrated in an article on the development of the Mu-lien story by Chao Ching-shen,[4] gathering together
several reports of modern performances in various country districts.

We know that performances on a generous scale took place already in
the Northern Sung capital of the early twelfth century.[5] It is here, if at
all, that we find a parallel to the early 'Tripitaka' cycles. Mu-lien's story
as known to us in the *pien-wen* texts (one dated 921)[6] is already constructed episodically upon the framework of a quest which has the
dignity of a sacred mission. In twelfth-century K'ai-feng it formed a
cycle whose performance could be sustained for seven days, and it is fair
to presume that, together with inherited elements of 'monkish folklore',
this cycle had its share of the boisterous *intermezzi* which have been
observed in later plays. Although there is no '*Mu-lien*' among the major
novels[a] of the sixteenth century and later, the story seems, particularly
in the earlier periods which form the background of the Kōzanji version, to have belonged to the same world as that of Tripitaka.[7]

In the material discussed above there are signs that certain features

---

[1] Waley (1960), p. 216.
[2] In Chinese, *Yü-lan-p'en*[b]: the festival, on the fifteenth of the seventh lunar month,
at which Buddhists were enjoined by the *Avalambana sūtra* (T. XVI, p. 779) to give
alms in pious remembrance of their parents and forebears. Eberhard (1941, pp.
175–6) resumes some of the background to the festival.
[3] Waley (1960), p. 216.
[4] Chao Ching-shen (1959a), pp. 81–8.
[5] *Tung-ching meng hua lu* 8:5b.
[6] *Tun-huang pien-wen chi*, p. 744.
[7] More about this association could be said. It is worth remarking that Tripitaka in
the Kōzanji version is summoned to ascend to heaven precisely on the fifteenth of
the seventh month, i.e. at the climax of the Avalambana season. (A:14ab, 1955: pp.
105–6; B 3:10b–11a, 1955: pp. 70–1.) But there is scope for further speculation as to
how far the 'Tripitaka' and 'Mu-lien' cycles were identified in the popular Avalambana celebrations. Certainly the long *hsi-wen* treatment of the 'Mu-lien' story by
Cheng Chih-chen makes free use of elements from the *Hsi-yu chi* tradition: cf.
above, p. 33, below, p. 165.

[a] 章回小說   [b] 盂蘭盆

used in the 'Tripitaka' cycle were known at least individually on the popular stages of the thirteenth century or before. The iron cudgel and the stolen peaches have been mentioned. We learn of more from the text of an edict issued in 1281, restricting dramatic performances:

From now on no-one, no matter who, is to...perform theatricals, to play wind or stringed instruments, to impersonate the four Lokapāla, or to wear skulls as necklace or headgear. Disobedience or infringement will be a criminal offence...[1]

The skulls slung about the neck of Shen-sha shen, which we meet in the Kōzanji version as well as in later *Hsi-yu chi* texts, have been discussed in the previous chapter (pp. 20–1). In the case of the Lokapāla it is possible to infer that Vaiśravaṇa, one of the group of four, may also have been represented individually in the special capacities which are described above. Evidence suggesting that Hou Hsing-che himself may have been a familiar figure on the stage of this period is introduced immediately below. That some version of the 'Tripitaka' cycle was enacted as a whole we can gather from the title *T'ang San-tsang*, which appears in the list of *yüan-pen*[a] of the twelfth and thirteenth centuries drawn up by T'ao Tsung-i (?1320–?1402).[2]

All this, together with the points of similarity which seem to associate the 'Tripitaka' and 'Mu-lien' cycles, can serve to remind us that in the thirteenth century and before we are dealing with story-cycles which were the shared preserve of both narrators and actors. The episodic material which receives such uneven synoptic treatment in the Kōzanji version may ultimately derive from a wide background of varied performances.

If, at the close of this very selective survey, we turn back to the content of the story as a whole, two characteristics stand out. Many elements of vaguely Buddhist origin are there, but there is certainly no monopoly of Buddhist themes, of whatever degree of orthodoxy. The episodes are

[1] *Ch'ung-chiao Yüan tien-chang*, 57:50a (18th year of Chih-yüan[b], 11th month, second day).

[2] *Cho-keng lu*, 25:14b. (The preface to this work is dated 1366.) *Yüan-pen* is a generic term used here by T'ao himself. There has been some debate as to what kind of performance it denoted and to what period it may be attributed. Cheng Chen-to (1954, vol. 2, pp. 37–8) suggests that it was in use from the twelfth to the thirteenth centuries. Hu Chi (pp. 6–10) deduces from contemporary references that the use of the word *yüan* implied performances by players ranked among the lowest orders in society.

[a] 院本   [b] 至元

bewilderingly varied. Secondly, such Buddhist (or sub-Buddhist) cults and traditions as are represented there lose most of their own significance and logic in the process. Kuei-tzu-mu and Shen-sha shen depart completely from their function in cult and legend; Vaiśravaṇa and Mahābrahmā retain the semblance of their Buddhist character but are forced in cavalier fashion to merge into a single story; Tripitaka trespasses rather unnecessarily into the story of the boy in the fish.

The Kōzanji version represents for us a cycle which is largely the preserve of the popular entertainer and his audience: it is not in fact surprising that so little written evidence of its earliest development appears in advance of this text, both editions of which are themselves transitory popular publications, preserved for us only by fortunate chance.

ALLUSIONS BY LIU K'O-CHUANG

The Kōzanji version is certainly the most significant evidence available to us of the 'Tripitaka' story in its pre-fourteenth-century form, but there is not a total lack of corroboration in other thirteenth-century sources.

There are two slight but interesting traces of literary evidence to be found in the work of the prolific poet Liu K'o-chuang[a] (1187–1269). Both occur in groups of epigrammatic six-syllable verse. The first, under the general heading of 'Buddhist and Taoist themes'[b], forms one line of the stanza:

> From one stroke of the brush it was possible to
>   learn the sense of the *Śūraṅgama* (*sūtra*),[1]
> Yet three letters accompanied the presentation of a
>   robe to Ta-tien[c].[2]

[1] Although the superficial sense of this line seems clear enough I am unable to identify the episode referred to.

[2] In his letter to Meng Chien[d] (see *Chu Wen-kung chiao Ch'ang-li Hsien-sheng wen-chi*, 18:6*ab*), Han Yüe[e], the famous leader of the T'ang Confucian revival, describes the circumstances under which he met and became friendly with the Buddhist monk Ta-tien, in the region of Ch'ao-chou[f] in AD 819. He admits to having presented him with a garment as a parting gift, but protests that this was a personal gesture, not a sign of assent to Buddhist doctrine. Apart from this, there remain three letters, not usually included in Han Yü's collected works, which were claimed by some to have been addressed by him to Ta-tien. The authenticity of the letters became a *cause célèbre* in the intellectual world of the Sung, with its jealous insistence on Confucian orthodoxy, because here the probity of its most highly regarded proponent was at stake. Ch'ien Chung-shu gives an erudite exposition of this great debate in *T'an-i lu*, pp. 77–82. The text of the letters is preserved in *CTW*, 554:14*a*–15*a*.

[a] 劉克莊　　[b] 釋老　　[c] 大顛　　[d] 孟簡　　[e] 韓愈　　[f] 潮州

> To fetch scriptures (it was necessary to) trouble the
> Monkey Novice-Monk (Hou Hsing-che).
> In composing verse (the Buddhists ?) do not rival
> Ho A-shih[a].[1]

My translation of this allusive and cryptic verse is both free and tentative, but it seems clear from this and the other nine quatrains of the group that a vigorous anti-Buddhist (and elsewhere anti-Taoist) lampoon is intended: the allusion to Ta-tien alone carries this implication, and it is possible to take all the other allusions in a similar sense. Fortunately the line concerning Hou Hsing-che is the least problematical of all: Liu K'o-chuang ridicules the degrading of Hsüan-tsang's great mission to the west into a story in which the traveller depends on the support of a fantastic monkey.

In itself this reference confirms what we infer from the Kōzanji source: that by the mid-thirteenth century there was in general currency a story, perhaps of long standing, of the scripture-seeking pilgrimage which already possessed this character, and under this name.

Further implications may be gathered from a similar line in a group of three epigrammatic quatrains entitled 'On holding up my mirror', in which the poet seems to take rueful stock of himself in his declining years (he speaks of himself as more than seventy years old). The first of the three runs:

> A back bent like a water-buffalo in the Szu[b] stream,
> Hair white as the silk thread issued by 'ice-silkworms',[2]
> A face even uglier than Hou Hsing-che,
> Verse more scanty than even Ho Ho[c]-shih.[3]

If Liu conceived of Hou Hsing-che as an epitome of ugliness he must have had good reason to be familiar with the figure in visual terms. Broadly speaking, this would imply either pictorial or theatrical rep-

---

[1] I am unable to explain this allusion, which recurs in modified form in the quatrain quoted immediately below.

[2] A breed of silkworm that flourished in icy conditions. The textile produced was remarkable for its fineness and durability.

[3] In spite of the slight graphic discrepancy there can be no doubt that we have here the same allusion as in the final line noted above, and the two references make it possible to discern something of what this character was known for. The ironical overtones of this line become clear when one takes even a glance at Liu K'o-chuang's immense output of verse: his *shih* alone occupy nearly fifty *chüan* of his collected works. Credit for drawing attention to this and the above references (to be found in *Hou-ts'un hsien-sheng ta-ch'üan-chi* 24:2*a* and 43:18*b* respectively) goes to Ch'ien Chung-shu, a notable authority on Sung poetry (cf. K'ung Ling-ching, p. 81).

[a] 鶴阿師   [b] 泗   [c] 何

resentation. The section which follows immediately below will show that the first alternative was certainly a possibility. But it has recently also been shown that Liu's verse bears the signs of a persistent interest in theatrical performances, often specifically those seen in country districts.[1] It could follow that he was referring here to some grotesque theatrical mask associated with Hou Hsing-che and comparable to the painted *lien-p'u* of Sun Hsing-che in modern stage conventions.

If these conjectures, based admittedly on extremely laconic evidence, correspond to the facts, the 'Tripitaka' stories, with their characteristic monkey-hero, may have been known among the popular entertainments of the South in the thirteenth century.

REPRESENTATIONS AT ZAYTON

The third group of reflections we find in a totally different quarter, in the form of carved figures preserved on the face of two granite pagodas which were built to stand in the grounds of a temple, the K'ai-yüan szu[a], in the medieval cosmopolitan port Ch'üan-chou[b], then known to Europeans as Zayton, in southern Fukien. This material received its definitive exposition in the monograph by Ecke and Demiéville:[2] any comment here is superfluous. But since it has to my knowledge received no attention from students of the *Hsi-yu chi* story,[3] it may be useful to quote here the passages of particular interest, where relevant adding observations in the light of current knowledge of the tradition.

About dating the structures there is little problem. The Western Pagoda, in its present stone form, was undertaken in 1228 or slightly earlier, and completed in 1237;[4] the Eastern Pagoda undertaken in 1238 and completed in 1250.[5] 'As an ornament within the architectural scheme of each pagoda, eighty panels with life-size figures carved in middle relief are inserted into the ashlar framework.'[6] In the carving of these figures Ecke discerns the influence of contemporary Buddhist painting. After describing a thirteenth-century monastic scroll-painting from the southern kingdom of Ta-li[c], he adds, 'one may perhaps

[1] Iwaki Hideo, pp. 124 ff.
[2] G. Ecke and P. Demiéville, *The Twin Pagodas of Zayton*, Harvard–Yenching Institute Monograph Series, 11, Cambridge, Massachusetts, 1935.
[3] I am grateful to Mr Piet van der Loon for drawing my attention to it.
[4] Ecke and Demiéville, pp. 90–1.
[5] *Ibid.* p. 92.
[6] *Ibid.* p. 11.

[a] 開元寺   [b] 泉州   [c] 大理

suppose that such more or less popular and often stereotyped representations and miniature legendaries existed in the libraries of the Sung monasteries and may have influenced the Buddhist sculptor of the time.' And slightly later: 'The reliefs of Guardians in particular may be adaptations of such scrolls and block-prints, which even now are affixéd to temple walls and doors, to embellish them on high festivals...Their primitive conception also reminds one of some of those fierce types in the popular fiction...Today they survive not only in the crude block prints, but even more so in certain types of the theatre.'[1] These comments, although speculative, leave us with a clear impression of where the carvings stand in iconographical terms. We are dealing with figures from a popular Buddhist pantheon, conceived and, essentially, executed in characteristically popular manner. It is within this context that we find reflections of an early *Hsi-yu chi* tradition.

Of most immediate interest is the figure described by Demiéville as follows:

[Western Pagoda, Story IV, NE] A Guardian with a monkey-head, holding with one hand a rosary which is hanging around his neck, and with the other a sword emitting a cloud from its tip. He wears a short tunic, travel-sandals, and a rope-belt from which are hanging a calabash and a scroll with the Chinese title of the *Mahāmāyūrīvidyārājñī* (T. 982–5, a text which was used as a charm against all calamities, dangers, wounds, and diseases). *Trad.*[2] Sun Wu-k'ung, the name of the monkey assistant...of Hsüan-tsang in the *Hsi yu chi* novel...In the upper right corner of the carving there is a small monk-figure with a halo, evidently Hsüan-tsang himself, appearing on a cloud, seemingly the same cloud as that which now emanates from the monkey's sword. In the version of the *Hsi yu chi* now extant, the monkey assistant's weapon is not a sword, but an iron rod with two golden rings, which he can reduce, whenever he finds it convenient, into a needle and so keep inside his ear. Also, he wears a tiger-skin over the lower part of his body, a detail which does not agree with our carving...[3]

In commenting on these various features Demiéville limits his references to the sixteenth-century novel (although he elsewhere, on p. 71, mentions the Kōzanji text and the *tsa-chü* version). In fact, however, the comments would apply almost as aptly to the monkey we find in the

---

[1] *Ibid.* pp. 15–16.

[2] By this is meant 'Temple Tradition,' in Demiéville's words—'the traditional identification of the figures, as recorded by the Rev. Hsing-yüan of the K'ai-yüan Temple. In most cases this tradition is either doubtful or manifestly wrong, but as it sometimes proved to be correct and helpful, it has seemed advisable to mention all the identifications suggested by the Rev. Hsing-yüan...' Cf. *ibid.* p. 29.

[3] *Ibid.* p. 35, and Pl. 26, reproduced here as Pl. 5.

Illustrations

1 Section of handscroll attributed to Li Kung-lin, depicting the story of Kuei-tzu-mu. The episode represented in this section is the attempt of demons in the service of Kuei-tzu-mu to raise the almsbowl under which the Buddha has imprisoned her son Priyaṅkara. Female attendants look on. See pp. 16 ff.

法師取經回程已次序界十大奉國
宗明皇聘當炎宴遂排大駕出百里之間迎
法師七人相見謝恩明皇共車与法師回至國
時六月末旬也日日朝中設齋勅下諸州造寺
奉迎佛法皇王恆得般若心經如護眼精肉小
道場香花迎請文值七月七日法師奏言曰啓
陛下日在香材受心經時空中有言曰僧此月
十五日午時为時至必當歸天唐帝國奏疲淘
薦衣天祢有限不可遷留法師曰取經歷歷龍
吳為東土眾生所有深沙神來國方

2 Kōzanji version, text A, p. 14a. See p. 27.

聞迎接明皇時當炎暑遂排大駕出百里
之間迎接法師七八相見謝恩明皇共
車与法師但朝是時六月末旬出日日
朝中設齋勅下諸州造去奉迎佛法皇
王牧得般若心經如護明糧内外道塲
香花迎請入值七月七日法師奏言臣
咨陛下臣在香林受心經時空中有言
臣僧此月十五日午時為時至必當歸
大唐皇帝聞奏淚滴龍衣天符有限不可
遲留法師曰取經歷盡魔難只當東土

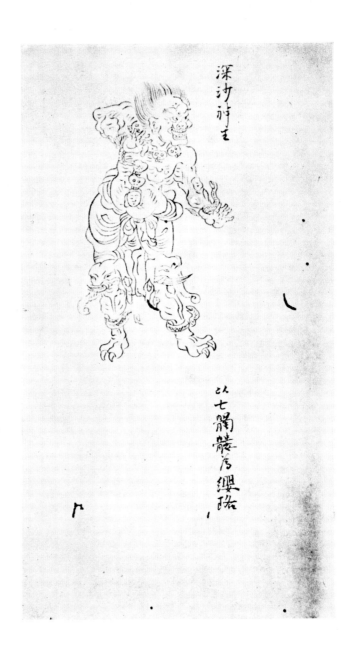

深沙神王

以七間藤房
櫻路

4   Shen-sha shen (*Jap.* Jinja-shin) as represented in a twelfth-century
    Japanese iconographical work, the *Shoson zuzō*. See pp. 18–20.

5   Monkey-headed figure carved in relief on the Western Pagoda of medieval
Zayton (Story IV, NE). See p. 48.

6 'Dragon-Prince' figure on the Western Pagoda at Zayton
(Story IV, NE). See p. 49.

Kōzanji version: there is no sign there of the traveller's garb in which the Zayton figure is so meticulously clothed; the sword is also not mentioned, although the 'iron rod with gold rings', as we have seen above, has not yet assumed its full distinctive role; similarly, the tiger-skin robe, while not described in as many words, seems faintly anticipated in the episode in which Hou Hsing-che slays a tiger-demon, and certainly this standard attribute of demonic figures in Tantric iconography[1] accords well with the description of the *yakṣa* in that same episode.[2] All this tends to suggest that the Zayton monkey-figure remains strangely distinct from that known to us in the literary sources. There is no reason, however, to attempt on these grounds to reject the identification attested by the local temple tradition. Certainly at this stage of their development, there seems to have been no obligation to uniformity in the enactment or representation of popular story cycles: the monkey seen, heard or read about by the northern public could well have differed from his southern counterpart. It may be that in this figure on the Western Pagoda we effectively see what confronted the septuagenarian Liu K'o-chuang in his mirror.[3]

A second important carving is described as follows:

[Western Pagoda, Story IV, NE] A figure dressed like a Guardian-deity, with a princely tiara. In the left hand the figure holds a ball; in the right hand, a spear from the tip of which a calabash is hanging. From the top of the calabash there emanates a cloud, on which a horse carrying on its saddle a lotus-flower (?) appears in the upper right corner of the carving. Epigraph:[a]. According to our present version of the *Hsi yu chi*, the name of this figure should be slightly different, as follows:[b]. The Dragon-king of the Eastern Sea[c], named Ao Kuang[d], was the person from whom the Monkey-attendant received his miraculous iron rod...

There follows a summary of the episodes in *HYC* chapters 8 and 15, in which the son of the Dragon-king of the Western Sea, condemned for causing a fire, is directed by Kuan-yin to escort Tripitaka on his journey, and eventually, after swallowing Tripitaka's white horse, himself turns into such a horse to serve as a steed to the pilgrim. Demiéville concludes:

[1] Cf. Getty, *The Gods of Northern Buddhism* (1928), pp. 52, 66, 69, 107, 125-6, 134, 145, 146, 149, 163 etc.; Waddell, p. 335; Waley (1931), pp. 55-6, 73-4, 147; *HYC*, ch. 14, p. 156.

[2] See above, pp. 35-6.

[3] Liu K'o-chuang's family home, at P'u-t'ien[e] (in modern Fukien), was only a matter of some fifty miles away from Ch'üan-chou.

[a] 東海火龍太子   [b] 西海玉龍太子   [c] 東海龍王   [d] 敖廣   [e] 莆田

Our carving is certainly a representation of the Dragon-prince with the white horse, but the inscription and several details of the carving do not agree with the text of the novel as we now have it.[1]

This identification is bold if it means to imply that a 'Tripitaka' story is being directly invoked in this carving. There is no mention of such a dragon in the Kōzanji version, and the white horse appears only insignificantly as a gift from the Queen of the Land of Women.[2] For confirmation of the presence of the dragon-horse story in the *Hsi-yu chi* cycle we have to wait for the *tsa-chü* version (where it raises complications which must be reconsidered below) and the hundred-chapter novel, with the discrepancies in detail described by Demiéville.

From ancient to medieval times, and beyond, there were countless legends and traditions centred around the archetypal dragon-horse myth in China.[3] The white horse was in its own right a central figure in Buddhist mythology, known to China above all in the famous legend of the introduction of Buddhism in AD 63 after the vision of the emperor Ming-ti[a].[4] The more humble story we meet here undoubtedly forms part of this great compounded tradition. The form, if not the detail, of the figure's name ensures that it bore some relation to the story which eventually joined the *Hsi-yu chi* tradition. What remains uncertain is whether it formed part of such a tradition in the thirteenth century. If it did, then that tradition would again seem distinct from what we see represented in the Kōzanji text. This is a matter for conjecture until further evidence comes to light.

Elsewhere in his iconographical analysis Demiéville has occasion to mention the *Hsi-yu chi* story a number of times.[5] In each case, however, there seems little direct relevance to the composition of the 'Tripitaka' cycle at this point in time: either the identifications are speculative, or the figures concerned are of very general significance—a representation of Hsüan-tsang, for instance, need carry no special implications for the development of a popular cycle. We shall therefore add no comment here.

---

[1] Ecke and Demiéville, pp. 35–6, and Pl. 24 (here: Pl. 6).

[2] B 2:9*a* (1955: p. 43).

[3] For a survey of this question in its world context, see Ishida Eiichirō, pp. 3 ff.

[4] For an analysis of the legend's early development, see H. Maspéro, 'Le songe et l'ambassade de l'empereur Ming', *Bulletin de l'École Française d'Extrême-Orient* 10 (1910), 95–130. Cf. Getty, *The Gods of Northern Buddhism*, pp. 94–5. The legend is found represented at Zayton in its own right: cf. Ecke and Demiéville, pp. 57–8.

[5] *Ibid.* pp. 30–1, 34, 70–1, 81.

[a] 明帝

The unique and authoritative material we find on the Zayton pagodas, although its interpretation is in some ways open to conjecture, leaves us with an important reminder: that the actual content of a popular cycle at various times and in various parts of China is by no means defined by the written sources which happen to be preserved. Our ideas about popular stories, certainly with regard to this stage in their development, should always allow for an essential flexibility.

3

A *Hsi-yu chi* Fragment in the *Yung-lo ta-tien*

In the case of this source there is little to be added to what is already known. The facts are mostly familiar and can be quickly resumed.

Survival

The *Yung-lo ta-tien*ᵃ was intended, in the words of the Ming Emperor Ch'eng-tsu'sᵇ commission, to 'make a full selection of the things recorded in each and every book, gather them into categories and organize them under rhymes'.¹ It was compiled in Nanking between 1403 and 1408 and recopied in 1562–7. In the eighteenth century only this later copy partially survived in the Han-lin Academy at Peking.² Subsequently the greater part of even that has been lost. A reconstitution of the surviving remnants (730 out of an original total of 22,937 *chüan*)³ has recently been published in facsimile.⁴

Among those parts recovered in recent years is the 13,139th *chüan* (originally listed among the survivals in 1773),⁵ which contains a fragment of an early *Hsi-yu chi*.⁶ The passage, just less than 1,100

---

1 *Ming shih-lu* (vol. 10), T'ai-tsungᶜ, 21:9a under the first year of Yung-lo, seventh month, *ping-tzu*ᵈ.
2 Cf. William Hung, 'The Transmission of the Book Known as *The Secret History of the Mongols*', *Harvard Journal of Asiatic Studies* 14 (1951), 433–5, citing a number of modern studies and discussing the problems of dating.
3 The initial total of 22,211 *chüan* in 1407 was brought up to 22,937 in 1408: cf. William Hung (1951), p. 435.
4 By Chung-hua shu-chü (Peking, 1960).
5 See the list compiled in preparation for the *Szu-k'u ch'üan-shu* project, reprinted in Yüan T'ung-li (1932), p. 117.
6 The original, no doubt part of the copy made in the 1560's, held by the Tōyō Bunkoᵉ, and a MS copy of that by the Peking National Library: see Yüan T'ung-li (1929), p. 241. Cheng Chen-to's study was based on a further copy made by Sun K'ai-ti from the Peking Library holding (1933, p. 270). This holding must presumably also be the 'manuscript copy' upon which the recent facsimile reprint is based, (*List of contents*, p. 27a).

ᵃ 永樂大典   ᵇ 成祖   ᶜ 太宗   ᵈ 丙子   ᵉ 東洋文庫

[52]

characters in length, is announced (p. 8 *b*) by the heading 'The dragon of the Ching river executed in a dream'[a]. (It is the first character *meng* which brings the extract into this part of the compilation, governed by the rhyme *sung*[b].) There follow, in red,[1] the words *Hsi-yu chi*[c], indicating the title of the source-work, then the extract itself, ending on p. 10*a*.

The episode and its antecedents

The preserved narrative[2] introduces the following story: A dragon king, enraged by the skill with which a Ch'ang-an soothsayer guides local fishermen to the best catching-grounds, challenges him in person. He elicits a forecast of the next day's rainfall and proceeds to fault it by making the rain fall late and in smaller quantity, although his instructions from Heaven meanwhile correspond exactly to the forecast. The soothsayer remains unmoved when subsequently menaced by the dragon, warns him that he has committed a capital offence and advises him to seek the protection of the Chinese Emperor T'ang T'ai-tsung. In a dream the Emperor receives a visitation from the dragon and learns that his own minister Wei Cheng[d] is the appointed executioner. He agrees to prevent the execution. The following day he has Wei Cheng play chess with him all day, but is unable to stop him falling asleep at the appointed hour and carrying out the celestial execution. A public commotion announces the descent of a dragon's severed head from the clouds.

The story is at once familiar as an episode found again in the sixteenth-century *Hsi-yu chi* (*HYC*, ch. 10, pp. 100 ff.), and from the later work we know that it formed a prelude to one major section early in the cycle. T'ai-tsung, for his breach of good faith, is first haunted by the unforgiving dragon, reduced to death and arraigned by the Ten Kings of Hell[e].[3] The charge is dismissed, and T'ai-tsung is granted an extension of life; he undertakes to send down a man with an offering of melons. While he is in Hell the ghosts of his slain brothers Li Chien-ch'eng[f] and Li Yüan-chi[g] accost him demanding reparation for their death;[4] and as he departs, progressing through all the scenes of the popular

---

[1] Cf. 'Explanation of the second reproduction', at the opening of the modern reprint.
[2] A full translation is given in App. B.
[3] For the origins and functions of these figures in Chinese popular Buddhism see Waley (1931), pp. xxvii–xxx.
[4] These notorious assassinations, by which Li Shih-min secured his own succession to the throne, took place on the fourth day[h] of the sixth month of the year 626: cf. *Tzu-chih t'ung-chien*[i], (*SPTK*) 191:15*b*.

[a] 夢斬涇河龍   [b] 送   [c] 西遊記   [d] 魏徵   [e] 十代冥王   [f] 李建成
[g] 元吉   [h] 庚申   [i] 資治通鑑

Buddhist Inferno, he is again challenged by a host of those wrongfully done to death. He agrees to hold a Grand Mass of the Dead[a][1] for the salvation of these aggrieved souls. Returned to the world of the living, he entrusts his consignment of melons to a commoner, Liu Ch'üan[b], who is anxious to follow his suicide wife Li Ts'ui-lien[c] in death. Husband and wife are granted leave to return to life when the offering has been made in Hell. The Emperor prepares to hold the Grand Mass. It is at this point that Tripitaka first enters upon his public career: he is made High Priest and subsequently entrusted with the mission of fetching scriptures from the West.

Since the *Yung-lo ta-tien* extract was drawn from a source named *Hsi-yu chi*, we are bound to assume that the story proceeded similarly through each of these subsequent stages before finally broaching the main narrative: apart from the relatively self-contained episode of Liu Ch'üan and the melons, there is no break in their sequence. Nevertheless, the elements of the story stand distinct:

(1) the dream-execution of the dragon;
(2) T'ai-tsung in Hell;
(3) Liu Ch'üan delivering the melons;
(4) the Grand Mass of the Dead, with Tripitaka as High Priest.

Among them, the story of T'ai-tsung has old and well-known precedents. According to a passage drawn from the *Ch'ao-yeh ch'ien-tsai*[d] of Chang Cho[e] (early eighth century):[2] T'ai-tsung at the threshold of death is summoned by a man who, though living, serves as a Judge[f] in the Underworld. He questions T'ai-tsung about the circumstances of his brothers' death ('the affair of the fourth of the sixth month'), then returns him to life. T'ai-tsung invests this man with secular office.

Here already we meet three basic figures in the story: apart from T'ai-tsung himself, the astronomer Li Ch'un-feng[g][3] (attendant at his

---

[1] The Buddhist ceremony dedicated to the salvation of the souls of the dead, traditionally instituted by the Liang[h] emperor Wu-ti[i]: cf. *Shih-men cheng-t'ung*[j], by Tsung-chien[k] (twelfth century), 4:401*b* (i) (in *Dai Nippon zokuzōkyō*, 11, 2, *t'ao* 3, *ts'e* 5); see also Eberhard (1941), p. 176.

[2] A six-*chüan* work of this name is known, but it contains material dating from after the death of Chang Cho. The original version appears to have been known as late as the thirteenth century, but thereafter the history of the text becomes confused: cf. Yü Chia-hsi, *tzu*, 7:8*b*–13*b*. The passage in question here is quoted in *TPKC*, 146:1050–1.

[3] Li Ch'un-feng: biographies in *Chiu T'ang-shu*, 79:5*b*–7*a*; *Hsin T'ang-shu* 204:1*ab*. Cf. notes on him by Waley (1952, p. 274). Legends about his powers of astrological insight are gathered in *TPKC*, 76:479.

a 水陸大會   b 劉全   c 李翠蓮   d 朝野僉載   e 張鷟   f 判官
g 李淳風   h 梁   i 武帝   j 釋門正統   k 宗鑑

bedside) and the mortal judge from the Underworld are both figures found in later versions. T'ai-tsung's arraignment for the death of his brothers is the exclusive occasion for this episode: the theme lived long in the popular memory.

In a manuscript fragment from Tun-huang[1] there is a prose treatment of the story with certain popular characteristics.[2] T'ai-tsung again faces the King of Hell on account of the death of his brothers and the thousands he has slain in battle. He bears a letter from Li (whose name is here corrupted to Ch'ien[a]-feng) to the Underworld official Ts'ui Tzu-yü[b],[3] who has been commanded to meet him (p. 210, ll. 8–9). Ts'ui arranges to extend T'ai tsung's mortal life by ten years (p. 212, l. 6). Much of the surviving text is concerned with his efforts to gain some official standing under T'ai-tsung's earthly administration. We meet this character again, under the name Ts'ui Chüeh[c], in the sixteenth-century *Hsi-yu chi* (*HYC*, ch. 11, p. 116), and T'ai-tsung there too bears a letter for him, now from Wei Cheng (*HYC*, ch. 10, p. 113).

Comparing these sources with the hundred-chapter version, and by natural extension with that earlier version used in the *Yung-lo ta-tien*,[4] we find that, despite a clear continuity in certain central features, the T'ai-tsung story has acquired its 'beheaded dragon' theme from elsewhere. I am however unable to trace the precedents for this theme in T'ang fiction to which Eberhard refers.[5]

Liu Ch'üan, bearing an offering of melons (to the Underworld ?), was the subject of an independent play, now lost, at least as early as the

[1] Stein 2630, in the British Museum. Cf. *Tun-huang pien-wen chi*, pp. 209–15; Waley (1960), pp. 165–74. No specific date is mentioned in either book, but Fu Yün-tzu (p. 192) has drawn attention to an inscription on the reverse side of the paper bearing a date equivalent to 11 February 907. It appears at the reverse of the text corresponding to *Tun-huang pien-wen chi*, p. 210, ll. 15–16. Such a date indeed falls within the period from which most of the *pien-wen* MSS seem to originate.

[2] Although there is no evidence of the more conspicuous formal characteristics of *pien-wen* texts (e.g. use of verse), the story contains elements of colloquial diction (e.g. p. 210, l. 13, p. 213, ll. 5, 7, 8, 11 etc.), and much of the narrative has a decidedly facetious tone. Cf. Waley (1960), p. 165.

[3] Also known as Ts'ui p'an-kuan[d]: one of the regular figures in the popular Buddhist Underworld (cf. Waley (1931), p. xxxii). A painting of Kshitigarbha[e] and the Ten Kings of Hell recovered from the Tun-huang cave-library represents him with the inscribed cartouche 'Ts'ui p'an-kuan' (Waley (1931), pp. 36–7).

[4] I have not had access to an article on the subject of T'ai-tsung's visit to Hell by Ch'en Chih-liang[f], listed in *Tun-huang pien-wen chi*, p. 922.

[5] 'Die Geschichte vom Drachen, der sich gegen das Gebot des Himmels versündigt, soll in t'angzeitlichen Novellen vorkommen; ein Beleg ist mir aber nicht bekannt.' (Eberhard (1948), p. 129.) He elsewhere (1941, pp. 174–5) cites a modern folk version of the legend (from Chekiang) unconnected with a 'T'ai-tsung in Hell' story.

[a] 軋   [b] 崔子玉   [c] 珏   [d] 判官   [e] 地藏王   [f] 陳志良

thirteenth century.[1] It is not made clear whether, in this case, there was an explicit connection with T'ai-tsung and his visit to Hell.

From the evidence there are two inferences to be drawn. (1) The 'T'ai-tsung' complex in chapters 10–12 of the present hundred-chapter *Hsi-yu chi*,[2] closely knit though it seems, was compounded of elements from a number of apparently distinct contexts, whose common feature was a connection with the popular Buddhist Hell. (2) The complex would seem to have reached this stage of development already in the early *Hsi-yu chi* used by the *Yung-lo ta-tien*. Liu Ch'üan is a possible absentee only because he does not offer a direct link in the story between the dragon's execution and the public debut of Tripitaka.

The text

The compilers of the *Yung-lo ta-tien* seem to have respected their sources: there is little reason to suppose that this passage has suffered any serious editing.

From its presence in the compilation we know that the source-book *Hsi-yu chi* was in existence before 1408. From the late fourteenth century no other vernacular prose fiction has come down to us, with the sole exception of the *Hsüeh Jen-kuei cheng Liao shih lüeh*[a] (an historical tale of the early T'ang hero Hsüeh Jen-kuei serving in T'ai-tsung's Korean campaign) also preserved in the *Yung-lo ta-tien*.[3] The date of this text's composition is however uncertain: Chao Wan-li[b], editor of the modern reprint,[4] has pointed out allusions in it which are common also to popular literature of the thirteenth and fourteenth centuries (specifically the *San-kuo chih*[c] *p'ing-hua*, among the group of five *p'ing-hua* from the 1320s).[5] This is at best an imprecise way of dating a text.

---

[1] A title 'Liu Ch'üan offers up melons'[d] is ascribed to the playwright Yang Hsien-chih[e], who is listed among 'gifted men of an older generation now dead, whose plays are still in circulation': see *Lu-kuei pu*, pp. 104 and 111. This catalogue of drama was first compiled by the Yüan dramatist Chung Szu-ch'eng[f] by the year 1330. The critical edition cited here uses as its basic text a version of Chung's work published by Ts'ao Ying[g] in 1706 (cf. p. 141).

[2] In the texts of Ming date (see, for instance, Dudbridge (1969), pp. 144–50) the complex in fact occupied chapters 9–12.

[3] *Chüan* 5,244, held by the Bodleian Library, Oxford.

[4] *Hsüeh Jen-kuei cheng Liao shih-lüeh* (Shanghai, 1957).

[5] *Ibid.* p. 76. The connotations of the term *p'ing-hua* at this period have been deduced largely from these same sources—a popular tale principally in prose and concerned with historical subjects treated in a free manner. A note in *SKCSTM* (54:1 *ab*) refers to the category *p'ing-hua* conserved in the *Yung-lo ta-tien*, ch. 17,636–17,661,

[a] 薛仁貴征遼事略   [b] 趙萬里   [c] 三國志   [d] 劉泉進瓜
[e] 楊顯之   [f] 鍾嗣成   [g] 曹寅

But in the *Hsi-yu chi* fragment there is even less internal evidence. The narrative proceeds simply, without incidental allusions. The extract is brief and offers little basis for comparison of formal or linguistic features.

Although there is no difficulty in recognizing here an early vernacular style, in some parts a stiff literary idiom prevails. The passage also happens to lack virtually all the more conspicuous particulars of diction and usage which we associate with colloquial Chinese of the fourteenth century, and which appear plentifully, if irregularly, in the *p'ing-hua* texts of the 1320s and the *Hsin-pien Wu-tai shih p'ing-hua*.[1] It does however at one point use the particle *ho*[a], equivalent to the literary *tse*[b],[2] which has been characterized as a usage of the fourteenth century.[3] And it once employs a construction in which *yeh*[c], emphasizing a new state of affairs, appears at the end of a sentence where *liao*[d] has been used to give a perfective aspect to the verb.[4] The usage is also found in colloquial texts of the Yüan period.[5] But these criteria are not precise enough in terms of time to be helpful in dating the text: it is by no means certain that they did not survive into early fifteenth-century usage, and the whole question of localization in any case remains obscure.

The text's formal characteristics present similar difficulties. It lacks

describing the contents as 'unrecorded traditions of bygone ages worked up into texts by performers and narrated orally'. The term *p'ing*[e] is possibly derived from *p'ing*[f] 'to comment on', hence perhaps 'enlarge upon, embellish'. Cf. Yeh Te-chün, pp. 40–1. Yeh claims (p. 41) that *p'ing-hua* did not treat non-historical subjects before the seventeenth century; but cf. below, p. 63.

[1] For tables giving the numbers and distribution of the most important expressions, see A. Lévy, 'Publications nouvelles intéressant l'histoire de la littérature chinois en langue vulgaire', *Bulletin de l'École Française d'Extrême-Orient* 53 (1966), 286–7, based on an article by Shōji Kakuichi[g]. Of the personal pronouns tabulated on p. 287 the *Hsi-yu chi* fragment uses *tsa* (singular) once, *wo* six times, *wu* twice, *ni* twelve times, *t'a* twice. On p. 286 Lévy sounds an appropriate warning note on the inadequacy of simple statistical evidence in forming conclusions on the early vernacular fiction.

[2] 'If this really is the case, I hope you can tell me clearly all about it.' (9*a*, ll. 15–16.)

[3] The early sixteenth-century Korean linguist Ch'oe Se-chin has the gloss: *Shih*[h] is as *tse*[b]: the old version [of the ?mid-fourteenth-century work *Nogŏltae*] used the character *ho*[a], but in the new this is replaced with *shih*[h], or sometimes with *pien*[i]. (*Tan-cha hae*, see *PTS*, p. 403.) For Ch'oe Se-chin and these references, see below, pp. 60–1. Cf. Yang Lien-sheng, p. 201.

[4] 'Sent down the wrong amount of rain'[j] (9*a*, l. 11).

[5] Cf. Yang Lien-sheng pp. 199–200. In illustration one may cite: 'The Emperor's uncle has fled'[k] in *San-kuo chih p'ing-hua*, 2 (p. 416); 'three of the Lü's have been made princes'[l] in *Ch'ien Han-shu*[m] *p'ing-hua*, 3 (p. 335).

a 呵   b 則   c 也   d 了   e 平   f 評   g 莊司格一
h 時   i 便   j 錯下了雨也   k 走了皇叔也   l 封了呂氏三王也
m 前漢書

any of the verse embellishments freely employed in the five dated *p'ing-hua*, whether straightforward *shih*[a],[1] descriptive 'set-pieces' in parallelistic rhythms,[2] or song-texts set to specified tunes.[3] It lacks also the conventional 'story-teller' clichés to be found throughout the same texts[4] and in the *Hsüeh Jen-kuei cheng Liao shih-lüeh*.[5] It leaves one clue in the form of a sub-heading embedded in the narrative: 'The Jade Emperor commands Wei Cheng to execute the dragon'[b], and the resumptive—'This indeed is what we call "Wei Cheng in a dream beheading the dragon of the Ching river"[c].' (9*b*, l. 16–10*a*, l. 1.) T'an Cheng-pi[6] was quick to identify this with the inscribed cartouches liberally scattered through the text of the *San-kuo chih p'ing-hua*. There is possibly a distinction to be observed here: the '*San-kuo*' cartouches are often placed indiscriminately in the midst of connected narrative, at times even in mid-sentence;[7] their purpose was evidently to attract the attention of the browsing reader and guide him to the passages he wanted to read. In the *Hsi-yu chi* text the sub-heading fulfils an additional role in dividing two distinct sections of the narrative. The brevity of the fragment makes it impossible to judge whether there was a real difference of purpose here.

The *Yung-lo ta-tien*'s uniform presentation has also denied us any impression of the original printed format: there is no indication of date, no publisher's name, no printing device (such as illustrations), to betray the provenance of a particular edition. We are in effect reduced to the modest conclusion that the fragment represents a publication probably of the fourteenth century. There is no doubt as to its popular nature, but the evidence is insufficient to allow more particular conclusions. One can however attempt to speculate on the length of the original: it gave more than 1,000 words to an episode which takes up less than one chapter of the hundred-chapter work and which represents only a minor preparatory incident. Although it would be dangerous to assume that

---

[1] *Ch'ien Han-shu p'ing-hua*, 1 (p. 282), *et passim*.

[2] *Ch'in ping liu-kuo*[d] *p'ing-hua*, 2 (pp. 237–8), 3 (pp. 257, 258).

[3] *San-kuo chih p'ing-hua*, 3 (p. 483).

[4] Cf. the Shōji-Lévy table (p. 286). The one exception is the phrase *chih-chien*[e], which appears in the fragment on p. 9*b*, l. 3.

[5] See 1957 reprint, pp. 1, 42: 'Our story goes . . .'[f]; pp. 48, 62, 67: 'But now we tell. . .'[g].

[6] T'an Cheng-pi (1935), pp. 265–6.

[7] E.g. *chüan* 1 (p. 398); 2 (p. 421). Cf. *Ch'i-kuo ch'un-ch'iu*[h] *p'ing-hua*, 3 (pp. 158, 166).

[a] 詩   [b] 玉帝差魏徵斬龍   [c] 正喚作魏徵斬涇河龍   [d] 秦併六國
[e] 只見   [f] 話說   [g] 却說   [h] 七國春秋

this earlier *Hsi-yu chi* ran to as many separate episodes as the sixteenth-century version, we can take it that there was at least a substantial presentation of the 'westward journey' story. The total length, while possibly not as great as 100,000 words, may well have exceeded, say, 60,000 (the approximate length of the *San-kuo chih p'ing-hua*).

A comparison with the corresponding section of the hundred-chapter novel shows up a striking uniformity: the story, as far as it goes, remains unchanged but for a slight recasting of the fishermen at the opening[1] and small adjustments in the timing and quantity of the rainfall.[2] The major innovation is a long debate in verse on the respective merits of the woodcutter's and the fisherman's life.[3] Aside from this, the later treatment is still more than three times as long (*HYC*, pp. 104–10), with leisurely excursions in parallelistic verse, fuller dialogue passages, more subsidiary characters. The comparison between these two versions is perhaps the nearest we come to evidence on the techniques of the sixteenth-century author: but even here the ground is uncertain. Some two hundred years were to pass before the long novel is known to have circulated: nothing guarantees that during that time the *Hsi-yu chi* story did not pass through further written versions.

[1] One of the fishermen, Li Ting[a], becomes a woodcutter (*HYC*, ch. 10, p. 100).

[2] *HYC*, pp. 105–7, cf. below, App. B, pp. 177–8.

[3] *HYC*, pp. 100–3. For a discussion of these comparative features, together with translation of parts of the text, see C. T. Hsia, *The Classic Chinese Novel, a Critical Introduction* (New York, 1968), pp. 119–22.

[a] 李定

4

Fragments of *Hsi-yu chi* Stories in *Pak t'ongsa ŏnhae*

The work 'Pak t'ongsa'

Since at least the late fourteenth century two popular manuals of colloquial Chinese have been current in Korea: their titles—*Nogŏltae*[a]— apparently referring to the Chinese by association with the Khitan;[1] and *Pak t'ongsa*[b]—'The Interpreter Pak'. A memorial submitted to the Emperor Se-chong[c] of the Yi[d] dynasty in the fifth year of his reign (*circa* 1424) proposed:

Since there are no printed editions of the books *Nogŏltae, Pak t'ongsa*, (. . .), and readers circulate and learn them in manuscript form, I request that a type-founder be commanded to print them. . .[2]

A later memorial in the eleventh year of Song-chong[e] (*circa* 1480), concerning the same two books, reported the opinion:

This is language from the period of the Yüan dynasty, quite different from modern Chinese, and there are many obscurities.

It went on to report and recommend:

Several sections were revised according to present-day speech, and all were intelligible and readable. I request that a speaker of Chinese be commanded to revise (the books) completely.

The Emperor responded with orders for prompt revision.[3]

Texts from the fifteenth century are not known to survive. The earliest edition of the *Pak t'ongsa* at present available is entitled *Pak*

---

[1] Cf. Yang Lien-sheng (1957), p. 197.

[2] See *Yicho Sillok*[f] (facsimile reproduction, Tokyo, 1953, of the 1933-4 ed. by the Seoul Imperial University), vol. 7, p. 298: under sixth month, *jen-sheng*[g] (*chüan* 20:26*b*, l. 4 ff.).

[3] *Ibid.* vol. 16, p. 480: under tenth month, *i-ch'ou*[h] (*chüan* 122:7*a*).

[a] 老乞大   [b] 朴通事   [c] 世宗   [d] 李   [e] 成宗   [f] 李朝實錄
[g] 壬申   [h] 乙丑

t'ongsa ŏnhae[a] ('*Pak t'ongsa* with vernacular renderings') preserved in the Kyu-chang-kak[b] collection of the Seoul Imperial University Library.[1] There is a preface, dated 1677, by a Korean academician Yi Tam-myŏng[c]. He presents the book as a reconstruction by members of the Interpreters' Academy of a work by Ch'oe Se-chin[d]. Ch'oe was a renowned Korean linguist, active in the first decades of the sixteenth century,[2] who prepared annotated editions of both the *Pak t'ongsa* and the *Nogŏltae*. According to this preface the books were lost in a fire and remained unknown until the seventeenth century, when a work named *No-Pak chip-nam*[e] ('A combined survey of *Nogŏltae* and *Pak t'ongsa*') was found in a library. With it was a collection of individual glosses—*Tan-cha hae*[f]—'also by Se-chin'. The *No-Pak chip-nam*, 'assembling the important expressions from the books and annotating them', was the basis of the present edition; it was separately appended, together with the *Tan-cha hae*, at the end.[3]

What the *Pak t'ongsa ŏnhae* now presents is a Chinese dialogue text in which each character is supplied with two phonetic transcriptions in Korean script; each sentence is rendered into Korean; and explanations of individual points in the dialogues are occasionally added in literary Chinese, set in double columns in the text. These notes are distinct from the dialogues and are presumed to be the work of Ch'oe Se-chin. The separate work to be found at the end is in fact entitled *Nogŏltae chip-nam*[g], in two *chüan*, and evidently represents that part of the original *No-Pak chip-nam* which dealt with *Nogŏltae*. The material concerned with *Pak t'ongsa* is distributed item by item throughout the text, where we meet it in the form of the annotations in literary Chinese.[4]

We are dealing here with three distinct sources: the original text of *Pak t'ongsa* as handed down, no doubt in versions modified along the lines of the 1480 memorial; the early sixteenth century annotations of Ch'oe Se-chin; and the editorial work of Yi Tam-myŏng's staff of

[1] Reprinted in *Keishōkaku sōsho*[h] (Seoul, 1943), no. 8. Even this modern reprint, however, is not generally available. I am indebted to Professor F. Vos of Leiden, who kindly lent his own copy and made it possible for microfilm to be prepared by the University Library, Cambridge.
[2] Biographical details on Ch'oe Se-chin are quoted by Ogura Shimpei[i] in *Zōtei Chōsen gogakushi*[j] (Tokyo, 1940), pp. 586-7.
[3] For the preface, which is the source of all this information, see *Pak t'ongsa ŏnhae* pp. 1-3.
[4] Cf. the postface[k] by the reprint editor Suematsu Yasukazu[l], p. 2.

[a] 諺解　[b] 奎章閣　[c] 李聃命　[d] 崔世珍　[e] 老朴輯覽
[f] 單字解　[g] 老乞大集覽　[h] 奎章閣叢書　[i] 小倉進平
[j] 增訂朝鮮語學史　[k] 解題　[l] 末松保和

academicians which, according to his preface, occupied twelve men for more than a year.[1] The bulk of this work, we may assume, consisted in supplying the Korean readings for each character and the translations of each sentence.

As to the date of the old *Pak t'ongsa*, there is the following evidence:

1. The memorial of 1424 (see above) records that it was then circulating in unpublished form.

2. The memorial of 1480 preserves a description of its language as belonging to the Yüan period and already—i.e. after less than 120 years—becoming unintelligible. Ch'oe Se-chin supports the point with certain of his comments in the *Tan-cha hae*.[2]

3. Certain internal evidence: although there are some Chinese place-names used in the text which belong to the Ming period,[3] there are others which were used under the Yüan and discontinued by the Ming.[4] They probably represent details which escaped modernization in the various revisions of the text.

There can be no reasonable doubt that the oldest versions of the *Pak t'ongsa* and *Nogŏltae*, probably also the bulk of the material in their later version, derived from the fourteenth century—perhaps even the period before 1368, which marked the end of Yüan rule in China.

Both works introduce their highly colloquial material in the form of everyday dialogues. *Nogŏltae* follows an imaginary party of Korean horse-dealers on their journey southward into China and towards Peking, showing how they deal with various personal situations and local conditions. *Pak t'ongsa* is set out in a large number of short, independent dialogues covering a broad range of domestic activities. The books incidentally present a valuable body of material on social conditions at the time, as well as a certain amount of linguistic data.

[1] *Pak t'ongsa ŏnhae*, p. 2.

[2] E.g. *ibid.* p. 404: on the particle *che*[a]—'Mongol speech used *che* as an expression of assent (?)[b]. The old versions of both books (*i.e. Nogŏltae* and *Pak t'ongsa*) record speech of the Yüan period and therefore frequently have the word *che*. In modern usage it is not employed, hence the new version exchanges *chao*[c] for it.'

[3] E.g. p. 335: Nan-ching[d], Ying-t'ien fu[e]—the early capital of the Ming; also p. 352: Shun-t'ien fu[f], the name of the Northern capital at Yen-ching[g] from the Ming Yung-lo reign on (1403–).

[4] E.g. p. 176: Tung-an chou[h], which was a *chou* only under the Yüan and became a *hsien* at the beginning of the Ming.

[a] 者   [b] 諸辭   [c] 着   [d] 南京   [e] 應天府   [f] 順天府   [g] 燕京
[h] 東安州

The fragments of a 'Hsi-yu chi' story

Two of the *Pak t'ongsa* dialogues allude to Tripitaka's pilgrimage: one in a generalized reference to Hsüan-tsang, offering him as an example in devout perseverance for the emulation of an unfortunate monk;[1] the other beginning with a brief discussion on buying books—among them a *T'ang San-tsang Hsi-yu chi*—and then retelling a complete episode from the story.[2]

It is this second dialogue which affords the more valuable material. In the first place, it presents a clear picture of ordinary people going out to buy popular stories in book form and confirms that a *Hsi-yu chi* was among those available. Since this story forms the substance of the whole dialogue, it must certainly have appeared thus in the earliest versions of the *Pak t'ongsa*; it is not likely to have been added incidentally later. The book quoted here was evidently known towards the end of the fourteenth century in Korea, and it is reasonable to assume that it was already established and popular at least in the northern regions of metropolitan China. A second point of interest is the friend's retort: 'What do you want with that sort of popular tale?' (in which 'popular tale' translates the phrase *p'ing-hua*[a]).[3] The group of five historical tales printed in the 1320s[4] are the only surviving works from a comparable period to bear the designation '*p'ing-hua*', and it has been assumed, on this evidence, to have been limited in application to stories on historical themes.[5] The *Pak t'ongsa* dialogue uses it in a loose general reference to cover both the *Hsi-yu chi* and a story about the Sung Emperor Chao T'ai-tsu.[6]

The dialogue then runs:

—The *Hsi-yu chi* is lively. It is good reading when you are feeling gloomy. Tripitaka led Sun Hsing-che to Ch'e-ch'ih kuo[b], and they had a contest in magic powers with Po-yen ta-hsien[c]. Do you know (that one)?
—Tell it, and I'll listen.
—When Tripitaka went to fetch scriptures . . . (etc.)[7]

---

[1] *Pak t'ongsa ŏnhae* (hereafter abbreviated to *PTS*), pp. 264–8.   [2] *Ibid.* pp. 292–309.
[3] *PTS*, p. 293. See below, App. B, p. 180.   [4] Cf. above, p. 10.   [5] Cf. above, p. 56, n. 5.
[6] *PTS*, p. 292. The title of this second book is given as *Chao T'ai-tsu fei-lung chi*[d], a title to which there are comparable references in the thirteenth century: *Tsui-weng t'an-lu* (p. 4), classing it under the category *han-pang*[e] ('club-fights') among the oral stories; and further in a number of sources for titles of early dramatic works. Later stories and plays treating this subject are extant: see T'an Cheng-pi (1956), pp. 31–2.
[7] *PTS*, pp. 293–4. See below, App. B, pp. 180–1.
[a] 平話   [b] 車遲國   [c] 伯眼大仙   [d] 趙太祖飛龍記   [e] 捍棒

The episode of Ch'e-ch'ih kuo is thus introduced as one selected casually for illustration and is told directly in the framework of the conversation. The narrative is quite consistent, in its thoroughgoing colloquial idiom, with the language of the other *Pak t'ongsa* dialogues. There is therefore every reason to believe that the text of the episode preserved here is one reworked to suit the purposes of a manual in colloquial Chinese; it is not likely to represent faithfully the words of whatever publication served as its source. Indeed, if such a publication at all resembled the five *p'ing-hua* of the 1320s or even the *Hsi-yu chi* quoted in the *Yung-lo ta-tien*, its prose almost certainly had a more literary flavour, less of a relaxed conversational fluency than the passage here. If it was originally interspersed with descriptive verses, the verses are absent here. The value of what we have lies in its presentation of the bare bones of the story, which can be compared directly with the later counterpart in the hundred-chapter novel.

The corresponding episode in the long novel extends from chapter 44 to chapter 46 and may be summarized as follows.

Tripitaka's party of pilgrims come to a city in Ch'e-ch'ih kuo where Buddhist monks are subjected to forced labour by three Taoist tyrants. These owe their favoured position at the royal court to their past services as rain-makers. Sun Wu-k'ung and his companions strike a blow at the Taoists by breaking up their ceremony, defiling and mocking their sacred images. The Taoists carry their protests to the king, who decides to make his arbitration depend on the result of a rain-making competition. The Taoists' invocation is effective, but Sun Wu-k'ung manages to delay the rainfall until Tripitaka's invocation has been made. He is able to convince the king of his success. After this initial defeat the Taoists issue a series of challenges to compete in performing miraculous feats. They begin with a meditation competition in which the first to move is the loser; then the competitors have to guess the contents of a chest sent out by the queen; finally, a series of ascetic feats—beheading and recovery of the head, self-disembowelling, bathing in boiling oil. The whole is a *tour-de-force* for Sun Wu-k'ung: he manages to contrive a victory in each case by dint of vigorous transformations, by outmanoeuvring his opponents and enlisting help from the spirit world. In the final rounds he succeeds in killing off all three Taoists, and they turn out to be animal-demons. The gullible king is at last convinced of his misdirected patronage, and Buddhists are reinstated in the royal favour.

The story as told in the *Pak t'ongsa* dialogue is strikingly close to this.[1] It anticipates clearly the structure of the episode—Buddhists under persecution through Taoist influence—the wrecking of a Taoist cere- mony—the case brought before the king—contests in magical powers,[2] including meditation, guessing hidden objects, the bath in boiling oil, the beheading—exposure of the leading Taoist as an animal-demon. Even much of the detail is alike: the agile byplay of transformation into insects which wins the meditation contest for Tripitaka;[3] the peach placed by the queen in the casket for the guessing-match;[4] Sun Wu- k'ung's deceptive disappearance in the vat of boiling oil;[5] his seizure of the Taoist's severed head to clinch the defeat.[6] In the whole series of contests only the initial summoning of rain and the feat of disem- bowelling are lacking in the *Pak t'ongsa* version.

There are points of difference in the names of characters: in this early version the single Taoist leader, named Po-yen ta-hsien (*PTS*, p. 294)[7] and further styled Shao-chin-tzu tao-jen[a] (*PTS*, p. 295),[8] is eventually shown up as a tiger-demon. He has a disciple named Deerskin[b] who assists him in the competition (*PTS*, pp. 300 ff.). There is mention of a 'Junior Taoist Master'[c] (*PTS*, p. 297) involved in the initial ceremony. The hundred-chapter novel has a group of three, with names that betray their animal identities—Hu-li ta-hsien[d], Lu[e]-li ta-hsien, Yang[f]-li ta-hsien.

The reader of *Hsi-yu chi* who turns to this passage in *Pak t'ongsa*

[1] For a full translation, see below, App. B, pp. 181–3.

[2] The archetype of this theme in Chinese literature may be traced to the famous story of Śāriputra and his successful battle of transformations against heretical spiritual powers in the kingdom of Śrāvastī: see *Hsiang mo pien-wen*[g] (*Tun-huang pien-wen chi*, pp. 378 ff.).

[3] *PTS*, pp. 300–1; cf. *HYC*, pp. 529–30.

[4] *PTS*, p. 302; cf. *HYC*, p. 531, where the incident is elaborated by introducing further objects to be guessed.

[5] *PTS*, pp. 305–6; cf. *HYC*, p. 537.

[6] *PTS*, pp. 307–8; cf. *HYC*, p. 535. Another, late example of this interrupted feat will be found in *Feng-shen yen-i* ch. 37, p. 338, where the severed head is borne off by a white crane.

[7] *PTS*, p. 294. In the hundred-chapter *Hsi-yu chi* there is a character Po-yen mo-chün[h], also named To-mu-kuai[i], who is associated with the episode of seven spiders (ch. 73, p. 838). Another character, Po-yen-kuei[j] appears in certain mythological *tsa-chü* plays of the fourteenth or fifteenth centuries—see below, ch. 9, p. 131.

[8] This name is taken up in one of the literary notes of *Pak t'ongsa ŏnhae*, which adds the detail—'With one breath he could turn bricks and tiles into gold. This amazed the King of the land, who honoured him as a *kuo-shih*[k] . . .' The relevance and im- portance of these notes will be discussed immediately below. It is worth noting meanwhile that such alchemical, rather than rain-summoning, abilities may have won favour for the Taoist in the early version represented here.

[a] 燒金子道人　[b] 鹿皮　　　[c] 小先生　[d] 虎力大仙　[e] 鹿　[f] 羊
[g] 降寬變文　　[h] 百眼魔君　[i] 多目怪　[j] 百眼鬼　　[k] 國師

will be surprised to find no mention of Sun Hsing-che's fellow disciples: all conversation takes place between Sun and his Master alone, beginning from the moment near the start of the dialogue when 'T'ang San-tsang led Sun Hsing-che to Ch'e-ch'ih kuo...'; there is even an explicit phrase: 'The two of them, T'ang-seng and his disciple...'[a]. We are not, however, entitled to argue from this that the other two disciples appeared only later in the tradition. The text here, it has been observed, is likely to contain less than its source-book. Moreover, this episode is in every respect Sun Hsing-che's triumph—a one-man show even in the hundred-chapter novel, which can keep the other two disciples present only in conversational asides. We may indeed take their absence here as a sign of how this hypothetical early *Hsi-yu chi* may have been simplified by presentation in a conversation manual.

A remaining and more fundamental discrepancy is the rain-making theme: which, although quite absent from the *Pak t'ongsa* version, carries some weight in the later novel by providing an occasion for the Taoists' power in Ch'e-ch'ih kuo[1] and the subject of the first competition. Tripitaka figures also as a rain-maker in the twenty-four-act *tsa-chü* sequence[2] at the outset of his public career: he gains the imperial favour by bringing rain to a drought-stricken capital. On the strength of this evidence, together with the *Pak t'ongsa* account, Ōta Tatsuo has suggested[3] that the theme was consciously removed by the author of the hundred-chapters from its established place in the story of Tripitaka's imperial commissioning (equivalent to *HYC*, chapter 12) to this much later point (*HYC*, chapter 45), in order to avoid duplicating the rainfall of the 'Ching-ho Dragon' episode (*HYC*, chapter 10). Such reconstructions bring their own problems. The implicit assumption here is that the sixteenth-century author was working from a given text—presumably that quoted in *Pak t'ongsa* or one based directly upon it. Ōta himself concludes that this probably differed from the version represented in the *Yung-lo ta-tien* fragment, which like the novel, but unlike the *tsa-chü* sequence, included the 'Ching-ho Dragon' story and would therefore be unlikely to have presented a drought within only a few pages. On these grounds Ōta postulates two distinct 'Yüan versions'.[4]

We are dealing here with a story that is in any case known to have

---

[1] The early *Hsi-yu chi* quoted in *Pak t'ongsa* may have accounted for this differently: cf. above, p. 65.
[2] *Tsa-chü Hsi-yu chi*, sc. 4, p. 20, sc. 5, p. 23. For this work, cf. below, ch. 5.
[3] Ōta (1959), p. 20.   [4] *Ibid.* p. 21.
[a] 唐僧師徒二人

attached itself to many other Buddhists of legendary stature.[1] When a theme circulates with such freedom its place in an extended, episodic story-cycle will hardly be subject to much rigour. Tripitaka the rain-maker may have appeared at many different points in oral versions of the cycle: the theme is simple, self-contained and no doubt more easily dislodged than a more precisely characterized episode. Variations in its use may readily have been reflected in popular publications, even when the 'Tripitaka' story was progressively settling into something like a generally accepted form.[2] We have no guarantee that the sixteenth-century author did not know some popular version in which the making of rain belonged already to the 'Ch'e-ch'ih kuo' episode.

The authority of the *tsa-chü* sequence as a source of insight into the tradition at large must be considered immediately below.

Our conclusions from this material in *Pak t'ongsa* are subject to some uncertainties. The story comes to us indirectly: it is impossible to judge clearly how the original version differed in form (e.g. in the use of verse and the choice of colloquial idiom) from what we read in *Pak t'ongsa*; nor can we judge accurately the scope of the original, beyond forming a general impression that the degree of detail introduced here suggests a text comparable in length at least to the *p'ing-hua* of the 1320s. The most positive and valuable assurance gained is that, some two hundred years before the long novel is known to have appeared, at least this episode—and we may reasonably expect, several others—formed part of a published *Hsi-yu chi* story in a form very close to that which is now familiar.

References to 'Hsi-yu chi' in annotations to 'Pak t'ongsa'

Among the literary Chinese notes appended to the *Pak t'ongsa* text in the sections described above, there are nine which contain significant and often extremely explicit references to a complete *Hsi-yu chi* story. They reflect a work which seems in form and content already remarkably close to the hundred-chapter novel. These notes are translated in full below, in Appendix B, where they are for convenient reference numbered Ni . . . Nix.

---

[1] Cf. Eberhard (1948), p. 138. Some outstanding examples appear in *TPKC*, 88:577, 90:595, 96:638 (cf. below, ch. 10, p. 142); also *Sung kao-seng chuan*, 1:711 *b*.

[2] A more spectacular example of such variation is presented by the story of Ch'en Kuang-jui[a] and the abandoned infant Tripitaka which, after a well-attested independent career, found its way into the *Hsi-yu chi* cycle at various different stages and in variant forms. See Ch'ien Nan-yang, p. 165, and Dudbridge (1969), pp. 170–84.

[a] 陳光蕊

Ōta Tatsuo (1959, pp. 6–19) has published a study of this material which compares many points of detail with the other known works in the *Hsi-yu chi* tradition. Such factual identifications require little further discussion and may be listed simply below.

Some general issues demand more consideration. The first is Ōta's assumption that both the dialogue account of Tripitaka's 'Ch'e-ch'ih kuo' adventure and the plot-summaries supplied in literary notes reflect a single *Hsi-yu chi* work of Yüan date.[1] From the facts we know about the work *Pak t'ongsa ŏnhae* it is clear that a large gap in time—at least as much as a century—separated the dialogue texts from Ch'oe Se-chin's notes. We may infer a fourteenth-century version from the 'Ch'e-ch'ih kuo' dialogue; but from the notes we have no right to look back further in time than the late fifteenth century. In the world of popular fiction there is hardly any comparable text which can be reliably dated to this strangely ill-documented period.[2] Yet it cannot be doubted that popular publication continued: we must certainly allow for the possible existence of several written versions, in various parts of China, within the two centuries which separate the early *Pak t'ongsa* and its sources from the known editions of the hundred-chapter novel. Ch'oe Se-chin may easily have known a well-developed, circumstantial prose-work which had not existed in the fourteenth century. There seem in any case to be two distinct titles involved here: the text of the original speaks of a *T'ang San-tsang Hsi-yu chi* (*PTS*, p. 292); Ch'oe Se-chin eight times refers simply to a *Hsi-yu chi* and in one case (Nv: *PTS*, p. 292) states outright that this was the title of the book he described. From his Nvii (*PTS*, p. 295) there is however no doubt that the book included a 'Ch'e-ch'ih kuo' episode, and that in it the Taoist Master was named, as in the dialogue text, Po-yen ta-hsien. Ch'oe supplies the detail—

There was a (Taoist) Master who came to Ch'e-ch'ih kuo. With one breath he could turn bricks and tiles into gold. This amazed the King of the land, who honoured him as a *kuo-shih*.

—none of which is made explicit in the dialogue account:

In that land there was a (Taoist) Master called Po-yen, also styled Shao-chin-tzu tao-jen. Seeing that the King honoured the Buddhist Doctrine he turned his black heart to the destruction of Buddhism . . . (*PTS*, p. 295).

[1] See in particular his page 21.
[2] Unless we except the 1498 edition of *Hsi-hsiang chi*[a] (reprinted in *Ku-pen hsi-ch'ü ts'ung-k'an*, First Series), at the head of which a vernacular short story is included.

[a] 西 廂 記

More positive conclusions and comparisons between these two sources are impossible because of the heavy modifications which the dialogue medium in one case, and the editor's selection in the other, have imposed upon the original.

A second issue concerns the order of subject-matter in Ch'oe Se-chin's source-book (raised and discussed by Ōta, pp. 6–9). Ch'oe's N ii (*PTS*, p. 266) is in the present text inserted after the words 'Master Tripitaka of the T'ang fetched the scriptures from the Western Paradise', and narrates the background to Tripitaka's mission: the Three Baskets of scriptures are created by the Śākyamuni Buddha—the Bodhisattva Kuan-yin agrees to travel to the East for a man to fetch them—in the guise of an old monk she (he?) witnesses a Buddhist Grand Mass of the Dead in T'ang T'ai-tsung's capital and invites the presiding monk Tripitaka to carry out the mission—Tripitaka accepts, with the Emperor's sanction. N viii (*PTS*, p. 307) adds names of the array of saints in attendance on the Buddha. In turn, N vi (*PTS*, p. 293) resumes in some detail the story of the monkey Sun Hsing-che and his war with Heaven, including: the monkey tribe's home beside the rushing waters of Hua-kuo shan—the monkey leader styled Ch'i-t'ien Ta-sheng[a]—his theft of peaches from the heavenly orchard, of elixir from the patriarch Lao-chün, and of embroidered robes from the Queen of the West—the army summoned by the Jade Emperor to exercise justice, under the leadership of the Devarāja Li—the invocation of Erh-lang's[b] assistance and the capture of Ch'i-t'ien Ta-sheng—the sparing of his life at the request of Kuan-yin—his imprisonment in a cleft on Hua-kuo shan—his release by the pilgrim Tripitaka and acceptance as a disciple—his services as a queller of demons and his final transfiguration with the other pilgrims.

It is clear at once that, aside from a few details, the stories here summarized correspond closely to their equivalents in the later novel. What is not clear is the order in which the older work introduced them. Ch'oe's annotations as such naturally referred to them only as required by particular expressions in the *Pak t'ongsa*—thus the note N vi was no doubt reserved until mention was made of Sun Hsing-che. If this older *Hsi-yu chi* resembled the hundred-chapter novel in structure, it must have begun with the story of Sun Hsing-che and left it at the point where he lay imprisoned on Hua-kuo shan, to move to the story of a scripture-seeking mission, opening with the first initiative from the

^a 齊天大聖   ^b 二郎

Buddha. Ōta argues that this is impossible, because the plea of Kuan-yin on behalf of the monkey's life includes the words:

on Hua-kuo shan let the lower half of his body be put in a crevasse in the rock, which should be sealed off...and so wait for me to go to the East in search of a man to collect scriptures; when I pass this mountain I shall see whether Ta-sheng is willing to go with him to the West and, if so, he can then be released... (*PTS*, p. 294).

The implication seems to be that Kuan-yin's purpose in going East is already settled, and hence that the scene with the Śākyamuni Buddha has already taken place. Ōta points also to the fully elaborated title in the 'Śākyamuni' scene (N ii)—'the Bodhisattva Kuan-shih-yin of Mount Potalaka in the Southern Sea'—which contrasts with the perfunctory 'Kuan-yin' of N vi. The suggestion is that such an extended designation belongs to the character's first introduction in the story, and that therefore the 'Śākyamuni' scene is more likely to have been the first in the book. Ōta concludes that the whole episode of the monkey's early career appeared most probably *after* the Bodhisattva Kuan-yin had accepted Śākyamuni's commission to find a scripture-seeker in the East, and *before* her actual journey to the T'ang capital was made. After the long digression, with the plot now fully prepared in advance, the story of the scripture-seeking mission could then continue.

This explanation accords with the facts apparently presented in *Pak t'ongsa ŏnhae* and cannot be categorically rejected. But it does depend upon the assumption that Ch'oe Se-chin's notes faithfully reproduced not only the summary contents of this early *Hsi-yu chi*, but also its wording. It may meanwhile be worth considering what the further implications are, and how far they are acceptable.

Ōta is surely right in suggesting (pp. 8–9) that the story of the monkey could not have been delayed until after the commissioning of Tripitaka. The objection is a literary one: it would be inconceivable for the action, having reached a forward-looking moment of progress, to pause for a long retrospective digression the timing of which should apparently fall at a given point in the previous 'scripture-mission' sequence. The words of Kuan-yin—'wait for me to go to the East'—would sound ill at a stage when the action itself was already past and settled. But to insert the story of the monkey at the point which Ōta favours—i.e. immediately before Kuan-yin's departure for the East—would raise an equally grave objection. It would require a character in the story—Kuan-yin—arbitrarily to delay a smoothly progressing action in anticipation of develop-

ments which only the author intends. Kuan-yin would have, in concrete terms, to accept Śākyamuni's errand and then sit in idleness until
the whole intervening 'Sun Hsing-che' episode reached its climax; she
would then appear to speak about her forthcoming errand to the East;
finally, at some arbitrary later time, she would perform it. It would be
difficult to find elsewhere in Chinese fiction parallel examples of a
situation in which the action were suspended, *not simply in terms of
narrative presentation, but in terms of its own internal progress*. Ch'oe
Se-chin certainly gives no ground, in the note concerned (Nii), to
assume this delay:

He (the Śākyamuni Buddha) asked all the bodhisattvas to go to the East and
seek a man to come and fetch the scriptures. But...none of that multitude
dared to volunteer lightly. Only the Bodhisattva Kuan-shih-yin of Mount
Potalaka in the Southern Sea, riding the clouds and mists, went to the Eastern
Land. She saw from afar...

Here she appears to respond with all promptitude.

In terms of the story's own logic, it would seem unacceptable to
interrupt the progress of this action with the rich and extended 'Sun
Hsing-che' episode. Indeed, the inevitable and satisfactory order of
events in this opening part of the *Hsi-yu chi* seems to be that which we
find achieved in the hundred-chapter novel. The monkey's adventures
come first, and their end itself dictates a pause and the passage of an
indefinite length of time. A protracted penance in the rock-prison of the
mountain makes Tripitaka's release of Sun Hsing-che into a more
meaningful act; and unless the imprisonment thus precedes the rest of
the action, Sun is confined for only a nominal period.

In judging these probabilities we are led to consider what kind of
authority Ch'oe Se-chin's testimony commands. His summaries of the
plot by no means bring out every detail. Much is left to implication. For
instance, the introduction of the two other disciples Sha Ho-shang and
Chu Pa-chieh is not accounted for in his notes—their names simply
appear in a sentence which describes the westward journey as a whole.[1]
Nor is it made clear what was the occasion for T'ang T'ai-tsung's
Grand Mass of the Dead in Ch'ang-an.[2] More particularly, the sequence
of events in which the monkey Ch'i-t'ien Ta-sheng is spared death and
locked in the mountain-cleft is accounted for only in the speech of
Kuan-yin discussed above: it is made to imply the fulfilment of all this
action, and indeed its wording in the original Chinese would equally

[1] See N vi (*PTS*, p. 294).   [2] See N ii (*PTS*, p. 266).

well suit a third-person narrative but for the closing phrases, which oblige the translator to render the whole as direct speech. It is conceivable that Ch'oe Se-chin's summary exposition here anticipated circumstances in the familiar eventual action which were not necessarily specified in an original speech by Kuan-yin. This older *Hsi-yu chi* could have resembled the hundred-chapter version in pronouncing a non-committal term for the monkey's release—

By the time his penance is fulfilled there will as a matter of course be one to save him. (*HYC*, ch. 7, p. 77)

—and the story could have proceeded to bear it out in the straightforward way which Ch'oe represents.

The evidence of Kuan-yin's grandiloquent title in the note (N ii) on the 'Śākyamuni' scene should not be accorded too much weight, if only because of the special circumstance that this is the prior appearance of the name in the fortuitous sequence of Ch'oe Se-chin's notes: he would be unlikely to extend himself in subsequent references. We may note, too, that the sixteenth-century novel employs this same full designation at a point where Kuan-yin, long since introduced to the story, reappears on the scene of action.[1]

This discussion cannot presume to be more than conjectural, because it tends to question the sole remaining source of information on a text that is not extant. The modern student is not in a position to tell Ch'oe Se-chin what he should have written. Yet the point in question, although it concerns only one feature of the text, serves to face Ch'oe's testimony with some of its direct implications and show up results which are not very convincing. This is not enough to show positively that he misreported the speech of Kuan-yin; but it can remind us that material such as this does not carry the same authority as would an original text and may not impose its own representation of the source.

The two notes considered above—N ii and N vi—represent between them the most important evidence on the content of this lost *Hsi-yu chi*. Of the remainder, only N iii (*PTS*, p. 267) makes important additions in providing a list of the perils through which the pilgrims passed on their westward journey. The dozen names cited are given below with, for the purpose of comparison, certain references to other works.[2]

---

[1] Cf. *HYC*, ch. 12, p. 134.
[2] This material is listed by Ōta (1959, pp. 15–19), with the exception of what is here added in footnotes.

Shih-t'o kuo[a] (N iii reads: 'when the Master went to the Western Paradise, he first reached the bounds of Shih-t'o kuo and suffered injury from fierce tigers and venomous snakes...') The hundred-chapter novel has an episode (chs. 74–7) involving this and a series of similar names, but where the demons are a group of three: black lion, white elephant, Great Roc[b] (*HYC*, p. 888). It is of course far from being the first adventure on the way.

Hei-hsiung ching[c]: apparently corresponding to Hei ta-wang[d] of Hei-feng shan[e] in the hundred-chapters (chs. 16–17): also a bear-spirit (*HYC*, p. 198).

Huang-feng kuai[f]: cf. hundred-chapter version ch. 20—Huang-feng ta-wang[g], referred to later in the novel as 'Huang-feng kuai' (*HYC*, ch. 59, p. 681): a 'Brown-haired sable'[h]. The *Hsi-yu chi tsa-chü* has a Yin-o chiang-chün[i] (sc. 11, pp. 48–50)—a tiger demon of *Huang-feng shan*[j] who abducts the daughter of the Liu family; but this is likely to be distinct from the Huang-feng kuai episode.

Ti-yung Fu-jen[k]: in the hundred-chapter version this is the true name of a female demon who seeks to seduce Tripitaka (*HYC*, chs. 81–3); she is associated by certain legendary relationships with Devarāja Li and his son Ne-cha (*HYC*, pp. 947–9).

Chih-chu ching[l]: this would seem to correspond directly to an episode in the hundred-chapter version (*HYC*, ch. 72): seven spider-demons in the form of women attempt to overpower the pilgrims by issuing silk threads to enmesh them.[1]

Shih-tzu kuai[m]: The hundred-chapter version mentions several different lion demons (*HYC*, ch. 3, p. 31; ch. 39, p. 455; chs. 74–7 *passim*; ch. 89, p. 1016 with many lions).[2]

To-mu[n] *kuai*: In the hundred-chapter novel this is the name of the Taoist (also called Po-yen mo-chün)[3] to whom the seven spider-demons appeal for help after being worsted by the pilgrims (*HYC*, ch. 73). In Ch'oe Se-chin's list the name is separated from the spiders and may belong to a quite different episode—perhaps even that in Ch'e-ch'ih kuo, where the Taoist leader was named Po-yen ta-hsien.

Hung-hai-erh[o] *kuai*: one of the best-known *Hsi-yu chi* characters, attested in both the *tsa-chü* version (sc. 12) and the novel (chs. 40–2); but in the former the Red Boy appears as the son of the popular Buddhist figure Kuei-tzu-mu, involved in the legend of her son's imprisonment beneath the Buddha's

---

[1] The theft of the women's clothes as they bathe, which is a central feature of this episode (*HYC*, p. 825), is a widespread folk motif: cf. Thompson, motif K1335: 'Seduction (or wooing) by stealing clothes of bathing girl', and F420.4.6.1: 'Water-women are powerless when their garments are taken'. Chavannes (vol. 4, p. 150) quotes a story from the *Hsien-yü ching*[p] (fifth century, by Hui-chüeh[q] and others) in which the same motif appears.

[2] The Kōzanji version (B 1:7*a*; 1955: p. 19) had also briefly featured a Lion King.

[3] Cf. above, p. 65.

[a] 師陀國　[b] 大鵬　[c] 黑熊精　[d] 大王　[e] 風山　[f] 黃風怪

[g] 大王　[h] 黃毛貂鼠　[i] 銀額將軍　[j] 山　[k] 地湧夫人

[l] 蜘蛛精　[m] 獅子怪　[n] 多目　[o] 紅孩兒　[p] 賢愚經　[q] 慧覺

almsbowl;[1] in the latter the two appear in quite separate incidents, and the Red Boy's mother becomes T'ieh-shan kung-chu[a].[2]

Chi-tiao (? = *kou*) *tung*[b]: no clear correspondence in other known versions. The hundred-chapter work has a Thorny Range[c] (*HYC*, ch. 64, pp. 731 ff.) —the place where Tripitaka was obliged to spend a night making elegant conversation with a group of tree spirits. There is no reference to a 'cave' (*tung*).

Huo-yen shan[d]: clearly attested in both the *tsa-chü* version (sc. 18, pp. 82–3) and the novel (*HYC*, ch. 59, pp. 676 ff.), where it is the obstacle which involves the pilgrims with T'ieh-shan kung-chu.

Po-shih tung[e]: the name seems to suggest the 'Road of Rotten Persimmons'[f] of the hundred-chapter version (*HYC*, ch. 67, p. 762).[3]

Nü-jen kuo: The Land of Women is attested in all known full versions of the story: Kōzanji text (B 2:6b–9b; 1955: pp. 38–44), *tsa-chü* (sc. 17, pp. 75–80), hundred-chapter novel (chs. 53–4, pp. 610 ff.).[4]

Ch'oe's N iii adds—

and demons and afflictions on every evil mountain and perilous river—I know not how many disasters and sufferings . . .

—which is enough to suggest that his list of episodes is by no means complete. Of the names in the list, more are to be identified in the hundred-chapter novel than in any other version. The same close relationship may be claimed of the material in N ii and N vi. The *tsa-chü* version, assumed (though not with any certainty) to date from the fourteenth century, shares a lower proportion of these known contents, the Kōzanji version least of all. As far as we may use the *Pak t'ongsa ŏnhae*'s sketch of a lost text as evidence of a trend, it appears that the *Hsi-yu chi* story, now well known in published form, was progressively assuming an accepted and less variable form. In terms of *written* versions, further developments were likely to be concerned more with what particular authors chose to modify or embellish, less with what external material might find its way into the story.

[1] Cf. above, ch. 1, p. 17.
[2] A character introduced in a later scene (sc. 19, pp. 84 ff.) of the *tsa-chü* version. This name also circulated widely: cf. *Nan-yu chi*, chs. 12–13, pp. 85–91; in the *Shui-hu chuan* (ch. 18, p. 259) it provides a nickname for Sung Chiang's brother Sung Ch'ing[g].
[3] The same page points out a pun on the words *shih*[h]: 'persimmon' and *shih*[i]: 'excrement' which is still known to popular speech of today. When the episode came to be adapted in the texts known as the 'Yang' and 'Chu' versions (for a discussion of which see Dudbridge (1969), pp. 155–70), both used the form[i] in writing the name (Yang, 4:26a; Chu, 10:16a).
[4] Cf. above, p. 14.

[a] 鐵扇公主   [b] 棘釣(鉤)洞   [c] 荊棘嶺   [d] 火炎山   [e] 薄屎洞
[f] 稀柿衕   [g] 宋清   [h] 柿   [i] 屎

5

Early Dramatic Versions
of the Story

There are records of the following stage works known or suspected to have appeared before the sixteenth-century novel:

1. *T'ang San-tsang*: title entered by T'ao Tsung-i in his list of *yüan-pen* (cf. above, p. 44, n. 2), under the section 'Buddhist monks'[a].

2. *Hsi-t'ien ch'ü ching*[b]: title attributed to the *tsa-chü*[1] playwright Wu Ch'ang-ling[2] in the fourteenth-century catalogue of drama *Lu-kuei pu*[3] and other sources.

3. *Hsi-yu chi*: title attributed to the fourteenth-century playwright and official Yang Ching-yen[c] (alternatively Ching-hsien[d])[4] in the catalogue *Lu-kuei pu hsü-pien*.[5]

4. *T'ang-seng*[e] *hsi-yu chi*: title listed in the section 'The present Dynasty'[f] of *Nan-tz'u hsü-lu*.[6] The dynasty in question was the Ming, and the drama was in the southern tradition.

[1] *Tsa-chü*[g]: this term is used here and subsequently to designate the lyrical dramatic genre based on northern tunes which became established in China in the thirteenth to fourteenth centuries.

[2] Wu Ch'ang-ling appears among the early *tsa-chü* masters 'of an older generation now dead' listed in the *LKP*, and may thus have been active towards the end of the thirteenth century (cf. above, p. 56, n. 1). It is also possible that he lived on into the early fourteenth century: cf. Sun K'ai-ti (1958), p. 72. He is described as a native of Hsi-ching[h], probably equivalent to Ta-t'ung[i] in modern Shansi.

[3] *LKP*, p. 109. This catalogue in its original form was first compiled by the Yüan dramatist Chung Szu-ch'eng by the year 1330. The text comes down to us in several variant versions, one of which, the so-called 'T'ien-i ko'[j] version, represents a revision by Chia Chung-ming[k] in the late fourteenth century including significant additional information on the listed titles. Cf. the preface to the work in *LKP*, which uses as its basic text a version of Chung's work published by Ts'ao Yin[l] in 1706 (*LKP*, p. 141).   [4] Cf. Sun K'ai-ti (1953), pp. 56–8.

[5] This work is still regarded as anonymous. Internal evidence suggests it belongs to the fifteenth century: cf. *Lu-kuei pu hsü-pien* (q.v.), pp. 277–8. For the reference in question here, see *ibid.* p. 284.

[6] *Nan-tz'u hsü-lu* (q.v.), p. 253. This work, by Hsü Wei (1521–93), is our earliest source of general information on drama in the southern tradition.

[a] 和尚家門　　[b] 西天取經　　[c] 楊景言　　[d] 賢　　[e] 唐僧　　[f] 本朝
[g] 雜劇　　　　[h] 西京　　　[i] 大同　　[j] 天一閣　　[k] 賈仲明　　[l] 曹寅

5. *Hsi-yu* (*chi*): title attributed to Ch'en Lung-kuang[a] in the *Yüan-shan-t'ang ch'ü-p'in*, a critical catalogue of drama by Ch'i Piao-chia (1602–45).[1] Conceivably the play may have appeared before the seventeenth century, but Ch'i's comment reads:

> It stolidly sets the whole *Hsi-yu chi* to music, without being able to miss out a single item or reduce its profusion of detail. This is simply due to mediocre talent and shallow ideas.

If he is here referring to the hundred-chapter novel as the source of the play, this item falls outside the scope of our present interest. What technical problems were involved in adapting this story for the stage may become clear from the discussion below.

6. *Hsi-yu chi*: a traditional ascription to Hsia Chün-cheng[b] is noted in *Ch'ü-hai tsung-mu t'i-yao*, a compendium of drama-synopses which date originally from the late eighteenth century.[2]

The editor of the extant *tsa-chü* sequence discussed immediately below wrote of plays by 'popular artists'[c].[3] A scene from one such play described as 'Popular[d] *Hsi-yu chi*' is quoted in the *Na-shu-ying ch'ü-p'u*, an eighteenth-century collection of dramatic texts with vocal pointing.[4] These references must represent only single instances from a long and prolific tradition of popular interpretations.

A preface to a sixteenth-century play, the *Tung-t'ien hsüan-chi*, describes a *Hsi-yu chi* 'with Buddhist overtones' which may correspond to any of the last four titles above.[5]

The twenty-four act '*tsa-chü*' sequence '*Hsi-yu chi*'

A printed sequence of plays in *tsa-chü* style, comprising a total of twenty-four distinct scenes, was discovered in Japan and first reprinted there in 1927–8.[6] The title-page reads: '*Hsi-yu chi*: annotated by Yang Tung-lai'[e]. The text was divided into six *chüan*, and full-page illustrations were distributed in pairs throughout the text.

---

[1] *Yüan-shan-t'ang ch'ü-p'in* (q.v.), p. 117.

[2] *Ch'ü-hai tsung-mu t'i-yao* (q.v.), p. 1941. Fu Hsi-hua (1959), pp. 326–7 includes the item in question, about which nothing definite is known.

[3] *Hsi-yu chi tsa-chü* (q.v.), *Tsung-lun*[f], p. 2.

[4] *Na-shu-ying ch'ü-p'u* (q.v.), *wai-chi*[g], *chüan* 2. The scene is headed 'Thinking of springtime pleasures'[h]. Its role in the *Hsi-yu chi* story is not apparent.

[5] This preface is quoted and discussed below in App. A, pp. 172–4.

[6] In the journal *Shibun*[i] 9,1–10,3. The circumstances of the discovery are described in the postface by Shionoya On[j].

[a] 陳龍光   [b] 夏均政   [c] 俗伶   [d] 俗   [e] 楊東來   [f] 總論
[g] 外集   [h] 思春   [i] 斯文   [j] 鹽谷溫

The work is prefaced by a *General Discourse*[a] signed Yün-k'ung chü-shih[b], and a *Short Introduction*[c] by Mi-ch'ieh ti-tzu[d], followed by a date corresponding to 1614.[1] None of these men have been identified.

The *General Discourse* attributes the work to Wu Ch'ang-ling, who is known to have written a play on this theme. This, as Sun K'ai-ti has shown in a well-known article,[2] was a mistaken or deliberately false ascription; Sun further argues that the play was really the work of Yang Ching-yen, a Mongol born under the Yüan, but who lived at least until the early 1400s.[3]

There can be no doubt that this is indeed not Wu Ch'ang-ling's work. The *Lu-kuei pu*, in the revised manuscript version of the 'T'ien-i ko' collection,[4] quotes in full Wu's original *t'i-mu* and *cheng-ming*[5]—

The Old Moslem calls to the Buddha from the East Tower;
Tripitaka of the T'ang collects scriptures from the Western Paradise.[6]

The short title derived from this second line reads *Collecting scriptures from the Western Paradise*; it reappears verbatim in the late fourteenth-century catalogue *T'ai-ho cheng-yin p'u*.[7] But the six-part *Hsi-yu chi* both has a different title and lacks any mention of a Moslem. It is therefore evidently not the same play. This part of Sun's case has never been challenged.

His identification of the extant work with the recorded play by Yang Ching-yen rests upon the apparent testimony of the sixteenth-century literary figure Li K'ai-hsien (1501–68) who in the anthology *Tz'u-nüeh*[8] quotes the 'fourth scene'[e] of a *Hsüan-tsang ch'ü-ching*[f] by Yang Ching-hsia[g]. The text corresponds, with only slight discrepancies, to that of the

---

[1] The cyclical signs *chia-yin*[h] are in fact filled in by hand.

[2] Sun K'ai-ti (1939).

[3] Cf. Sun K'ai-ti (1953), pp. 56–7.

[4] See above, p. 75, n. 3.

[5] *T'i-mu*[i] and *cheng-ming*[j]: conventional names for the parallelistic resumptive titles set at the end of *tsa-chü* texts and from which the short, familiar titles were usually derived.   [6] *LKP*, p. 172, n. 334.

[7] The preface to this work by the author, Chu Ch'üan (d. 1448) is dated 1398 (*T'ai-ho cheng-yin p'u* (q.v.), p. 11). For the reference in question here, see *ibid.* p. 37.

[8] Sun K'ai-ti (1939), pp. 378–9 satisfactorily attributes this work to Li K'ai-hsien. For the material in question here (which he quotes in 1939, pp. 381–2) he relies on a manuscript version preserved in the Ch'uan-shih lou[k] collection (Sun (1939), p. 378) which is not acknowledged by the editors of the recent critical edition (*Tz'u-nüeh* (q.v.), p. 261). This material does not appear in the extant printed versions of *Tz'u-nüeh*. Sun suggests (1939), p. 379, that the manuscript may represent an early draft of the eventual published work, for which he postulates a date later than 1557.

a 總論	b 蘊空居士	c 小引	d 彌伽弟子	e 第四出
f 玄奘取經	g 夏	h 甲寅	i 題目	j 正名	k 傳是樓

extant play's fourth scene. The short title *Hsüan-tsang ch'ü-ching* could be pieced together with the words *Hsi-yu chi*—which appear under Yang's name in the *Lu-kuei pu hsü-pien* as well as at the head of the extant play—to form a plausible *cheng-ming*. On these grounds it is claimed that the play known to Li K'ai-hsien and attributed by him to Yang Ching-yen[1] (at a distance of 150 years) was the same as the six-part *Hsi-yu chi* that survives.

This ascription has been accepted, rather unenthusiastically, by the majority of subsequent editors and critics of the work, but it remains in several respects vulnerable: dependent upon a single piece of evidence, a century and a half removed from the period in question, in a manuscript of doubtful provenance and identity, and complicated by a graphic ambiguity in the very name which forms the key to the whole. It is not surprising that there have been attempts to reinterpret the evidence in broader terms. If the results have been unconvincing, it is partly because the material itself is not explicit enough to allow useful conclusions to be drawn, partly also because attempts at analysis have been too boldly speculative and sometimes even careless.[2] It will not be of much service to the reader to lead him through a critique of various theories which neither answers the important questions nor yields any other result of value. Here it is sufficient just to acknowledge the 'amalgamation' theory put forward principally by Yen Tun-i (1954), whose sceptical attitudes towards the dating of dramatic literature are well known. He observes that no source links Yang's name explicitly with a six-part or twenty-four-scene *Hsi-yu chi*; also that the present text betrays considerable unevenness in its distribution of incident throughout the twenty-four scenes. His solution is to suggest that it may be the result of expanding an original *tsa-chü* by Yang, presumably in the conventional four scenes, at some much later period. It is implied that a good deal of material was introduced into the sequence from other sources.

Whether or not this conjecture is substantially true, one thing at least is clear from the excerpts in the manuscript *Tz'u-nüeh*: they are drawn from a scene which resolves the story of Tripitaka's adventures in early infancy,[3] which is described as the fourth in Yang's play, and which

---

[1] This attribution of course depends on the assumption that the discrepancy in the names implies no more than a graphic slip (Sun (1939), p. 378).

[2] Chang Wei-ching's study (*q.v.*) is so full of misconceptions and factual mistakes that I shall not detain the reader with it here. For a discussion of his arguments, see Dudbridge (1967), pp. 132–8.   [3] Cf. the summary in App. C, pp. 193–4.

corresponds closely to the fourth in the extant sequence. A play in four scenes designed to end at such a point would naturally not have been called *Hsüan-tsang collects scriptures* or *Hsi-yu chi*. The source of this quotation must therefore have been a play which gave an adequate treatment of the 'westward journey' story *after four introductory scenes about Tripitaka's adventures in infancy*.[1] This in itself testifies to an exceptionally broad conception. There can be little doubt that, aside from the question of authorship, the play known to Li K'ai-hsien closely resembled our present version, and had therefore assumed this extended form at least before 1568 (the year of Li's death).

Before considering the questions of most relevance to this present study, i.e. the characteristics of the extant text and its value as a reflection of the *Hsi-yu chi* tradition, it is important to explain the assumptions upon which the argument rests. The first is that, irrespective of what elements were derived from the work of various different authors and what kind of derivation was involved, the play-sequence *in its final form* was essentially from one hand. There is enough uniformity of style and presentation in the extant version to make this seem almost certain. And certainly, unless we know exactly which parts came from which sources, we are unable to draw any conclusions from the work as a whole except in terms of the author (or compiler, or editor) of the text we now have. In that sense the single author is a logical necessity. If Yen Tun-i is right, this man may not have done his part before the sixteenth century.[2] It is unlikely, however, that at the early extreme he anticipated the opening of the Ming period in the latter part of the fourteenth century. The lines of conventional eulogy of the reigning dynasty which appear in the play's final scene correspond to features in several other plays, all of which appear to derive from the Ming period.[3] This is certainly something which we do not find in the few plays of undeniable Yüan provenance.[4] More specific than this rather circum-

---

[1] The final song in the quoted scene carries an allusion to the coming westward journey, a characteristic which recurs here and throughout the extant six-part sequence: sc. 4, p. 20 (reference to the fetching of the scriptures), sc. 8, p. 36 (to the coming experience at Hua-kuo shan), sc. 12, p. 55 (to the coming rescue by Erh-lang), sc. 16, p. 73 (to the Land of Women and Huo-yen shan), sc. 20, p. 90 (to the imminent end of the journey). In each case these allusions fall at the close of one of the six sub-plays into which the sequence is divided.

[2] Yen Tun-i (1954), p. 149 ff.

[3] Cf. Yen Tun-i (1954), p. 149; (1960), pp. 46–7; and below, ch. 9, pp. 130–3. For the passage in the original text, cf. sc. 24, p. 104.

[4] Thirty plays extant in Yüan printed editions: reproduced in *Ku-pen hsi-ch'ü ts'ung-k'an*, Fourth Series; critical punctuated edition, Cheng Ch'ien (1962).

stantial point is a remark from the preface to a late Ming anthology, *Wan-huo ch'ing-yin*[a], in which four scenes are quoted from a source named as *Hsi-yu chi*. Two of the four correspond to scenes in the present sequence.[1] In his preface the anthologist, styled Chih-yün chü-shih[b] and writing in 1624, explains:

Here, for the most part, I have not selected works by Yüan authors for inclusion, but have picked out the best among the famous writers of our present Dynasty to edit and print.[2]

If, finally, Sun K'ai-ti was right in laying the entire sequence at the door of Yang Ching-yen, it remains likely that the work was completed under the Ming: Yang is known to have died at some point after the beginning of the Yung-lo[c] reign (1403–), and therefore knew more than thirty years of Ming rule.[3]

One further point is more in the nature of a reservation than an assumption. Whatever conclusions may be drawn about individual scenes as quoted in different sources, nearly always in the form of song-suites devoid of dialogue, the very explicit prose dialogue of the present twenty-four-scene version carries no guarantee of belonging in the same form to earlier versions of the play. Students of *tsa-chü* drama are familiar with the discrepancy in dialogue between the thirty plays preserved in Yüan prints and their equivalents in later collections, principally the *Yüan-ch'ü hsüan* (*q.v.*). What appears in the Yüan editions specifies not much more than stage cues for the convenience of spectators or actors. It seems most likely that the long and often wordy sequences of dialogue in later texts were supplied, or at least greatly expanded, by actors or editors of a much later age.[4] In the case of the *Hsi-yu chi* play the implications are clear. So much of the action and circumstantial detail of the story is entrusted to the dialogue alone that the play as a whole offers no authoritative insight into the story-tradition in society at large before the sixteenth century. We can certainly note variants in the episodes and their contents: we cannot use them to construct a meaningful chronology of development.

---

[1] Sc. 4 and 10, the latter quoted under a slightly different heading: cf. Sun K'ai-ti (1939), pp. 396–7. The question of the two remaining scenes will be introduced at the end of this chapter.

[2] Quoted by Yen Tun-i (1954), p. 150. The original text is not available to me.

[3] Cf. *Lu-kuei pu hsü-pien*, p. 284; Sun K'ai-ti (1953), pp. 56–7.

[4] Cf. Cheng Ch'ien (1961), p. 207.

[a] 萬壑清音   [b] 止雲居士   [c] 永樂

Characteristics of the twenty-four act 'Hsi-yu chi'

This sequence of plays is uniquely long in *tsa-chü* literature: only the five-part *Hsi-hsiang chi* often attributed to Wang Shih-fu is of comparable length. At the same time it has been accepted that the verse-writing is of some quality, and the fact that Yün-k'ung chü-shih devoted most of his *General Discourse* to the citation of fine lines from it suggests that for him the play's main attraction lay in its verse.[1] Within the play itself there are scenes whose only *raison d'être* is to carry a quantity of verse and which make virtually no contribution to the progress of the action.[2] Much about this play becomes clear when it is seen as a literary work, set in a particular dramatic form. The author's handling of his material shows signs of being dictated by the well-developed lyrical medium in which he was working.

The inherited convention of *tsa-chü* drama was that all sung numbers in a given *che*[a] (act, or scene) were to be rendered by one actor, male or female, specified in each case as the 'lead' (*cheng-mo*[b] and *cheng-tan*[c]). The acts frequently took the form of sustained expression of a single dominant emotion. Although the leading actor was free, at the change of scene, to reappear as another character in the play, he could represent only such characters as accorded with his own general style of performance. To a certain extent there was a conventional range of hero and heroine types.

The *Hsi-yu chi* story, so well suited to the flexibility of prose narration (and particularly, as the hundred-chapter novel shows, that form which can resort at will to the use of descriptive verse), rarely affords scope for concentrating and sustaining climaxes of individual feeling. The novelist resolutely stresses this by introducing rude bathos at certain moments of potential emotional climax: the small local tragedies are incidental to the drift of the whole story and are seldom allowed to declaim in their own right.[3] With such a subject the *tsa-chü* poet is hard-pressed to

---

[1] *Hsi-yu chi tsa-chü, Tsung-lun*, pp. 2 ff. Chao Ching-shen (1935), p. 274 adds his own selection.

[2] E.g. sc. 18, with the songs of the Taoist; sc. 20, with little more than the songs of Mother-Lightning; sc. 21, with the homiletic songs of the Poor Woman.

[3] In illustration one may briefly cite the intended dignity of the close of the 'Land of Women' episode (*HYC*, ch. 54, p. 630), where the Queen seems almost about to become a Dido, but which is dramatically broken up by the female demon who bears away Tripitaka; or again, the sharp contrast between the despairing Ch'en[d] household, whose two small children are to be sacrificed to a monster, and the gay preparations of Sun Wu-k'ung and Chu Pa-chieh to take their place (*HYC*, ch. 47, pp. 542 ff.).

[a] 折   [b] 正末   [c] 旦   [d] 陳

DHY

find suitable lyrical material and suitable characters to render the different suites of songs. In the event, the author of this six-part version has met his difficulties by giving priority to the *tsa-chü* requirements.

He allots the first four scenes to the story of the abandoned child Chiang-liu—a theme of proven dramatic value which is known, from the testimony of Hsü Wei, to have inspired a Southern drama in what he terms the 'Sung-Yüan' period.[1] This *tsa-chü* sequence thus becomes the first known work in which the story was related to the Western Pilgrimage. The centre-point of these emotionally charged scenes is the mother, who sings throughout, in one sweep.

The lyrical dramatist's real problem begins with the westward journey. His main resource in treating it is the 'abducted maiden' theme, which he invokes at three different points and which provides him with singers for five of the remaining acts—(sc. 9, 11, 13, 14, 15). Here again is tested dramatic material: in the context of the White Ape legend[2] this 'abduction' theme was itself the subject of an early Southern play.[3] In giving the stage to a heroine in distress it naturally supplies the needs of a lyrical medium. The disadvantage is that in doing so it makes of itself a self-contained unit not easily subordinated to the progress of a larger whole. Thus, while it is relatively successful in the episode of Chu Pa-chieh (sc. 13–16), where it fills the dimensions of a whole conventional play and becomes a complete independent episode,[4] it drags heavily in the scene in which Sun Hsing-che is captured (sc. 9). This is a key episode of sufficient narrative interest in itself—yet the battle which forms its natural climax has here to wait while the abducted Princess sings appropriately to her own situation, and the scene can resume only when she has been dismissed.[5]

Among the 'leading actors' who sing in other scenes a surprising number have no significant role in the story as a whole. Some, as suggested above, are there to sing a text of no particular dramatic value— effectively a stylistic demonstration by the author (e.g. the Taoist in sc. 18). Others are harder to account for: such as the Mountain Spirit

---

[1] *Nan-tz'u hsü-lu*, p. 251. Cf. above, p. 67, n. 2.

[2] See below, ch. 8, pp. 114 ff.

[3] *Nan-tz'u hsü-lu*, p. 250.

[4] There is reason enough to believe that an 'abduction-rescue' story was associated with the capture of Chu Pa-chieh even in traditional versions of *Hsi-yu chi*. Certainly the hundred-chapter novel makes use of a comparable theme (ch. 18).

[5] Needless to say, this scene, free of any abduction motif, fills the first eight chapters of the novel. There is no positive evidence that Sun Hsing-che abducted a wife in other traditional versions.

in sc. 10 ('Sun is caught, the charm rehearsed'), an important scene involving three principal characters—Sun Hsing-che, Tripitaka and Kuan-yin. The author must have had his own good reason for passing over all three to give the songs to a completely dispensable secondary figure.

Of the three, Sun Hsing-che is not eligible to sing a full suite because he is evidently created for one of the non-singing 'buffoon' roles—*ching*[a] or *ch'ou*[b]—of the *tsa-chü* drama. This shows clearly in his dialogue (the facetious remarks in sc. 15, p. 68; the comic battle of words in sc. 21, pp. 93–4), in his acrobatic turns (the somersault required in sc. 19, p. 88); and in his four single songs, distinct from the mode and sequence of the suite proper, which he announces himself, usually adding the name of the tune.[1] Two of the songs are ribald, another obscene. That he is cast in such a role may also help to explain why, in this version, he is unexpectedly represented as an abductor.

Tripitaka fails to sing at any point in the twenty-four scenes. For such an important character in the play this certainly seems paradoxical, and can surely be only explicable again in terms of the actor-types. The eighteenth-century anthology *Chui po-ch'iu* (*q.v.*), quoting a scene from another *Hsi-yu chi* play, marks all dialogue attributable to Tripitaka to be spoken by the *lao-tan*[c] actor.[2] This example, while not offering direct access to earlier *tsa-chü* casting conventions, at least demonstrates that Tripitaka was not necessarily easy to cast in a conventional male role, nor, of course, in the 'heroine' style of role. The figure of an exemplary monk can rarely have occupied so important a place in any dramatic action;[3] such a hero in the *Hsi-yu chi* was plainly ill-suited to the resources of a *tsa-chü* dramatist. His failure to sing either here, in scene 10, or at other such suitable moments as his departure in scene 5 (where the singing is done by a more orthodox venerable male character in Yü-ch'ih Kung), may thus be explained simply in terms of *tsa-chü* conventions of casting.

The same can only be supposed of Kuan-yin, who also has no song throughout the play. The Mountain Spirit thus gains the hardly de-

---

[1] Sc. 9, p. 42, sc. 15, pp. 66 and 70, sc. 17, p. 80. Chao Ching-shen (1959*b*), pp. 11–12 cites other examples of single songs from subordinate characters inserted into particular scenes in Yüan *tsa-chü*. In the case of one of Sun's songs, the *Chi-sheng-ts'ao* in scene 17, Chao suggests (1935), pp. 274–5, that this, a universally popular tune in the mid-sixteenth century, may have been inserted by later actors.

[2] i.e. an older female role. Cf. *Chui po-ch'iu*, eighth collection, 3:116 ff.

[3] The abbot Tan-hsia in scenes 3 and 4 of this play, for instance, is naturally subordinate to the leading female role.

[a] 淨   [b] 丑   [c] 老旦

served distinction of singing scene 10 by default, because the material of the *Hsi-yu chi* story can provide no more suitable singer.

A further embarrassment confronting the dramatist must have been the sheer wealth of incident traditionally associated with the story. The account given in *Pak t'ongsa ŏnhae*[1] specifies a dozen incidents on the journey alone, most of which survived in some form to reappear in the hundred-chapter novel. In spite of the broad canvas the playwright was using here, the *tsa-chü* genre was too slow-moving to permit him the same lavishness with incidents and characters as the author of an extended narrative work. Some discrepancies in the organization of the plot are accountable as ill-concealed adaptations for the sake of economy.

In scene 9 the capture of Sun Hsing-che is carried out by the Devarāja Li with his Third Son Naṭa, assisted by the Seven Sages of Mei-shan[a]. In the course of the scene the Devarāja Li commands his son:

Comb this mountain thoroughly, together with the Seven Sages of Mei-shan.[2]

One unique feature of this account is that the monkey's captor is Naṭa and not Erh-lang, who is invoked only for the capture of Chu Pa-chieh in scene 16. (The traditional story as reflected in both the *Pak t'ongsa ŏnhae* (p. 293) and the later novel (*HYC*, p. 61) calls in Erh-lang expressly to clinch the campaign.) The Seven Sages of Mei-shan in fact belong essentially to the Erh-lang legend: the place lay in the neighbourhood of Chia-chou[b], a Szechuan sub-prefecture where one of the Erh-lang legends had its origin.[3] Elsewhere in *tsa-chü* literature the Sages appear only in company with Erh-lang.[4] Their appearance in this scene without him is unprecedented and must suggest that Erh-lang did originally belong there, only to be removed by the dramatist. The same is true of the phrase 'comb the hills' (*sou-shan*[c]), a hunting expression used characteristically of Erh-lang in his search for demons. When Erh-lang does enter in scene 16 he is attended by his hunting hounds[d]—familiar attributes of this hunter-figure; his other attendants are named in the same passage—Kuo Ya-chih[e], Chin-t'ou nu[f],[5] but not the Seven Sages. Various elements of the Erh-lang legend are thus divided between the two parallel scenes 9 and 16. The author has apparently decided to spread his material, either to avoid a duplication of Erh-lang in different

---

[1] See above, pp. 73–4.   [2] *Hsi-yu chi tsa-chü*, p. 42.
[3] Huang Chih-kang, p. 40.
[4] For a discussion of the relevant plays, see below, ch. 9, pp. 129 ff.
[5] For variants of these names, see below, p. 131.

[a] 眉山七聖   [b] 嘉州   [c] 搜山   [d] 細犬   [e] 郭壓直   [f] 金頭奴

scenes (in the gloss to *Pak t'ongsa*[1] we are not told whether Erh-lang figured in the latter), or to thin out an unmanageable stage-full of colourful characters in the earlier scene. If so, it is no longer anomalous, when we compare the various extant versions, that Erh-lang should capture the monkey both in the (? fifteenth-century) version cited in *Pak t'ongsa ŏnhae* and in the sixteenth-century novel, but not in this *tsa-chü*; conversely, it may also be true, and explicable, that only in the *tsa-chü* sequence is Chu Pa-chieh captured by Erh-lang.

Still more economy seems to have been exercised in treating the role of Kuan-yin. In the *Pak t'ongsa ŏnhae* (p. 294) it is said to be her (? his) intercession before the Jade Emperor which secures a reprieve for the monkey; he is then sent under escort to be imprisoned under the mountain. In the play (sc. 9, p. 42) she assumes the whole responsibility herself:

I have come expressly to convert this ape so that he may be a disciple to Tripitaka and go to the Western Paradise to fetch scriptures. Don't kill him!

This is again apparently the result of reducing and redistributing the material. In scene 7 ('Moksha sells a horse') Kuan-yin responds to cries for help from a Dragon of the Southern Sea. Then she explains:

Just now by the way I met the Fiery Dragon Third Crown Prince. For 'causing insufficient and delayed rainfall' he was guilty of a capital offence. I went up to the Nine Heavens and submitted a memorial to the Jade Emperor. I have succeeded in saving this spirit and have had him change into a white horse to attend Tripitaka and bear the scriptures for him from the Western Paradise back to the East. After that he will be able to return to the Southern Sea and to his life as a dragon.[2]

The Fiery Dragon-Prince who becomes a horse is a figure we meet already on the face of the Western Pagoda at Zayton. The dragon of the Ching River who offends by disregarding the precise terms of his orders to send down rain appears independently in the *Yung-lo ta-tien* fragment. The hundred-chapter novel treats them as two distinct and quite unrelated characters, duly reserving the title Crown Prince for the dragon who is to become a horse. The second dragon, who appears in chapters 10 and 11, provides the occasion for T'ai-tsung's visit to Hell and is then simply dismissed from the story. Such an inconclusive departure suggests in itself that this dragon and its episode not only had come independently into the *Hsi-yu chi* tradition but also had never been

---

[1] *PTS*, p. 294 (N vi): cf. below, App. B, p. 184.
[2] *Hsi-yu chi tsa-chü*, p. 30.

fundamentally involved with other parts of the cycle. But the play here fuses the two dragons into one: the beheading of the dragon from the Ching River is suppressed outright, and the offender is identified directly with the Third Crown Prince, who then becomes a white horse. The dramatist contrives this by means of Kuan-yin's intercession: the beheading and the subsequent implication of T'ai-tsung in the story are neatly by-passed, the dragon receives its pardon, Tripitaka acquires the services of a magic horse. The story is brought up to date within a few lines, but at the expense of a distinction between two dragon figures which seem traditionally to have had quite different functions.[1] If the dramatist seems reluctant to complicate his action with another appeal by Kuan-yin in the scene of the monkey's capture but chooses to have her assume instead the full role of *deus ex machina*, it is perhaps for similar motives as were suggested above—a distaste for repetition and an urgent need for simplicity in handling a story which had not been framed for such a discipline.[2]

To sum up: there is reason to suppose that demands of the *tsa-chü* medium led the dramatist into various adjustments of his material—particularly the unfamiliar emphasis in his choice of episodes and the strange prominence given to minor characters in the various singing roles. His organization of the plot seems in certain respects at odds with what other sources testify about the tradition. Too little traditional material remains for the point to be judged conclusively; but the treatment characteristic of this *tsa-chü*, in at least one case (Erh-lang) cited above, involves the modification of an independent legend which, whether in *Hsi-yu chi* works or elsewhere, never appears treated in a similar way. About the 'beheaded dragon' theme we cannot speak with as much confidence, beyond saying that here the play is at odds with the one well-attested *Hsi-yu chi* version of the fourteenth century.

In other scenes, particularly at points where action is stressed in stage direction and spoken dialogue, the play offers confirmation of popular themes known to us from other sources. Such are the entry of the Red Boy (Hung-hai-erh), weighing intolerably on the back of Sun Hsing-che,

---

[1] It should be noted that the summaries supplied in *Pak t'ongsa ŏnhae* make no mention of either dragon.

[2] It may be convenient to add in reminder that the hundred-chapter version exposes the monkey Sun Wu-k'ung to a would-be execution, under sentence from the Jade Emperor; after his subsequent escape he is re-sentenced and effectively confined beneath Wu-hsing shan by the Buddha. Kuan-yin is concerned in this action only later, when the question arises of his release.

ordered to carry him;[1] Sun Hsing-che's masquerade as bride of the
abductor Chu Pa-chieh;[2] Sha Ho-shang's adornment of skulls, remnants
from previous incarnations of Tripitaka;[3] the iron fan of T'ieh-shan
kung-chu, able to quench the flames of Huo-yen shan.[4] These were
themes clearly entrenched in the tradition: but on the strength of the
play alone we cannot presume to draw any more precise conclusions
about them.

Wu Ch'ang-ling's play and the extant single scenes

To his article Sun K'ai-ti appends a survey of isolated scenes from
plays on the *Hsi-yu chi* theme found in various dramatic anthologies.[5]
The greater number of the scenes correspond to individual scenes in
the extant six-part *Hsi-yu chi*. In two of the anthologies the source is
described as *Hsi-yu chi*, in a third as *Hsi-t'ien ch'ü ching*. Of all the
quoted scenes only the two appearing in *Wan-huo ch'ing-yin* (cf. above,
p. 80) give dialogue as well as songs.

There remain two frequently quoted scenes which are not to be
found in the present sequence of plays. One represents the meeting
between Tripitaka and two Moslems; the other is equivalent in subject
to scene 5 of the extant play (the scene of Tripitaka's departure, attended
by an aged Yü-ch'ih Ching-te) but has a completely different text. We
know from the titles given in Chia Chung-ming's revision of *Lu-kuei pu*
that Wu Ch'ang-ling's *tsa-chü* had an episode on an old Moslem as one
of its central features.[6] Sun K'ai-ti goes so far as to conclude that both
this stray 'Moslem' scene and the variant 'departure' scene derive from
Wu Ch'ang-ling's lost play.[7]

Both appear in the *Wan-huo ch'ing-yin*, where the source is named as
Hsi-yu chi: superficially the same as the source of the other two quoted
scenes discussed above.[8] Later anthologies variously give the titles *T'ang
San-tsang*, *Lien-hua pao-fa*[a], *An-t'ien hui*[b] as their sources.[9] One even
attributes the two scenes separately, one to a *T'ang San-tsang*, the other
to *Lien-hua pao-fa*.[10]

---

[1] Sc. 12, p. 51. Cf. *HYC*, ch. 40, pp. 463–4; *PTS*, p. 267 (N iii).
[2] Sc. 16, p. 70. Cf. *HYC*, ch. 18, p. 209. The same device is found in the *Shui-hu
chuan* in a scene between Lu Chih-shen and Chou T'ung (*SHC*, ch. 5, pp. 83 ff.);
cf. also *Nan-yu chi*, ch. 6, p. 69.
[3] Sc. 11, p. 47. Cf. above, ch. 1, p. 21.   [4] Sc. 18, pp. 82–3. Cf. *HYC*, pp. 677 ff.
[5] Sun K'ai-ti (1939) pp. 388–98.   [6] Cf. above, p. 77.
[7] Sun K'ai-ti (1939), pp. 368 and 373.   [8] Cf. above, p. 80.
[9] Sun K'ai-ti (1939), p. 396.
[10] *Na-shu-ying ch'ü-p'u*, *cheng-chi*[c] 2 and *hsü*[d]*-chi* 2.

[a] 蓮花寶筏   [b] 安天會   [c] 正集   [d] 續

Of these titles, only *T'ang San-tsang* offers any sign of relevance to Wu Ch'ang-ling: the words appeared in the full title of Wu's play as given in the revised *Lu-kuei pu*, and could conceivably be derived from it as a short title. But this point is far too tenuous for comfort. The other titles all bring some problem in their wake, although fortunately none which seems to affect the Wu Ch'ang-ling question at all closely.[1] To judge from a lengthy dramatic treatment of the 'Tripitaka' story entitled *Sheng-p'ing pao-fa*[a], one of a series of adaptations from earlier plays made by Chang Chao[b] (1691–1745),[2] in which both these stray scenes are to be found,[3] the various other works in question here are likely to have been derivative or composite versions of the story, drawing at least some of their material from older plays. This would account straightforwardly for the fact that essentially identical scenes are attributed variously to them in the eighteenth-century anthologies.

In the case of the source used in *Wan-huo ch'ing-yin*, Sun K'ai-ti argues plausibly that the editor Chih-yün chü-shih could himself have met the four scenes as anthology pieces with a life of their own, or as single scenes copied out by players for purposes of individual performance. There are parallel examples to confirm both possibilities.[4] The quoted title *Hsi-yu chi* could then represent simply the story to which the episodes obviously belonged, not necessarily a specific single work.

The hard information that emerges from this confusion of sources is unspectacular:

(1) No evidence points unambiguously to the full title and author of the play, or plays, from which the 'Moslem' and 'departure' scenes were taken. Only the feature of a Moslem's participation associates the former with Wu Ch'ang-ling's play; only stylistic intuition[5] the latter. It is therefore far from axiomatic that Wu Ch'ang-ling's work is represented here at all.

---

[1] *An-t'ien hui*, given in *Chui po-ch'iu*, eighth collection, 3:115, has not been identified. *Lien-hua pao-fa* resembles the title *Lien-hua fa* which appears with a summary in *Ch'ü-hai tsung-mu t'i-yao*, 35:1651–4, but the story involved is completely different. It seems likely that we have here an alternative version of, perhaps even a mistake for, the title *Sheng-p'ing pao-fa*[a].

[2] Cf. A. W. Hummel (ed.), *Eminent Chinese of the Ch'ing Period* (Washington, 1943–4), p. 25 a.

[3] Cf. the reprint in *Ku-pen hsi-ch'ü ts'ung-k'an*, Ninth series: scenes 16 and 18 in the second volume. The scenes are taken from this source to appear in an appendix to Chao Ching-shen (1956), pp. 163–72.

[4] Cf. Sun K'ai-ti (1939), p. 368.

[5] Cf. *Na-shu-ying ch'ü-p'u*, 2:2b; Sun K'ai-ti (1939), p. 374.

[a] 昇平寶筏   [b] 張照

(2) There is no known trace of either of the two scenes before the anthology *Wan-huo ch'ing-yin* in 1624. As they remain now, quoted in various later anthologies, they sustain an independent existence.

(3) While it is fully possible that various scenes in the extant *Hsi-yu chi* sequence—e.g. scene 12: 'Kuei-mu is converted'—were under the influence of a play by Wu Ch'ang-ling, nothing suggests a textual indebtedness.

6

Reflections in the *Hsiao-shih Chen-k'ung pao-chüan*

Sawada Mizuho, author of currently the longest and most discriminating account of the popular religious and literary genre known as *pao-chüan*[a],[1] has divided the available corpus into two broad periods—'old' and 'new'. Within the former category he discerns three stages: the 'primitive'[b] works, of which no reliably datable examples are available,[2] known to us through a few titles quoted in a printed edition of 1509;[3] it is probable that these represent a form of popular literature akin to Buddhist liturgical texts,[4] current by the end of the fifteenth century but not necessarily much earlier. The second stage begins with the 'scriptures' of the Patriarch Lo[c] (cf. note 3), representing the earliest dated specimens. Within it falls the greater part of a spate of homiletic and expository texts in which the *pao-chüan* medium served as the mouthpiece of many popular sects on the fringes of orthodox Buddhism and Taoism.[5] This 'sectarian'[d] stage took the genre into the seventeenth century. Thereafter, under repressive policies of the Ch'ing government in the early eighteenth century, the *pao-chüan*'s influence as a primarily religious vehicle declined. The class of 'old' *pao-chüan* terminates in the early nineteenth century.[6]

The manuscript text *Hsiao-shih Chen-k'ung*[e] *pao-chüan* belongs within this general class and has indeed played a part in discussions on the origins of the genre. It has attracted an unusual degree of attention

---

[1] 'Hōken sōsetsu'[f], included in Sawada Mizuho (1963).
[2] Both Sawada (1963), pp. 1–2, 6 and Li Shih-yü (*q.v.*), p. 174, cast doubt on the texts which were claimed by Cheng Chen-to (1954), vol. 2, pp. 308, 318, to date from the fourteenth century or before.
[3] The five 'scriptures'[g] attributed to Lo Ch'ing[h]: cf. Sawada (1963), pp. 6, 15, 76.
[4] Sawada (1963), p. 12.
[5] *Ibid.* pp. 15–17.   [6] *Ibid.* pp. 17–18.
[a] 寶卷   [b] 原初   [c] 羅祖   [d] 教派   [e] 銷釋眞空   [f] 寶卷總說
[g] 經卷   [h] 羅清

because it contains in particular a passage alluding to the pilgrimage of Tripitaka. From the time of the text's publication in 1931[1] this has been recognized as a reflection of a *Hsi-yu chi* story. Although by no means long (twenty-eight lines of largely decasyllabic verse), the passage contains a number of proper names which can be related, or at least distantly associated, with episodes known to us from other sources.

Potentially this material is of great interest, but, as with each of the above sources, no useful evaluation is possible without first ascertaining both the period of the work itself and the nature of this allusive passage in particular. About both questions there is disagreement.

Date

The work first became known in connection with a group of texts in the Tangut (Hsi-hsia[a]) script, recovered from Ninghsia and bought by the Peking National Library in 1929. It was listed in a catalogue of this material published in May/June 1930, under the heading 'Appended list of old prints of scriptures and miscellaneous texts in the Library's collection'.[2] It was there described as a manuscript 'Buddhist volume'[b], of fifty-nine pages[c]. (The opening of the manuscript is missing.)

Hu Shih, in an article[d] concerned formally with the text's date,[3] pointed out that it had been assigned to the 'Sung or Yüan' periods by association with the early Hsi-hsia prints with which it had been discovered.[4] (This represents the most explicit published information we have concerning the text's origin.) Hu's retort—that nothing prevents texts of widely differing periods from being together in one place, as they were at Tun-huang—is sound. More precise criteria of dating are needed than this.

The first and most substantial internal clue is the title applied to Confucius in the twenty-fourth line:[5] Ta-ch'eng chih-sheng wen-hsüan wang[e]. This name was conferred by the Yüan emperor Wu-tsung[f] in the year 1307[6] and modified into a new form (Chih-sheng hsien-shih[g]) only in 1530.[7] The dates define roughly a span of time within

---

[1] In *Kuo-li Pei-p'ing t'u-shu-kuan kuan-k'an*, 5,3 (1931), pp. 13–47. The passage relevant to Tripitaka's pilgrimage runs from line 30 to line 56.
[2] *Kuo-li Pei-p'ing t'u-shu-kuan kuan-k'an*, 4,3 (1930), p. 339.   [3] Hu Shih (1931).
[4] *Ibid.* p. 1.   [5] Line references follow the lineation marked in the 1931 printed version.
[6] *Yüan shih*, 22:9*b*. Cf. Hu Shih (1931), p. 1.
[7] *Ta Ming hui-tien*[h] (revised edition of 1587 by Shen Ming-hsing[i] and others), 91:19*b* and 22*a*. Hu Shih (1931), p. 1.

[a] 西夏   [b] 梵帙   [c] 頁   [d] 跋   [e] 大成至聖文宣王
[f] 武宗   [g] 至聖先師   [h] 大明會典   [i] 申明行

which we may presume the *pao-chüan* to have been written: from the early fourteenth to the mid-sixteenth centuries. This period encompasses the time at which the first dated *pao-chüan* appeared—i.e. the early sixteenth century.

The second stage in Hu Shih's argument—inferring that the work's allusive passage derived its material from the hundred-chapter novel and dated in fact from the end of the sixteenth or early seventeenth century[1]—rests so obviously on fallacious assumptions and has been so laboriously refuted by Yü P'ing-po (*q.v.*) that it need not detain us here.

Yü P'ing-po alone claims that the manuscript in places observes the taboo on Sung imperial names, but he qualifies this at once by allowing for scribal errors.[2] Only small sections of the text have been photographically reproduced:[3] in present circumstances it is impossible to judge this point. Until there is confirmation one way or the other it should not affect our argument.

Considering the *Hsiao-shih Chen-k'ung pao-chüan* as a text, one is bound to recognize that it shares many characteristics of form and content with *pao-chüan* of Sawada's 'sectarian' stage, in the sixteenth century and later.

Although the opening of the text as such is missing, the first passages of the manuscript fragment clearly belong to an introductory section. Lines 1–12 represent all but the first three or four lines of an exhortation to turn to the Three Jewels[a]—Buddha, Dharma and Saṅgha. Lines 13–14 are an invocation to the Buddhas, announcing the burning of incense: both were almost universal introductory features of *pao-chüan* in the 'sectarian' stage.[4] The words of this invocation are moreover virtually identical to those used in the *Hsiao-shih Ta-sheng*[b] *pao-chüan*, printed in 1584.[5] They are followed immediately by the 'Opening *gāthā*'[c] (also a universal feature), whose text here corresponds almost exactly to that used in the *Yao-shih pen-yüan kung-te*[d] *pao-chüan* of 1543.[6] Precisely the same verses are used again in the lines immediately preceding the 'Opening *gāthā*' of the 1584 *Hsiao-shih Ta-sheng pao-chüan*.[7]

---

[1] Hu Shih (1931), pp. 4 ff.   [2] Yü P'ing-po, p. 182.
[3] Lines 31–55 and 586–8, reproduced in *Kuo-li Pei-p'ing t'u-shu-kuan kuan-k'an*, 4,6 (1930) and 5,3 (1931). The passages offer no evidence helpful on this point.
[4] Cf. Sawada (1963), p. 26.
[5] Quoted by Sawada Mizuho (1963), p. 27, l. 7.
[6] Quoted by Cheng Chen-to (1954), vol. 2, p. 312. On *K'ai-ching chieh*, cf. Li Shih-yü, p. 170, Sawada (1963), pp. 26 ff.   [7] Sawada (1963), p. 27, ll. 13–14.
[a] 三寶   [b] 銷釋大乘   [c] 開經偈   [d] 藥師本願功德

There follows a passage of verse (seven syllable lines) reviewing the Three Doctrines of the Buddhas, Lao-chün and Confucius and finding them reducible to a transcendent One.[1] The syncretic theme is equally familiar in extant early *pao-chüan* literature.[2] The pilgrimage of Tripitaka appears at this point (line 28), to add an elaborate illustration to the author's religious apologia. Simultaneously the verse-form shifts from a seven-syllable line to the 3–3–4 rhythm of the standard *pao-chüan* metre[3] and sustains this throughout the catalogue of names and incidents on Tripitaka's journey. The religious exposition which forms the *pao-chüan*'s substance is introduced subsequently partly in prose, partly in further passages of the decasyllabic verse. Near the close of the work are two sets of songs for the Five Watches[a] of the night, set to the popular tunes *Wu-yeh-erh*[b] and *Huang-ying-erh*[c] respectively.[4] Sawada has suggested that the use of such tunes in *pao-chüan* may not have become usual until after the period (early sixteenth century) at which the earliest dated texts appeared.[5]

Although its specific sectarian allegiance remains unidentified,[6] the work shows a high degree of uniformity with those from the most flourishing period of the 'old' *pao-chüan* upon which our knowledge of the genre is based. When Sawada Mizuho ventures an opinion that Hu Shih was after all most probably right in his assessment of the *Hsiao-shih Chen-k'ung pao-chüan*,[7] he is by implication speaking of this formal correspondence with the genre as it evolved in the sixteenth century. Clear and positive evidence would be necessary to allow the assumption that it dated from a period long before this, and such evidence is not forthcoming.

[1] Lines 19–27.   [2] Cf. Li Shih-yü, pp. 171–2; Sawada (1963), pp. 43–4.
[3] Cf. Li Shih-yü, p. 170; Sawada (1963), p. 31.
[4] Lines 534–67.
[5] Sawada (1963), p. 14; cf. p. 32. Fu Yün-tzu, in a study of the popular song sequences known as *nao wu-keng*[d], associates the phenomenon in its secular context specifically with the Ming period (Fu Yün-tzu, pp. 249 ff.). Chao Wei-pang, analysing the information on *pao-chüan* to be gathered from the unique work *P'o-hsieh hsiang-pien*[e] by Huang Yü-p'ien[f] (early nineteenth century), draws attention to his mention of the tune *Huang-ying-erh* in this connection (Chao, p. 111).
[6] The figure Chen-k'ung Lao-tsu[g], whose name appears recurrently throughout the text, was the highest god in the pantheon worshipped by the Hung-yang sect[h], founded in 1594 (Chao Wei-pang, pp. 96–8). But more detailed evidence will be required before the question is decided.
[7] Sawada (1963), pp. 1–2. But he does not subject the work to any more detailed examination.

[a] 五更   [b] 梧葉兒   [c] 黃鶯兒   [d] 鬧五更   [e] 破邪詳辯
[f] 黃育楩   [g] 眞空老祖   [h] 紅陽教

References to a 'Hsi-yu chi' story

The passage reflecting a *Hsi-yu chi* narrative may be rendered as follows:[1]

l. 30   It is told how Tripitaka[a], in the royal palace of the Chen-kuan[2] Emperor,

Vowed to go to the Western Paradise to fetch scriptures.

31   The sage ruler of the T'ang burned precious incense, bowed thrice, and circumambulated nine times.

32   Having burned incense, he brought out the Imperial coach and saw him off from the Golden Gate.[3]

33   He (Tripitaka) brought under control Sun Hsing-che—Ch'i-t'ien Ta-sheng,

34   Chu Pa-chieh[b] and Sha Ho-shang: these 'four sages' kept company together[c].

35   And indeed they encountered Huo-yen shan[d], and passed through Hei-sung lin[e].

36   They met demons and ghosts, fiends in droves.

37   Lo-ch'a nü[f]—the Iron Fang—bringing down the sweet[4] dew.

38   Liu-sha ho[h]—the Red Boy[i]—Ti-yung Fu-jen[j].

39   Niu Mo-wang[k]—the spider demons—snatching him away into[l][5] a cavern.

40   Kuan-shih-yin of the Southern Sea rescuing Tripitaka.

41   They tell of the Master, devoted to the Buddhist Law, great in supernatural powers.

42   Who would have dared to go to the Buddha's land and fetch the holy scriptures?

43   In Mieh-fa kuo[m] he displayed his supernatural powers: Buddhists and Taoists competed in magic.

44   The brave Master's power defeated the evil demons: they were robed and tonsured as monks.

45   The Maitreya Buddha in the Tuṣita Heaven—they desired to hear his holy teaching.

---

[1] In this translation I avoid imposing a single interpretation upon disjointed lines except where the sense is immediately clear.

[2] The original characters read *Cheng-kuan*[n]. I emend *cheng* to read *chen*[o], and hence the phrase to correspond to T'ai-tsung's reign title.

[3] An allusion to the Golden Horse Gate[p] of the Han royal palace. Cf. *Shih-chi* 126:8*b*.

[4] The original character[q] strictly means 'frost', but in the context it seems as if the homophonous *kan-lu*[r] is intended, a phrase which serves as the equivalent of *amṛta*, the Buddhist ambrosia.

[5] For this emendation see Ōta Tatsuo (1965), p. 21.

a 唐僧	b 豬八界	c 根=跟	d 火焰山	e 黑松林
f 羅利女	g 鐵扇	h 流沙河	i 紅孩兒	j 地勇夫人
k 牛魔王	l 設人=攝入	m 滅法國	n 正觀	o 貞
p 金馬門	q 雷	r 甘露		

46 The Land of Perfect Happiness[1]—the Fiery Dragon-horse—a white horse to bear the scriptures.

47 From the Eastern Land to the Paradise in the West[2] was more than 100,000 *li*.

48 Hsi-shih tung[a]—the Land of Women—Tripitaka was hidden away.

49 They reached the Western Paradise and gazed on the sage, attentively doing obeisance.

50 They addressed the Buddha, who extended his merciful kindness, and opened [the great gate].[3]

51 The precious store was opened and they took the holy scriptures, doctrinal texts of the Three Vehicles.

52 In a brief space of time, a moment, they had left the Thunderclap[b] (Monastery).

53 Taking the holy scriptures, they returned to the Eastern Land to have audience with the Emperor.

54 They addressed the Buddha, begging to offer repentance, and he gave out great illumination.

55 They came to the Eastern Land and offered up the holy scriptures. The T'ang Emperor was highly pleased.

56 At the assembly of Golden Spirits (?)[c] they opened the precious store. Every single character was distinct.

The passage presents some peculiar characteristics. Line 47, after the catalogue of perils overcome, sums up the distance of the complete journey (already anticipated in the earlier line 28—'Tripitaka went to the Western Paradise to fetch scriptures: in one journey a distance of 108,000 *li*'); in line 48 yet more incidental perils appear; in line 49 the pilgrims 'reach the Western Paradise', in line 50 'address the Buddha', and by lines 52–3 they are returning to Ch'ang-an; but in line 54 they are again, in the same terms, 'addressing the Buddha' and in line 55 again returning to the East. These repetitions suggest that the author was moved less by a regard for the original story's strict narrative sequence than by a sense of the emotive weight of various key points in it, reinforced by the declamatory rhymed verse in which the whole was here being rehearsed.

More serious puzzles emerge when one considers the content in more

[1] Chi-lo[d] kuo, apparently the Buddhist Chi-lo shih-chieh[e], i.e. Sukhāvatī, the Paradise of the Amitābha Buddha. It is not clear whether this is here distinct from the Western Paradise for which the pilgrims are bound.

[2] In the MS the order of words here appears to be *hsi tao t'ien*, not *tao hsi t'ien* as given in the typeset reprint.

[3] Ta Sha-men[f] is an expression equivalent to the Sanskrit Mahāśramaṇa—i.e. the Buddha. Here the treatment of its final syllable as a word for 'gate' makes the line meaningless.

[a] 戲世洞   [b] 雷音   [c] 金神會   [d] 極樂   [e] 世界   [f] 大沙門

detail, and Ōta Tatsuo has devoted a recent article (1965) to their tentative elucidation. The simple identification of individual names and episodes is straightforward, and nothing need be added, on this level, to his tabular summary (1965, p. 28). If, however, this material is to yield more than a random list of names we must face the problems of relating together various individual names which find themselves grouped together.

Line 38—in which Liu-sha ho, the Red Boy and Ti-yung Fu-jen keep company, although in all known versions of the story they belong to quite different episodes;

line 39—where the three allusions seem, in the light of other versions, equally unrelated;

lines 43–4—presenting in outline an episode which incorporates features from two independent episodes (as we know them in the *Pak t'ongsa* and hundred-chapter sources);

lines 45–6—introducing two Buddhist heavens which have no significant place in the known versions;

line 48—three allusions again unexpectedly brought together.

Ōta Tatsuo has expended some ingenuity on a series of elaborate explanations; and he claims with some confidence to have shown the work serving as the source for these allusions to be 'in the same tradition' as the 'Yüan' version of the story used in *Pak t'ongsa ŏnhae*, and to be probably earlier than it.[1] His case rests upon these assumptions:

1. That the *Pak t'ongsa ŏnhae* reflects, in its annotations, a *Hsi-yu chi* of Yüan date.
2. That the *pao-chüan* may, regardless of its own date, represent a Yüan source.[2]
3. That the text of the *pao-chüan* reproduces with reliable accuracy the order and episodic elements of its *Hsi-yu chi* source.[3]

The first has been challenged above (p. 68): nothing *guarantees* a date earlier than the late fifteenth century for this particular source. The second assumption is less dangerous: the *pao-chüan* could theoretically reflect a source anticipating its own time of composition by several centuries. But in the light of the discussion above (pp. 91 ff.), suggesting that this *pao-chüan* is unlikely to date from before the sixteenth century,

---

[1] Cf. Ōta (1965), p. 29.
[2] Ōta (1965), pp. 20 and 26 (remarks in connection with the Maitreya cult of Yüan times).   [3] Cf. Ōta (1965), p. 29.

it seems also unlikely, and certainly not necessary, that in practice its author would be using a *Hsi-yu chi* version from two centuries before. The discussion of this material in abstraction from its own external context opens the way for special-pleading.

The crucial decision affecting our understanding of this *pao-chüan* source is that implied in Ōta's third assumption. It requires an act of faith both in the author's memory (unless we imagine him leafing hastily through his *Hsi-yu chi* as he wrote) and in the discipline of his exposition. Ōta accepts the first in, for instance, being willing to interpret lines 43–4 as representing the 'Ch'e-ch'ih kuo' episode in a kinder and hence probably 'older' form: the tonsure administered as a mild alternative to the extermination of the Taoists in *Pak t'ongsa* and the hundred-chapter *Hsi-yu chi*.[1] In the hundred-chapter work, however, Mieh-fa kuo is the scene of a quite different episode in which Sun Wu-k'ung contrives to shave the head of every citizen in the realm, from the king down.[2] Could these two lines not equally reflect a confusion between two different episodes, prompted by an equivocal place-name? In the case of line 38 Ōta advances an even more radical reconstruction: proximity in this line is given as ground for inferring that Ti-yung Fu-jen[3] was in this hypothetical version the mother of the Red Boy—a relationship neither attested nor indicated in any other source. Yet Ōta stops short of implicating either of these characters with Liu-sha ho (in all versions the habitat of Sha Ho-shang), although it claims a place in the same line.[4]

Inevitably, these juxtapositions raise the question of the *pao-chüan*'s authority. Even in the prosaic annotations of Ch'oe Se-chin, expressly intended to summarize aspects of a story for the reader, occasion has been found to question the literal accuracy of his account.[5] In the (infinitely more perfunctory) *pao-chüan* passage informative summary was clearly less important to the author than the rhetorical flight of allusion in lines of ten-syllable verse. Sawada Mizuho has written in a similar connection of the 'self-intoxication' of many *pao-chüan* writers.[6] The genre was of a nature to disregard logic and clarity in the interests of emotive effect and rhetorical formula. Seen in this context Ōta's third and central assumption comes to seem gratuitous. There are no grounds for unfaltering trust in the true reproduction of original episodes, which in

[1] Ōta (1965), pp. 25–6.   [2] *HYC*, ch. 84, pp. 962–3.
[3] Cf. above, p. 73.   [4] Ōta (1965), pp. 23–4.
[5] Cf. above, pp. 69–72.
[6] Sawada (1963), pp. 32-3.

several cases are not even made explicit. Used as the sole basis for re-constructing stories in a radical and unprecedented form, these allusions offer no more than fantastically thin evidence.

We are bound to conclude that the *Hsiao-shih Chen-k'ung pao-chüan* is a source of only limited value. In date it carries no guarantee of antici-pating the sixteenth century. Its authority is so scant as to make any speculative reconstruction—beyond a mere list of individual names—open to serious question. It nevertheless has a contribution to make to our knowledge of the *Hsi-yu chi* tradition. We are of course not obliged to return to Hu Shih's long since discredited proposal that the *pao-chüan*'s allusions were to the hundred-chapter novel. Its author, in writing this passage, was mentally recalling the salient features of an episodic story he might have known in many different forms. He could indeed have had in mind a given prose version of the fifteenth or six-teenth century; and some of his allusions may yet have intruded from other—perhaps oral or dramatic—sources. Although these uncertainties cannot be escaped, the references in lines 45–6 (to the teachings of Maitreya Buddha, and to the Sukhāvatī heaven) offer us traces of epi-sodes which no other source preserves.

APPENDIX

A note on 'Shuo-ch'ang Hsi-yu chi'[a][1]

The editors introduce this text as a manuscript of unknown authorship and date held by the Peking City Library. They describe it as a recasting of the novel *Hsi-yu chi* into a simple *chantefable* form, with about one million words, two thirds consisting of song-texts.

In its present published form it has been subjected to severe editing: several episodes are suppressed (including two which do not occur in the hundred-chapter work), and much of the text itself has been revised. It naturally becomes more difficult for the reader to judge the work's true characteristics than for the editors.

The text as it stands certainly seems to bear out their report. The verse is written in an insistent, jingling metre basically of seven syllables to the line, but in some cases preserves particular wording from the hundred-chapter version.[2] The narrative, in a fluent and essentially modern colloquial idiom (how much the editors' work?), follows so closely the sequence of

---

[1] Edited by Lo Yang[b] and Shen P'eng-nien[c] (Peking, 1956, 2 vols.).

[2] See, for instance, the woodcutter's song (vol. 1, p. 5), clearly related to the text in *HYC*, ch. 1, p. 8.

[a] 說唱西遊記   [b] 羅揚   [c] 沈彭年

names and events in the hundred chapters that one is readily able to take it provisionally as a later revision of the novel. Technically it must therefore count as falling outside the scope of this study.

It merits at least a note in passing for the sake of the new episodes said to be introduced in the manuscript. They are designated in the editors' prefatory note as 'the fight with the White Ape' and the 'Five Demon Women'[a]. The White Ape figure will be considered independently below. What is of interest here is that a text corresponding so closely in content to the hundred-chapter version presumed to be its original could yet include extraneous episodes. It is impossible to judge, especially when the episodes themselves are not available to be read, whether they were derived from current oral traditions or from clear-cut written sources. The simple fact of their presence reflects back on the *Hsi-yu chi* tradition as a whole: even at the advanced stage represented by the hundred-chapter novel the constitution of the cycle was open to variation.

The Japanese manuscript 'Genjō Sanzō toten yurai engi'[b]

Ōta Tatsuo has recently drawn attention to this manuscript text, preserved in Ryūkoku University Library.[1] It is described as a version, in 98 pages and about 100,000 words, of the *Hsi-yu chi*. Although closely resembling the story as told in the hundred-chapter Chinese novel, it is distinct from it in two important ways: (1) certain episodes differ in their content, sequence, and situation in the story; (2) the work as a whole takes the form of a script[c] for popular religious exposition as used by the Amidist Shinshū[d] sect. Internal evidence suggests a period *circa* early nineteenth century for the text as such. Ōta nonetheless finds in it grounds for a more far-reaching hypothesis: that it ultimately reflects a version of the story earlier than the hundred-chapter novel.[2]

I have not seen this text and am not in a position to form a separate judgement. In the sense that the defined scope of this study concerns evidence 'known to antedate' the hundred-chapter work, the present manuscript claims no place here. It seems sufficient to refer the reader to Ōta's study, at the same time pointing out the main assumptions which underlie it. They include those which have been questioned above in chapters 4 and 6. Ōta posits (*a*) a distinct Japanese translation (of which no other trace survives), serving as a basis for the present 'sectarian' script;[3] (*b*) the Chinese original of that hypothetical translation, conceived as an antecedent to the hundred-

---

[1] Ōta Tatsuo (1967).

[2] The early Ming, i.e. late fourteenth century, is suggested as a tentative date (Ōta (1967), p. 9).

[3] Ōta (1967), p. 9.

[a] 五㒵女   [b] 玄奘三藏渡天由來緣起   [c] 台本   [d] 眞宗

chapter work. The assumptions involved here are—first, that the form of those episodes slightly at odds with the hundred-chapter version necessarily implies a distinct original text and cannot be the result of editing and revision by the author of *Genjō Sanzō toten yurai engi*;[1] secondly, that when one version of a story is written with less sophistication than another, it is by that token to be regarded as older than the other.[2]

[1] See, for instance, Ōta (1967), pp. 5–6.
[2] See, for instance, Ōta (1967), p. 6.

7

Putting the Sources to Use

It is now possible to say something about the collective value of the sources described above. They give us a basic assurance that published treatments of popular 'Tripitaka' cycles were appearing from the thirteenth down to the sixteenth centuries; but by no means all represent with equal fidelity what the public from time to time would have seen and read. In this respect certainly the greatest value lies in the 'Kōzanji' text which, apart from being the earliest source, is unquestionably first-hand material. The fragment in the *Yung-lo ta-tien* is likely to stand close to the text of its original, but we lose, both by lacking the remainder of the text, and by being unable to see the original printed format. The same disadvantages apply again to the testimony of the *Pak t'ongsa ŏnhae*, but there is also some ambiguity as to how many versions are involved, and a further suspicion that here the material has suffered some distortion in reaching us at second hand. The *tsa-chü* play in twenty-four acts, at best of questionable authorship, is in any case subject to all the uncertainties that attach to the text—in particular the dialogue—of a belated, seventeenth-century dramatic edition; it also shows signs of some manipulation in the interests of literary expediency. The names and episodes listed in the *Hsiao-shih Chen-k'ung pao-chüan*—in all likelihood a sixteenth-century text—give insufficient grounds for useful speculation.

With these reservations in mind we may attempt an estimation in general terms of what the sources testify about the tradition as a whole.

The *Hsi-yu chi* is the story of a journey and by its nature lends itself to episodic treatment: it exactly meets the needs of the professional teller of tales, who naturally desires freedom to expand or suppress his material at will and, as an individual performer, is likely also to specialize in certain episodes which best suit his talents and his public. Theoretically we should be prepared for a complete lack of congruity between different versions appearing at different times. In fact, the sources which have here been examined reflect on this question in two distinct ways.

1. Between the Kōzanji version and all its known successors there is an extreme discrepancy in content. Many episodes are simply not to be found in any later text; there are certain names (e.g. Kuei-tzu-mu) which, although they do reappear, are involved in utterly different episodes. In a few cases (the monkey-disciple, the spirit of the sands, the Land of Women, the Heart Sūtra), a semblance of the original feature persists in all later sources, but strongly developed in a way which, altogether, leaves the Kōzanji version clearly dissociated from what seems a more closely knit group of later texts. For a period of centuries before the probable appearance of this version, we lack coherent written evidence of popular story-cycles on the 'Tripitaka' theme. The twelfth and thirteenth centuries—the closing part of this period—were the very time during which the oral and dramatic arts of the Sung capitals were so abundantly attested by contemporary witnesses. It begs no controversy to regard the period as one in which popular traditions were carried on more universally in the oral medium than in writing. The background of the Kōzanji version, so much of whose material can be identified with themes in the broad field of later popular fiction and in that of Asian folklore at large, lay in the comparatively free oral traffic of this period. Much of the material may have been derived from what the original compiler had himself seen and heard in his own locality; it can by no means be expected to represent even a substantial part of the 'Tripitaka' legends abroad elsewhere in China. Nor should every episode be regarded as permanently associated with a 'Tripitaka' cycle. The central topic of Wu Ch'ang-ling's lost play *Hsi-t'ien ch'ü-ching*—an encounter with a Moslem—suggests another such episode, evidently associated with 'Tripitaka' cycles in the north during the thirteenth century,[1] of which there is no sign in subsequent prose works.

The Kōzanji version is so placed as to reflect both the freedom with which the old traditions were circulating and, dimly, the coming shape and some of the more permanent features of the developed cycle known to us in later versions. It shares with them a simple but characteristic framework, in which a formal imperial commission replaces the embarrassing secrecy forced upon the historical Hsüan-tsang at the outset of his journey, and the returned, triumphant pilgrim, after completing his immediate mission, is borne up promptly to the heavens and

[1] On the assumption that Wu Ch'ang-ling was a northerner. Cf. above, p. 75.

installed in the Western Paradise. This framework, together with the small group of figures and episodes noted above as remaining with the story throughout the sequence of later versions, give some rudimentary substance to the idea of a '*Hsi-yu chi* tradition': certain basic characteristics imposing themselves upon tellers of the story as necessary and indispensable to it.

2. The versions to which the *Yung-lo ta-tien*, the *Pak t'ongsa ŏnhae* and the long *tsa-chü* sequence testify must be judged by a quite distinct scale of values. In each case we are already within clear sight of the story told in the hundred-chapter work of the sixteenth century. With this material, the idea of a comprehensive *Hsi-yu chi* tradition gains greatly in significance: but it is important that the implications should be judged with care. The early versions are linked to the hundred-chapter novel (and, in various ways, to one another) by a considerable similarity of detail, in some cases also of structure. The uniformity is most evident in the opening scenes of the story: the circumstances of T'ai-tsung's descent to Hell; the imperial commissioning of Tripitaka; the introduction and early adventures of the monkey-hero. About the complex of adventures taking place on the journey the evidence is not so full. There is no means of judging, for instance, whether the sheer quantity of distinct episodes in the hundred-chapter work was fully anticipated in any earlier version. One must be content to observe that the 'Ch'e-ch'ih kuo' story used in *Pak t'ongsa* corresponds remarkably closely to its counterpart in the hundred chapters, and a high proportion of the episodes named by Ch'oe Se-chin (*PTS*, p. 267, N iii) and even in the *Hsiao-shih Chen-k'ung pao-chüan*, have equivalents in other versions. Nevertheless, as far as can be judged, the affinities stop well short of an identifiable textual relationship, and indeed when finer points of detail are compared there are signs of many individual discrepancies. In content the old versions closely resemble the major sixteenth-century work, but they are fully distinct from it.

One must resist the impulse to conclude that, since traces of older written versions are known, these versions necessarily served as direct sources for the long novel. Cheng Chen-to was so impressed with what at the time seemed the unique evidence offered by the *Yung-lo ta-tien* fragment that he dignified its source as an *Urtext*, for two centuries awaiting embellishment at the hands of a sixteenth-century master.[1] Valuable as the fragment is, there are other factors which should be

[1] Cheng Chen-to (1933), p. 273.

acknowledged before so confident a conclusion may be drawn. The existence of further evidence at once complicates the scene: although it may theoretically just be conceivable that the early prose versions discussed above were in fact all one, we have no guarantee that this was so, or even likely. It is an open possibility that yet others appeared in the course of those intervening two hundred years. And even if more complete and easily identified printed specimens from this strangely obscure period were available, one would also be bound to allow at every stage for the contingent role of living oral traditions. In the late sixteenth century the author of the *Chin P'ing Mei*[a] could still write of a 'strolling monk, waving his noisy cymbals, recounting tales of Tripitaka...'[1] Local performers must yet have been capable of adding episodes or effecting variations in the formless body of adventures which made up the bulk of the *Hsi-yu chi*: those who worked in the written medium, artists or hacks, must at times still have been open to such influences.

The early versions will not necessarily bring us straight to the workshop in which the hundred-chapter work was drawn up, but from their degree of uniformity there is a clear inference to be drawn. From the fourteenth century onwards there was a general, and no doubt progressive, standardization of the cycle, and this was a process we may associate with a growing number of printed editions. One can imagine a situation in which the *Hsi-yu chi* had become a story which everyone knew, and knew increasingly in a particular form. The studies which follow below offer some evidence of this familiarity and its effects.

The author of the hundred chapters did indeed inherit a story much of whose content was already determined; but his knowledge of it was almost certainly derived from a range of sources extending well beyond one particular written version handed down from two centuries before. One is forced to recognize that attempts to assess his creative achievement in terms of how he used earlier material will be overshadowed by many uncertainties.

Our discussion hitherto has considered the content of the *Hsi-yu chi* tradition only in passing, where it has had light to throw on some text or on individual, external problems. Study of the content for its own

---

[1] *Ching P'ing Mei*, ch. 15 (Dai-an (1963) ed. vol. 1, p. 343), cited by Yeh Te-chün, p. 55. For the dating of the novel see P. D. Hanan, 'The Text of the *Chin P'ing Mei*' in *Asia Major*, New Series, 9 (1962), p. 39, n. 45.

[a] 金瓶梅

sake involves difficulties which hardly need to be stressed: not only are we far removed from the original, characteristically oral, medium of its transmission. We are further bound to recognize that the very substance of the old stories was to a large degree volatile and subject to no clear-cut discipline. Research, even conjecture, in such a field is valid only when it accepts and allows for these general limiting conditions.

There are in this story, however, certain features which pose their own insistent questions—in particular those linked with the *Hsi-yu chi* tradition from its earliest known stages. Among them the figure of Sun Wu-k'ung stands out as demanding particular attention. He is not only the effective hero of the cycle as it is above all known in the hundred-chapter *Hsi-yu chi*—the novel's most brilliantly and sympathetically realized character; he has at the same time found a place in the pantheon of popular spirit-worship and in some parts of the world is the centre of cults down to the present day.[1] One is impelled, whether as folklorist, literary historian, or simply as reader of the novel, to ask what reasons lie behind the monkey's prominence in the story and the mark he has made on Chinese life. What indeed were the origins of the figure that somehow came to be permanently adopted in the legend of Tripitaka ? What implicit coherence can be found in his versatile adventures throughout the story ?

These questions have often been asked, and there is no lack of suggested answers to some or all of them. Editors of the hundred-chapter novel from the sixteenth to the nineteenth centuries[2] had no hesitation in identifying the monkey as a symbol of the restless human mind and the whole story as an appropriate allegorical structure to accommodate it.[3] Twentieth-century scholarship has in turn been preoccupied with the task of identifying the monkey's origin in Chinese or alien legend. Almost every critic to produce a general survey of the novel and its problems has felt bound to express an opinion on this issue: it has become a major topic in the field of *Hsi-yu chi* studies.[4]

---

[1] For a study of one, see A. J. A. Elliott, *Chinese Spirit-Medium Cults in Singapore* (Monographs on Social Anthropology 14, London School of Economics, London, 1955). For other cults, see Eberhard (1948), pp. 125 and 147–8.

[2] For details of the various editions involved, their prefaces and commentaries, see Dudbridge (1969), pp. 144–55.

[3] The question of this and other allegorical devices used in relation to the traditional *Hsi-yu chi* story will be discussed separately in App. A.

[4] See, for instance, Hu Shih (1923), pp. 368–72; Lu Hsün (1924), p. 19; Cheng Chen-to (1933), pp. 291–3; Ōta and Torii (1960), pp. 356–7; Uchida Michio, pp. 33 ff.

The studies which go to form the remainder of this book are concerned with material falling into two overlapping categories—those legends and traditions which have from time to time been cited as sources for the Sun Wu-k'ung figure; and a group of popular stories and plays which at some stage in their development show evidence of connection with the *Hsi-yu chi* monkey. The questions asked are—How far does this material take us in a search for the origins and function of Sun Wu-k'ung? If not far enough, what kind of evidence does it in fact provide? And where are we to look for a truer idea of the figure's background?

To concentrate so much attention on this single inquiry is not a wholly arbitrary procedure. It is clear that the *Hsi-yu chi* tradition in its richness faces the student with a task of unlimited size and complexity. If he is to achieve anything at all, he must select, and selection must be governed by two principal factors: the breadth and availability of material relevant to any individual topic, and the usefulness of that topic in reflecting back on the wider tradition, its nature and environment. In both respects the *Hsi-yu chi* monkey has an importance which matches its own inherent claims on our attention. As we trace Sun Wu-k'ung's progress through the pre-sixteenth-century sources, we find the popular literary milieu grow clearer even as the monkey himself becomes more elusive.

Material from the 'Hsi-yu chi' tradition

In the chapters that follow it will be necessary to characterize a number of independent traditions individually and to reconsider certain factual evidence, particularly questions of dating. For convenient reference, however, relevant features of the early *Hsi-yu chi* versions are first summarized here.

Verses by Liu K'o-chuang:

To fetch scriptures one had to trouble the Monkey Novice-Monk...
A face even uglier than the Monkey Novice-Monk...

It is suggested above[1] that these references may reflect stage representations in thirteenth-century southern China.

The Kōzanji version:

Section 2: 'On their journey they meet the Monkey Novice-Monk'

They had already passed through one country when, one day about noon, they saw a *hsiu-ts'ai* graduate in plain clothes come from due east...The

[1] Ch. 2, p. 47.

hsiu-ts'ai said, 'Monk, in previous lives you have twice been to fetch scriptures and fallen into difficulties on the way. If you go this time ten thousand deaths (await you)! The Master asked, 'How do you know?' The *hsiu-ts'ai* said, 'I am none other than the king of 84,000 bronze-headed, iron-browed monkeys of Tzu-yün tung on Hua-kuo shan. I come now to help you fetch the scriptures . . .' His name was thereupon changed to Hou Hsing-che.[1]

Section 3: 'They enter the palace of Mahābrahmā Devarāja'
Asked about his age, the monkey replies:

'Nine times I have seen the Yellow River run clear.' Involuntarily the Master laughed. He felt very incredulous and asked, 'You are still young: how can you talk so extravagantly?' Hsing-che said, 'My years may be few, yet I have lived through thousands and thousands of ages. I know that you, Master, in previous lives twice made for the Western Paradise to fetch scriptures and came to grief on the way.'. . . The Master said, 'If you have seen the Yellow River run clear nine times, do you know all about Heaven and Hell?' Hsing-che said: 'How could I fail to know?' The Master asked, 'What is going on in Heaven today?' Hsing-che said: 'Today Vaiśravaṇa of the North, the Mahābrahmā Devarāja, is giving a feast for religious in the Crystal Palace' . . .

The monkey then takes them, by magic arts, to meet Vaiśravaṇa.[2]

Section 11: 'They enter the Pool of the Queen (of the West)'

The Master said, 'Have you been here?' Hsing-che replied: 'When I was eight hundred years old I came here and stole some peaches to eat. Twenty-seven thousand years have passed since then, and I have not returned until now.' The Master said, 'I wish that today the peaches could bear fruit, and then we could steal a few to eat.' Hsing-che said, 'It was because I stole ten peaches when I was eight hundred years old that I was seized by the Queen and sentenced to eight hundred strokes from an iron cudgel on my left side and three thousand on the right, then banished to Tzu-yün tung on Hua-kuo shan. It still hurts down my side even now.'[3]

Later, trying to overcome the monkey's scruples, the Master uses the phrase 'your spiritual powers are mighty'[a].[4]

Section 17: 'They reach Shensi, where the wife of a householder, Wang, kills his son'
After the narrative proper comes to an end, the text concludes with this line:

T'ai-tsung afterwards conferred on Hou Hsing-che the title Great Saint of Bronze Sinews and Iron Bones[b].[5]

[1] Cf. above, p. 31.   [2] Cf. above, p. 32.
[3] Cf. above, p. 36.   [4] B 2:11*a* (1955: p. 47).
[5] A 15*a* (1955: p. 107); B 3:11*b* (1955: p. 72).
[a] 神通廣大   [b] 銅筋鐵骨大聖

Elsewhere in the work the monkey serves as a guide, giving warning of each new hazard, supplying information on the various supernatural phenomena on the way and in a few cases personally intervening to solve difficulties, either by appealing to Vaiśravaṇa of the North, or by taking action himself.

Briefly: this monkey is associated with a fixed home in the east—Tzu-yün tung on Hua-kuo shan—to which he was banished by the Queen of the West for stealing peaches, and where he ruled over a tribe of monkeys; he is of immense age, has insight into supernatural mysteries and himself wields powers of transformation and magic combat. His relationship to Tripitaka is that of assistant and guide.

The 'T'ang San-tsang Hsi-yu chi' quoted in 'Pak t'ongsa'

Although only one episode—the adventure in Ch'e-ch'ih kuo—is given, the monkey plays a prominent and distinctive role. He is introduced as apparently the sole companion of Tripitaka,[1] now named Sun Hsing-che; he takes into his own hands the routing of the Taoist usurpers in the land and contrives to win the decisive contests in magic powers. Apart from his resourcefulness, Sun Hsing-che has a characteristic facetiousness and love of posturing, brought out clearly in this passage:

Sun Hsing-che said, 'Now I am getting in to have a bath!' He took off his clothes, turned a somersault and jumped into the oil. On the point of taking his bath he disappeared. The King said, 'General, lift him out! Hsing-che must be dead!' The General went to lift him out with a hook. Hsing-che changed into a monkey only five inches or so in size. When (the hook) came to the left-hand side to lift him out he dodged across to the right, when it came to the right he dodged to the left: no device succeeded in fetching him out. The General reported, 'The oil has boiled away all Hsing-che's flesh!' Seeing (all this), Tripitaka wept. When Hsing-che heard him he jumped out and cried, 'Great King, do you have any soap for me to wash my head with?' The crowd applauded: 'The Buddhists have won!'[2]

The 'Hsi-yu chi' described in annotations to 'Pak t'ongsa'[3]

N vi is devoted exclusively to the monkey's part in the story. I quote it here in full:

According to the *Hsi-yu chi*, there was in the Western Regions a Mountain of Flowers and Fruit[a]; below the mountain was a Water-curtain cave[b]; before the cave was a bridge of sheets of iron, beneath the bridge was a torrent ten

---

[1] This point is discussed above, pp. 65–6.   [2] *PTS*, pp. 305–6.
[3] Cf. above, p. 67: full translation below, App. B.
[a] 花菓山   [b] 水簾洞

thousand *chang* deep, beside the torrent were ten thousand small caves, and in the caves a multitude of monkeys. There was a monkey-spirit styled Ch'i-t'ien Ta-sheng, of mighty spiritual powers, who entered the orchard of magic peaches in Heaven and stole the fruit. He likewise stole Lao-chün's holy elixir and made off with the Queen (of the West)'s embroidered robes from her own palace. He held a party in celebration of the robes. Lao-chün and the Queen both appealed to the Jade Emperor, who summoned the Devarāja Li to lead 100,000 heavenly warriors and all the spirit-commanders against the Mountain of Flowers and Fruit and engage Ta-sheng in combat. But they lost their advantage, and a Strong Spirit[a] who patrolled the hills reported to the Devarāja that if they raised the spirit of Kuan-k'ou near Kuan-chou, called Erh-lang the Small Saint[b], the capture could be effected. The Devarāja sent his Crown Prince Moksha[c] and the Strong Spirit to go and ask the spirit Erh-lang to lead his celestial army and surround the Mountain of Flowers and Fruit. The monkeys all came out to fight but were defeated, and Ta-sheng was captured. He was about to die when Kuan-yin submitted a request to the Jade Emperor to spare his life: 'Let Chü-ling shen[d] be ordered to hold him in custody and take him to the world below; on the Mountain of Flowers and Fruit let the lower half of his body be put in a crevasse in the rock, which should be sealed by drawing the mark of Tathāgata Buddha; let the mountain spirits and local gods keep guard over him; when hungry let him eat iron pellets, when thirsty drink molten bronze, and thus wait for me to go to the East in search of a man to fetch scriptures; when I pass this mountain I shall see whether Ta-sheng is willing to go with him to the West, and, if so, he can then be released.' Subsequently T'ang T'ai-tsung commissioned the Master Hsüan-tsang to go to the West and fetch the scriptures. The route ran past this mountain, and he saw the monkey-spirit confined in the rock-crevasse, removed the seal of the Buddha and brought him out. He made him a disciple, gave him the religious name Wu-k'ung[e], changed his style[f] to Sun Hsing-che, and set off together with him and Sha Ho-shang[g] and a black pig-spirit called Chu Pa-chieh[h]. On the way it was wholly through the agency of Sun Hsing-che's spiritual powers that demons were defeated and the Master saved from difficult situations. When the Master reached the Western Paradise he received the Three Baskets of scriptures and returned to the East. The Master reaped his spiritual reward by becoming the Candana Buddha Tathāgata[i], Sun Hsing-che by becoming the Strong King Bodhisattva[j], Chu Pa-chieh the cleanser of altars at the Assembly of Incense and Flowers.[1]

Amidst all this circumstantial detail, there are the following points of innovation in the monkey's story: the cave has the new name 'Shui-lien tung'; the name Ch'i-t'ien Ta-sheng has appeared, only vaguely adumbrated in the title quoted in the final line of the Kōzanji texts; the theft

[1] *PTS*, pp. 293–4.
[a] 大力鬼   [b] 小聖二郎   [c] 太子木叉   [d] 巨靈神   [e] 吾空   [f] 號
[g] 沙和尚   [h] 朱八戒   [i] 栴檀佛如來   [j] 大力王菩薩

of elixir and an embroidered robe are now among Sun's crimes; he is subject no longer to the Queen of the West's arbitration, but to that of the Jade Emperor; there is an elaborate celestial war against Hua-kuo shan; the monkey's release is explicitly bound up with Tripitaka's mission to the West; he receives the name Wu-k'ung; at the end, together with Tripitaka, he is canonized in the Buddhist pantheon.

The six-part tsa-chü 'Hsi-yu chi'

Two full scenes introduce Sun Wu-k'ung into the action. His appearance is first anticipated in Moksha's song of the previous scene 7 (p. 33). Hsing-che then opens scene 9 himself with a conventional self-introduction in eight lines of verse and the following speech:

We are five brothers and sisters: my elder sister is Li-shan Lao-mu[a], my second sister Wu-chih-ch'i Sheng-mu[b]; my elder brother is Ch'i-t'ien Ta-sheng, I myself am T'ung-t'ien Ta-sheng[c], and my younger brother Shua-shua San-lang[d]. When in good spirits I climb in the creepers and vines, when angry I cast the seas and rivers into commotion. I made the girl from Chin-ting-kuo[e] my wife; I have had the precious wine from the Jade Emperor's Palace to drink. I stole from T'ai-shang Lao-chün[f] his fully-refined elixir of gold. Through nine alchemical reactions (I have been) refined until my sinews are bronze and my bones iron, my eyes fiery and metallic, my anus of brass, my penis of tin. I have stolen a hundred of the Queen's fairy peaches and a set of her robes for my wife to wear. Today I am holding a party in celebration of the robes.[1]

The Devarāja Li, who in the same scene leads the punitive force against him, names the monkey's home as Tzu-yün lo-tung[g] on Hua-kuo shan (p. 38). At the end of the scene he is imprisoned on the orders of Kuan-yin below Hua-kuo shan, and a character is 'painted' on it (p. 42). In scene 10 Sun is released by Tripitaka and his murderous reaction is curbed by Kuan-yin with an iron hoop binding his head (p. 46); he is given the name Sun Hsing-che. One of the songs in this scene (p. 45: *K'u-huang-t'ien*[h]), alludes to the monkey's kinship with Li[i]-shan Lao-mu and Wu-chih-ch'i.

The monkey's characterization throughout this sequence of plays has been determined, it was suggested above,[2] by the habitual stage manner of the *ching* role: there are strains of bawdy humour, comic verbal

---

[1] Sc. 9, p. 37.   [2] P. 83.

[a] 離山老母   [b] 巫支祇聖母   [c] 通天大聖   [d] 耍耍三郎   [e] 金鼎國
[f] 太上老君   [g] 紫雲羅洞   [h] 哭皇天   [i] 驪

patter and acrobatic agility which are no better than crude equivalents to some of the characteristics we find, for instance, in the sixteenth-century novel.

The hundred-chapter novel 'Hsi-yu chi'

One cannot hope to reduce to the dimensions of a note the complexities of Sun Wu-k'ung's adventures in the early chapters of this book, nor the many nuances of character drawn out in the course of the whole. This monkey stands among the earliest rounded characters in the Chinese popular novel, in the sense that he is constantly able to surprise the reader with, for instance, unexpected traits of warm feeling or even of sentimentality.[1]

For the purposes of the discussion here, which is concerned with the figure inherited from tradition at large, we must be content to record the principal features of his story which can be related, or at least compared, with the remnants of that older tradition.

The monkey is born from a primeval stone egg. He leads a tribe of various simian creatures in the discovery, penetration and colonization of a stone lair concealed behind a curtain of falling water. The mountain on which this takes place is again called Hua-kuo shan; the cave—again Shui-lien tung. The Monkey King, crowned in recognition of his leadership, tires of the primitive, innocent life of his tribe and departs on a raft in search of a teacher to guide him towards immortality. He finds a master in the Patriarch Subhūti[a] on Ling-t'ai[b] mountain (chapter 1). He there learns esoteric techniques and eventually returns to Hua-kuo shan to organize his subjects into an army (chapter 2). He equips them with stolen arms and visits the palace of the Dragon King to demand a weapon for himself: he is given the famous iron cudgel, bound by golden rings, adaptable in size. In a drunken sleep he dreams a visit to Hell, where he fights himself free of arrest and strikes the names of his tribe from the Register of Life and Death. Complaints are made in Heaven, and he is summoned to take office there (chapter 3). He is employed as a groom in the heavenly stables, with the punning title Pi-ma-wen[c];[2] he returns disgruntled to Hua-kuo shan, lays claim to the title Ch'i-t'ien Ta-sheng and resists attempts to take him by force. Again he is received into Heaven (chapter 4). He is appointed to guard

---

[1] Compare his nostalgic tears, provoked by the sight of the Eastern Ocean immediately after his first dismissal by Tripitaka (HYC, ch. 27, p. 314); his access of bitter emotion in ch. 33 (p. 381); his tears of shame and outrage in ch. 34 (pp. 390–1).

[2] Homophonous with an expression meaning 'proof against horse diseases'[d].

[a] 須菩提祖師   [b] 靈臺   [c] 弼馬溫   [d] 避馬瘟

the Queen of the West's peach orchard, but himself consumes the fruit, then steals elixir from the Taoist patriarch Lao-chün, drinks celestial wine intended for a celebration among the immortals, and finally returns again to Hua-kuo shan (chapter 5). He resists the efforts of celestial armies sent to arrest him and falls only to the god Erh-lang (chapter 6). All methods of execution fail: he is enclosed in the furnace of Lao-chün, but survives to burst out and again run wild. The Tathāgata Buddha uses a simple stratagem to pin him beneath a mountain—now named Wu-hsing shan[a]—formed from the Buddha's own five fingers (chapter 7). He is in due course released by the traveller Tripitaka (chapter 14), who gives him the name Sun Hsing-che. He kills a tiger and robes himself in the skin. The Bodhisattva Kuan-yin provides a set of three steel bands for Tripitaka's use, one of which is set on the monkey's head: only its tightening—in response to Tripitaka's recitation of a spell—controls the monkey's actions. Henceforth he serves as Tripitaka's protector and as leader of the other disciples. In the general canonization of the final scene (*HYC*, ch. 100, pp. 1129 ff.) his title is Tou-chan-sheng Fo[b].

Recurrent features

In the tradition represented by the above sources the monkey's career is from first to last divided between two contrasting roles—the celestial delinquent and the protector-guide. He is invariably overshadowed by some figure representing divine discipline: in the thirteenth-century text this is the Queen of the West, in later versions the Bodhisattva Kuan-yin, representing the final authority of the Buddha; only in the sixteenth-century novel is the Buddha accorded an active role in asserting this authority, and here too Kuan-yin remains a prominent figure.

The monkey's name changes in time from Hou Hsing-che to Sun Hsing-che and Sun Wu-k'ung; in all but the thirteenth-century text he bears the title Ch'i-t'ien Ta-sheng (although there is some irregularity in the *tsa-chü* version). In the *tsa-chü* sequence alone he has as kinsfolk Li-shan Lao-mu and Wu-chih-ch'i. In every source he is associated with a mountain named Hua-kuo shan; and in all but the sixteenth-century novel this is not only his home during the initial delinquent phase, but also the site of his punishment by confinement. The novel introduces a new theme with the Buddha and his Wu-hsing shan.

Of the misdeeds committed by the monkey in his delinquent phase, the stealing of celestial peaches is attested in all the sources. In all but

[a] 五行山   [b] 鬪戰勝佛

the thirteenth-century text he also steals wine from a heavenly banquet and elixir from the Taoist Patriarch; in two sources (the *tsa-chü* sequence, and the work described in *Pak t'ongsa ŏnhae*) he steals a fairy robe from the Queen. Only in the *tsa-chü* text does he specifically abduct a princess and make her his wife. The war against Heaven, with a fairly constant *dramatis personae* drawn from Chinese legend at large, is integral to all but the thirteenth-century version. The 'refinement' of the monkey in Lao-chün's furnace is found only in the *tsa-chü* and the sixteenth-century novel. The metal band about his head is likewise common to the same two sources. In all but the thirteenth-century text (with its strange investiture at the hands of T'ai-tsung) the monkey is finally transfigured and canonized in the Buddhist Heaven.

A considerable proportion of the familiar story is known to us in the hundred-chapter novel alone: it comprises the whole detailed account of the creation myth, the monkey tribe's earthly paradise, the Monkey King's quest for immortality, his discipleship with a religious master, his visits to the Dragon Palace and to the Underworld, his appointment as groom in the heavenly stables. We can only guess at how far these elements formed part of earlier *Hsi-yu chi* traditions.

8

The White Ape[1]

This title designates a long and well-defined Chinese tradition at the centre of which stands the T'ang literary tale *Pu Chiang Tsung Po-yüan chuan*[a]. The theme is simple: a supernatural ape-like creature at large in the hills of southern and south-western China abducts the wives and daughters of travellers and maintains its own mountain seraglio. In the later versions, one husband is successful in tracing his lost wife and eliminating the ape.

In recent years several minor studies have been devoted to different aspects of this legend and its accumulation of literary treatments. They range from the bold attempt of Lin P'ei-chih (*q.v.*) to trace a relationship with the *Rāmāyaṇa* epic of classical India to the more recent politico-literary assessment by Liu Yeh-ch'iu (*q.v.*). The early literary sources culminating in the *Po-yüan chuan* receive their fullest and most sensitive discussion in a longer study by Uchiyama Chinari (*q.v.*), who has successfully established a detailed and illuminating context for the T'ang tale. But the legend as such becomes most obviously relevant to the *Hsi-yu chi* tradition in the form of a later vernacular prose story, pre-served in the sixteenth-century collection now known as *Ch'ing-p'ing-shan t'ang hua-pen*[b],[2] in which the ape-demon shares certain specific features with the early Sun Wu-k'ung.

Among commentators on *Hsi-yu chi* material, Ōta Tatsuo in particular has sought to identify the figures more closely, finding in the traditional white ape a close parallel to the monkey-hero of what are termed the 'Yüan' versions of *Hsi-yu chi*, and suggesting that they were eventually

---

[1] This is merely a conventional rendering of the term *po-yüan*[c], which is that used in the T'ang source discussed here. For the role of this creature—tentatively identified as the Silvery Langur—in T'ang literature, see E. H. Schafer, p. 232.

[2] After the studio of Hung P'ien[d] (mid-sixteenth century), who originally brought out a collection apparently of sixty vernacular stories under the general title *Liu-shih chia hsiao-shuo*[e]. See André Lévy, pp. 97–106.

[a] 補江總白猿傳　　[b] 清平山堂話本　　[c] 白猿　　[d] 洪楩　　[e] 六十家小說

dissociated only through radical and sophisticated changes in characterization by the sixteenth-century novelist.[1] With questions such as these
at issue the most confident theories may be advanced only on a hypothetical basis, and they are useful only in so far as they take into account
whatever facts are relevant. I take up the discussion here not in the hope
of pronouncing definitively on matters which are bound to remain to
some extent uncertain, but in order to work towards a more complete
and precise picture of how the known sources stand—what form of
useful evidence they provide and in what original context they should
be seen.

Early literary references

We are not here concerned to spell out the richness of traditional motifs
put to use in the T'ang *Po-yüan chuan,* and do not need to reconsider
the full range of material discussed by Uchiyama in this connection.
The need is rather to characterize the central legend in its early stages,
as a background to the ape figure which emerges in later popular sources.

An early, almost archetypal statement of the theme is found in the
Han text *I-lin*[a], with verses for each of the hexagram permutations in
the *Changes.*[2] Under *po*[b] in the section *k'un*[c] are the lines:

> A great ape from the southern mountains
> Robbed me of my beloved wife.
> For fear, I dared not chase him.
> I could but retire, to dwell alone.[3]

We find more detail in a prose passage which purports to date from the
third or fourth century AD:[4]

In the high mountains of southwestern Shu[d] there is an animal resembling
the monkey. It is seven feet in height, it can imitate the ways of human

---

[1] Ōta Tatsuo (1959), pp. 9–12. Cf. also Uchida Michio, pp. 35–6.
[2] Traditionally the work is attributed to Chiao Yen-shou[e], who lived in the first
century BC (cf. *SKCSTM,* 109:13 *ab*). But Yü Chia-hsi (*tzu,* 3:29 *a*–40 *a*) has shown,
by comparing internal evidence with biographical data, that the work we have
comes more probably from the hand of Ts'ui Chuan[f] (first century AD) and would
in this case have been written *circa* AD 25 (cf. Yü, p. 39 *b*).
[3] *I-lin (SPTK),* 1:25 *b*–26 *a.*
[4] It is attributed to the *Sou-shen chi*[g], a collection of marvels ascribed to Kan Pao[h]
(*circa* AD 300). Yü Chia-hsi's researches (*tzu,* 8:1 *a*–5 *a*) disqualify the confidence of
the *Szu-k'u* editors in the *CTPS* version as an integral text (cf. *SKCSTM,* 142:12 *a*–
13 *b*), but support the likely authenticity of many individual excerpts cited in various
compendia, among them the present passage. An almost identical passage is in other
sources attributed to the *Po-wu chih*[i] of Chang Hua[j] (third century): see, for instance,
TPYL, 910:5 *b*–6 *a.*

[a] 易林　　[b] 剝　　[c] 坤　　[d] 蜀　　[e] 焦延壽　　[f] 崔篆　　[g] 搜神記
[h] 干寶　　[i] 博物志　　[j] 張華

beings and is able to run fast in pursuit of them. It is named *chia-kuo*[a] or *ma-hua*[b]; some call it *chüeh*[c].[1] It watches out for young women travelling on the road and seizes and bears them away without anyone being aware of it. If travellers are due to pass in its vicinity they lead one another by a long rope, but even this fails to avert disaster. The beast is able to distinguish between the smell of men and of women and can thus pick out the women and leave[2] the men. Having abducted a man's wife or daughter it makes her its own wife. Women that fail to bear it children can never return for the rest of their lives, and after ten years they come to resemble the beast in appearance, their minds become confused, and they no longer think of return. Those that bear sons return to their homes with the infants in their arms. The sons are all like men in appearance. If any refuse to rear them, the mothers die. So the women go in fear of the beast, and none dares refuse[3] to bring up her son. Grown up, the sons are no different from men, and they all take the surname Yang[d], which is why there are so many people by that name now in the southwest of Shu: they are mostly descended from the *chia-kuo* or *ma-hua*.[4]

In these two early sources we find the core of the *Po-yüan chuan* story and its vernacular successors, and already certain significant motifs emerge. The locality is fixed in the mountainous country of the southwest, in particular of Szechuan, a region which to several has suggested a connection with tribal myths of the Tibetan peoples that for centuries lived there.[5] Even in its more developed later forms the 'white ape' story was never to leave the traditionally barbarous regions of south-western China, although the exact situation varied according to the particular circumstances described in each new version. The ape-creature himself is seen to be not only an abductor, but one whose preoccupation is above all with the generation of offspring. It is this, together with the distinctive comments on the Yang surname and its background, that carries the strongest suggestion of influence from an ancestral myth. These features play an important role in the *Po-yüan chuan*.

About the T'ang prose tale[6] a good deal has been written, yet the

---

[1] The passage attributed to *Po-wu chih* in *TYPL* has *hou-chüeh*[e] in place of *chia-kuo* and *chia*[f] in place of the final *chüeh*. *Chüeh* is glossed in the *Shuo-wen chieh-tzu*[g] (*SPTK*), 10:6a as a 'large monkey', in the *Kuang-yün*[h] (revised version of early eleventh century) (*SPTK*), 5:36b as a 'large ape'. *Chia* in its variant graphs[i] is universally glossed as a male or female pig.

[2] Preferring the wording preserved in the *CTPS* version of *Sou-shen chi*, 12:6b–7a.

[3] *Ibid.*   [4] *TPKC*, 444:3629.

[5] Eberhard (1942), pt. 2, pp. 27–9, draws attention to this, pointing out that the Tibetans claimed descent from a monkey ancestor. See also Ishida Eiichirō, pp. 131–3, with a discussion of this passage from an ethnic point of view.

[6] The title *Pu Chiang Tsung Po-yüan chuan* appears in the bibliographical section of the *Hsin T'ang-shu* (59:12b). Other early bibliographical references are cited by Wang

a 猳國   b 馬化   c 玃   d 楊   e 猴玃   f 猳   g 說文解字
h 廣韻   i 猳豭

basic circumstances of its authorship and period remain obscure. Uchiyama Chinari, much of whose study is devoted to a refutation of earlier theory and speculation, leaves a clear impression that this is not a product of the early T'ang, but dates more probably from the eighth or ninth century.[1]

The story now concerns a particular victim of the ape's depredation, a military commander Ou-yang Ho[a] involved in a southern border campaign of the sixth century,[2] whose wife is spirited away at night from the heart of the army encampment. She is discovered, after a month of fruitless searching, as a member of an ape-demon's seraglio. Ou-yang lies in wait in the monster's sumptuous mountain residence while the other wives, all stolen from human society, contrive an orgy which reduces it to helplessness. The husband then binds and slays it. Assuming the form of a white ape, the demon speaks the dying words:

It is heaven that has killed me. How could it lie within your power? But your wife is with child: do not kill her son, for he will come before the Sage Emperor and bring honour on his ancestors.

And the captive women report an earlier speech:

I have reached the age of one thousand years without siring a son. Now that I have one, the term of my life has come.[3]

In spite of Uchiyama's strictures on the ape's personality and its lack of coherence,[4] certain dominant motifs now show up more clearly through the medium of conscious fiction. The ape's concern for off-spring is intensified by the failure of all his wives but one to bear him a son. He inherits the brutish instincts of his predecessors in legend, maintains the household of a rich collector in which he leads a de-bauched existence, but combines this with an unexpected literacy:

he would read slips of wood (inscribed in) a seal-script like that used on Taoist charms, completely unintelligible . . .[5]

P'i-chiang, p. 17. The text is preserved in *TPKC*, 444:3629–31, under the title *Ou-yang Ho* and with the final note 'From the continuation of Chiang's story'[b]. A Sung edition once in the collection of Ku Yüan-ch'ing[c], a sixteenth-century bibliophile, is reproduced in the collection *Ku-shih wen-fang hsiao-shuo*[d] (10 vol. edition (Shangai, 1934), vol. 8); Wang P'i-chiang's text is based on this.

[1] See in particular his summary of the evidence on p. 252.
[2] Uchiyama has shown that the ostensibly historical background of this story amounts to no more than a random and inaccurate reconstruction of a complicated original state of affairs: see his pp. 248–51.
[3] *TPKC*, 444:3631.
[4] Uchiyama, pp. 256–7.   [5] *TPKC*, 444:3631.

[a] 歐陽紇   [b] 出續江氏傳   [c] 顧元慶   [d] 顧氏文房小說

Several other such characteristics, in their turn inspired by precedents in supernatural legend, attach themselves to the traditional ape figure in this fictional treatment, yet they leave the ape's central motivation, the starting point of the whole story, clear and intact. In so far as we can judge the progress of an old legend through these scanty sources, its shape has up to this point not suffered great distortion.

That the legend continued to be known in virtually the same form is confirmed in the miscellany *Ling-wai tai-ta*[a] by Chou Ch'ü-fei[b], whose preface to the work is dated 1178. He records there a variant in which a monkey with magic powers is said to dwell below a cliff in Ching-chiang fu[c] (in present Kwangsi) and steal beautiful women; once more a robbed husband surnamed Ou-yang is successful in killing the demon and regaining his wife; the other women all become nuns. The dead monkey is said to continue haunting the place of its burial.[1]

A vernacular short story

The story *Ch'en Hsün-chien Mei-ling shih-ch'i chi*[d] appears in the third volume of the fragment from the *Ch'ing-p'ing-shan t'ang hua-pen* collection preserved in the Naikaku Bunko[e].[2] The title (without the final character *chi*) is noted in the *Pao-wen-t'ang shu-mu*[f].[3] A revised version, under a slightly different title and with a few alterations and excisions, forms *chüan* 20 of the anthology *Ku-chin hsiao-shuo*[g] edited by Feng Meng-lung[h] and first published *circa* 1620.[4]

The story is now set in the years 1121–4. The *chin-shih*[i] graduate Ch'en Hsin[j] is appointed to the post of *hsün-chien*[k] in the market-town of Sha-chiao[l] in Nan-hsiung fu[m], Kwangtung. Before he sets out a powerful Taoist saint Tzu-yang chen-jen[n] gives him a serving boy, in fact a disguised Taoist, whose secret responsibility it is to prevent

---

[1] *Ling-wai tai-ta* (PCHSTK), 10:11b. The compendium *Lei-shuo*[o] by Tseng Hao[p], completed in 1136 but now known only in seventeenth-century editions, quotes another version of the legend allegedly from the *Chi-shen lu*[q] of Hsü Hsüan[r] (917–92), but which is absent from the text of this work preserved in CTPS: see *Lei-shuo*, facsimile reprint (Peking, 1955), 12:15b.

[2] Cf. André Lévy, pp. 97–8.

[3] A catalogue of the titles in the library of Ch'ao Li[s] and his son up to *circa* 1560, offering evidence of the published works of fiction available to enthusiasts at this period.

[4] Sun K'ai-ti (1957), p. 91. For the nature of the revision, see André Lévy, p. 142.

a 嶺外代答	b 周去非	c 靜江府	d 陳巡檢梅嶺失妻記
e 內閣文庫	f 寶文堂書目	g 古今小說	h 馮夢龍	i 進士
j 陳辛	k 巡檢	l 沙角	m 南雄府	n 紫陽眞人
o 類說	p 曾慥	q 稽神錄	r 徐鉉	s 晁瑮

the coming disaster. On the road south with his wife Ch'en dismisses this attendant and thus unwittingly loses his magic protection. Now, as they approach the Mei-ling range, (on the border of Kiangsi and Kwangtung), the wife is seen by the powerful monkey-demon Shen-yang Kung[a] and abducted by supernatural means. She refuses to yield to his advances and is condemned instead to fetch and carry for him. Ch'en sees through the three years of his appointment without further news of his wife—an unrelated incident, the defeat of a bandit, Yang Kuang[b], is all that intervenes—and on his way back to the capital comes upon a Buddhist monastery where the monkey is a frequent visitor. He fails in his first rash attempt to kill the demon, but is able to enjoy a secret meeting with his wife. Finally the Taoist Tzu-yang chen-jen must intervene to capture the monkey and deliver him to Hell (Feng-tu[c]) for trial.

Certain details in this story directly recall older versions of the legend. The *Chia-kuo* fragment says, for instance, of the women detained by the ape:

after ten years...their minds become confused and they no longer think of return...

which becomes, in the words of one of Shen-yang Kung's women:

It is five years since I too was captured and brought to the cave by Shen-kung. He looks repulsive to you—I was the same at first. But later on you get used to him, and then life is much easier. (p. 127)[1]

The basic features of the plot—particularly the revenge wrought on the ape, its white colour (p. 130), the community of stolen wives—betray some kind of relationship with the T'ang *Po-yüan chuan*; but it may be too bold to claim that an affiliation is acknowledged in the closing couplet of the story:

Although this is a famous anecdote in the world of letters, We have made it into a pleasant tale for the present-day. (p. 134)

In this vernacular version two kinds of change are apparent. It employs the more diffuse narrative techniques that we associate with the genre. There is an abundance of incidental verse, secondary detail and even some inessential incident (the battle with Yang Kuang). More significantly, the characters become more articulate and more is made of their potential sentimental value: the stolen wife now refuses to yield,

---

[1] This and the subsequent page-references are to T'an Cheng-pi's critical edition *Ch'ing-p'ing-shan t'ang hua-pen* (Shanghai, 1957).

[a] 申陽公   [b] 楊廣   [c] 酆都

and her chastity becomes an issue in the story. In particular, the personal distress of the ape now takes a different form: he comes to the abbot of the Hung-lien monastery with this problem:

I cannot rid myself of sexual desire.[1] Through this worldly mind[a] my True Nature[b] has been charmed and beguiled. (p. 131)

An appeal to the values of Buddhism appears as an innovation in this legend. It is balanced both by the importance given in the story to the Taoist Tzu-yang chen-chün and, in the closing scene, to details of Taoist transformations and exorcism ritual.

From the brief passages of characterization it becomes clear that the ape-figure itself is compounded of strangely matched elements:

His spiritual powers mighty, his transformations manifold, he can quell the mountain demons from every cave, he governs the savage beasts of every mountain; raising spirits and practising magic rites, he snatches away beautiful women that suit his fancy; screaming at the moon and wailing to the wind, he intoxicates himself with wines better than any on earth. (pp. 124–5)

then later:

This demon is a white ape spirit, developed through a thousand years, his powers of transformation unfathomable...the man's name is Shen-yang Kung, he often comes to the monastery to hear discourses on the Ch'an mysteries or to discuss Buddhist doctrine. (p. 130)

The paradox of this personality is perhaps the story's most outstanding feature. But what concerns us more particularly here is that the ape bears the additional name Ch'i-t'ien Ta-sheng (p. 124) and belongs to a characteristic family of demons:

There were three brothers: one was T'ung-t'ien Ta-sheng[c], one Mi[d]-t'ien Ta-sheng, and one Ch'i-t'ien Ta-sheng; the younger sister was Szu-chou Sheng-mu[e]. (p. 124)

With no apparent precedent in the white ape tradition, these names[2] at once recall the Sun Wu-k'ung of the *tsa-chü* sequence *Hsi-yu chi* and of the prose work referred to by Ch'oe Se-chin. It becomes important at this point to know more about the background of the *Ch'en Hsün-chien* story.

---

[1] *Ai-yü*[f]. In orthodox Buddhist usage this phrase would no doubt be better rendered simply as 'desire', but in the present context both this phrase and *se*[g] immediately following have obvious sexual overtones.

[2] Szu-chou Sheng-mu is cognate with the demon Wu-chih-ch'i, to be discussed below in ch. 10.

[a] 色心   [b] 本性   [c] 通天大聖   [d] 彌   [e] 泗州聖母   [f] 愛慾   [g] 色

It has been accepted almost unanimously by those who have previously written on this question as a version of 'Sung', or at the latest 'Yüan' date.[1]

The meagre evidence cited in support of this view includes the following points:

1. An expression in the opening line runs:

Going to[2] this[a] Eastern Capital Pien-liang town...(p. 122)

Nagasawa Kikuya (1937), p. 166, cites two other examples in the same collection of the same expression, each introducing a Sung place name, and cautiously infers that these stories were originals of the Sung period from the places in question. The three occurrences seem rather to suggest that the formula was a conventional one, not a graphic evocation of a present situation, and indeed Nagasawa goes on (1937), p. 167, to quote an example of 'this' (che[b]) deliberately used retrospectively.

2. The narrative proper opens (p. 122) with a statement of the date:

In the third year of the Hsüan-ho period under Hui-tsung of the Great Sung

(i.e. 1121). Yen Tun-i (1955), p. 6, quotes the words 'Great Sung'[c] and by implication seeks to use them in support of a Sung dating. But it is at least of passing interest to note that this very date appears verbatim, in exactly the same way, in another story—*Shen Hsiao-kuan i niao hai ch'i ming*[d] [3]—which has been convincingly dated to the Ming period.[4]

In itself, the simple statement of a date cannot be accepted as sound evidence. It is meanwhile worth remarking that the action of the subsequent story covers three years and therefore allows for the year 1124. The Northern Sung dynasty collapsed in 1126, only two or at the most three years after this. It is most improbable that the present version of the story was composed in K'ai-feng precisely within that brief interval of time. On this account Nagasawa's suggestion must again lose conviction.

---

[1] Cheng Chen-to (1933), p. 292; Ch'ien Nan-yang, p. 173; Liu Ts'un-yan (1962), p. 139; Liu Yeh-ch'iu, p. 50; T'an Cheng-pi (1956), p. 63; Yen Tun-i (1955), p. 6 and (1960), p. 48; Uchida Michio, p. 35; Uchiyama Chinari, p. 241.

[2] The original text has yün[e], 'say', but this must be a misprint: the analogous passages in these stories (quoted by Nagasawa (1937), p. 166) all read ch'ü[f], 'go', which differs in only one stroke and makes clearer sense. Feng Meng-lung corrected to ch'ü in his version (facsimile, 20:1a, cf. T'an Cheng-pi, Ch'ing-p'ing-shan t'ang hua-pen, p. 134, n. 4).

[3] *Ku-chin hsiao-shuo* 26, p. 391.

[4] Ma Yau-woon and Ma Tai-loi, p. 26, n. 14.

[a] 去這   [b] 這   [c] 大宋   [d] 沈小官一鳥害七命   [e] 云   [f] 去

3. The closing words of the text run:

Our tale is told: for the time being we must break up the session[a]. (p. 134)

Yen Tun-i (1955), p. 6, uses these words as his clinching evidence of a Sung dating, describing them as 'technical expressions of the old narrative art'. Bearing in mind the ambiguities discussed above in chapter 1, we should hesitate before pronouncing so confidently on rhetorical features which could as easily be the stylistic devices of writers from a later age.

All three points seem equally inconclusive. They cannot amount to a satisfactory demonstration that the present written version of the story (as distinct from any oral or written antecedents) is of Sung authorship. The matter is still open to examination.

Ch'en Hsin's official appointment is described (p. 122) as *hsün-chien* of the *hsün-chien-szu*[b] at Sha-chiao chen[c], Nan-hsiung in Kuang-tung. Later in the story he is summoned by the Prefect of Nan-hsiung fu[d] (p. 129) to bring the bandit Yang Kuang to order. Under the Sung, however, the name Kuang-tung was not yet in official use, and indeed this particular provincial designation was not adopted until the Ming.[1] More significantly, the Nan-hsiung administration was a 'chou'[e] under the Sung, a 'lu'[f] under the Yüan, and did not become a 'fu' until the opening of the Ming dynasty in 1368.[2] From the 1824 gazetteer of Nan-hsiung chou we learn details of more specific relevance: first, that no *hsün-chien* officers were attached to this administration until the opening years of the Ming period; secondly that the *hsün-chien* of Sha-chiao in particular was one of four such appointments created in the year 1369 in a county subordinate to Nan-hsiung fu—Pao-ch'ang[g] hsien, with a view to maintaining public security in the bandit-ridden neighbourhood of the mountain pass. The gazetteer further notes that the Sha-chiao appointment had been 'long since discontinued', whereas the remaining three persisted for more than 270 years.[3]

---

[1] For the relevant passages in the dynastic histories, see *Sung shih* 90:1 a, *Yüan shih*, 62:25 b, *Ming shih*, 45:8 b.

[2] *Sung shih*, 90:1 a, *Yüan shih*, 62:25 b, *Ming shih*, 45:12 b. Only Průšek has previously taken account of this: see his 'New Studies of the Chinese Colloquial Short Story', *Archiv Orientální* 25 (1957), p. 489.

[3] *Chih-li Nan-hsiung chou chih*[h], 3:1 b, 4:20 b. It is pointed out on 4:20 b–21 a that older editions of the gazetteer had omitted to give names of the officials who held the posts throughout this period. As an official title the term *hsün-chien* was known in the Sung, Yüan and Ming dynasties, in each case concerned with maintaining local order: cf. *Sung shih*, 167:32 b; *Yüan shih*, 91:16 a; *Ming shih*, 75:22 b.

[a] 話本説徹權作散場   [b] 司   [c] 鎮   [d] 南雄府尹   [e] 州   [f] 路
[g] 保昌   [h] 直隸南雄州志

The anachronism of these features in the story must weigh heavily against the arguments which have been questioned above. The evidence of the *hsün-chien* appointment may lead us to doubt whether even the story itself, in this form, was conceived before the late fourteenth century; but certainly the dating of the text now available to us must be reconsidered. The earliest extant edition is that published around 1560 by Hung P'ien. An abundance of faults suggests that not much careful editorial attention was devoted to the stories in the collection, and they can be regarded as very much in their original form.[1] It therefore seems virtually certain that the *Ch'en hsün-chien* story as we know it was of Ming date. In this case there are no longer clear grounds for the suggestion several times advanced that it provided a precedent, or even served as a model, for the *Hsi-yu chi tsa-chü* version.[2] In both works the name Ch'i-t'ien Ta-sheng and the family of ape demons appear only incidentally; and to judge from the available evidence neither work demonstrably preceded the other—both date at the earliest from the latter part of the fourteenth, at the latest from the mid-sixteenth century.[3] There is more to be said in later chapters on the role of the names and the 'family' motif.

There was, in addition to this vernacular story, a southern dramatic version on the same theme. Its title is listed in the *Nan-tz'u hsü-lu* under the heading 'Old pieces from the Sung and Yüan' as *Ch'en hsün-chien Mei-ling shih ch'i*;[4] again, the anthology *Hui-tsuan yüan-p'u nan-ch'ü chiu-kung cheng-shih*[a] [5] quotes several fragments from a *Ch'en hsün-chien* play, attributing each to a '*ch'uan-ch'i*[b] of the Yüan'. The early fifteenth-century *Yung-lo ta-tien* also featured the title—*Ch'en hsün-chien ch'i yü pai-yüan-ching*[c]—as one in a list of twenty southern plays[d]:[6] this may possibly represent the same work. Both this title and that quoted by Hsü Wei, as well as the abbreviated source-titles given under extracts

[1] Cf. Lévy, p. 102.
[2] Cf. Yen Tun-i (1954), p. 149, (1960), p. 48; Liu Ts'un-yan (1962), p. 139, n. 129.
[3] The *Hsi-yu chi* sequence appears to have been known to Li K'ai-hsien, d. 1568.
[4] *Nan-tz'u hsü-lu*, p. 250. Cf. Ch'ien Nan-yang, p. 173.
[5] Hereafter abbreviated to *Cheng-shih*. Facsimile reprint (Peking, 1936). According to the 1596 preface by Yao Szu[e] the work is attributable jointly to Niu Shao-ya[f] (aged eighty-eight that year) and Hsü Tzu-shih[g].
[6] Listed among the contents of the lost *chüan* 13,981. Cf. Wang Hsiao-ch'uan, Preface, p. 9.

[a] 彙纂元譜南曲九宮正始   [b] 傳奇   [c] 妻遇白猿精   [d] 戲文
[e] 姚思   [f] 鈕少雅   [g] 徐子室

in several anthologies of dramatic verse,[1] specify Ch'en's rank as *hsün-chien*. We have noted that a version of the story committing itself to this detail is for historical reasons unlikely to anticipate the last decades of the fourteenth century. It would certainly be unwise to work from an assumption that the surviving fragments in southern verse represent a composition of the thirteenth or early fourteenth century. Their value to us here is that they allow us to glimpse a distinct treatment of the '*Ch'en hsün-chien*' tradition which, however it relates in time to the vernacular prose story, throws certain features of its characterization and plot into relief.

The most striking difference in treatment is the apparent absence from the dramatic version of the Buddhist abbot and his monastery. No preserved song intervenes between Ch'en Hsin's departure from office (marked in a song sung apparently by well-wishers in Nan-hsiung)[2] and the sung dialogue which runs as follows:

—May a stranger tell his woes? Urgent matters have brought me to the summit of this mountain, and fate has granted me to meet with you, Immortal Saint.
—What matter is it, Sir? Please tell me all.
—When I, Ch'en Hsin, and my wife left home and made for Nan-hsiung, she was violated on the Ta-yü Ridge[a] by a demon.
—Now you may hear, Sir, that this baleful visitation is none other than the black art of one named Shen-kung[b], who falls within the category of the trigrams *k'un*[c] and *tui*[d];[3] he has the form of a monkey, his countenance is ferocious.[4]

The words 'immortal saint'[e] are certainly addressed to a Taoist, whose reply here supplies the information entrusted in the vernacular story to the Buddhist abbot. To judge from the one remaining song that appears to follow this scene,[5] the Taoist executes retribution on the ape personally (contrast the condemnation to Hell in the vernacular story,

---

[1] See Ch'ien Nan-yang, pp. 174–9. Three further songs to the tune *Tsao-lo-p'ao*[f] can be found in the collection *Feng-yüeh chin-nang*[g] (B. 20, 2*ab*). Cf. J. J. Y. Liu, 'The *Feng-yüeh chin-nang*', *Journal of Oriental Studies* 4 (1957–8), p. 85.

[2] *Feng-chien-ts'ai*[h]: Ch'ien, p. 178. The *Tsao-lo-p'ao* songs in *Feng-yüeh chin-nang* probably belong to this part of the story, but their function is to express the feelings of Ch'en bereft of his wife and they do not illuminate the plot.

[3] The two trigrams together form the hexagram *ts'ui*[i]. Although this category is not the same as in the *I-lin* (see above), the constituent *k'un* is common to both.

[4] *Cheng-shih, ts'e* 2; Ch'ien, p. 179.

[5] *I-p'en-hua*[j], describing a magic sword for exterminating demons: *Cheng-shih, ts'e* 3; Ch'ien, p. 179.

[a] 大庾嶺　　[b] 申公　　[c] 坤　　[d] 兌　　[e] 神仙　　[f] 皂羅袍　　[g] 風月錦囊
[h] 風檢才　　[i] 萃　　[j] 一盆花

p. 134). It seems also, as Ch'ien Nan-yang points out (p. 178), that a previous connection between ape and Taoist is implied in the song *Ts'ai-ch'i-erh*[a]:

I bow my head in humble devotion,
O saint[b], deign to hear me.
Recall that when last you caught me
You granted a special pardon to your lowly servant.
I reverently burn incense of aloeswood,
I bow before you, I kneel low;
I place flowers [on your image?],[1] I offer up water, burn paper money.
I crave your mercy.
How happy I was in my cave—a universe in a pot.[2]
How was I to know that today I would meet this beauty?
Nor did I consider what retribution might overtake me.[3]

These two passages give some idea of certain features of the southern dramatic plot and of the ape-figure as he appeared in this context. From the old tradition he inherits the practice of abduction and a skill in occult arts. He resembles the figure in the vernacular story in being obliged helplessly to obey a powerful Taoist saint. The vocabulary of Buddhism finds an inconspicuous place in the wording of the songs, but this is no more than a hint at what becomes a major characteristic in the prose story. The ape seems here to repent his lapse primarily out of fear for his past captor, and the force of *karma* is mentioned almost as an afterthought; the prose story shows him attentive to the intellectual problems of Buddhism and genuinely caught in a personal religious conflict. In neither of these later versions does the bearing of offspring play any part: the course of the legend and its preoccupations appear to have changed completely.

Between them, these two popular versions of the *Ch'en hsün-chien* story provide virtually the only relevant insights into the characterization of this white ape between the thirteenth and the sixteenth centuries. The story was widely known, as allusions elsewhere testify. An anonymous *tsa-chü Shih chen-jen szu-sheng so pai-yüan*[c],[4] refers in three places to it and shows

[1] Cf. the suggestion by Ch'ien Nan-yang, p. 178.
[2] An allusion to the story of Shih Ts'un[d], who hung up a pot and slept in it, making it his universe complete with sun and moon.
[3] *Cheng-shih, ts'e* 2; Ch'ien, p. 177. The use of the term *yeh-yüan*[e] in the last line is conspicuous as one of the few Buddhist terms to be found among the fragments of the play.
[4] A play apparently of Ming date preserved in a MS version from the Mo-wang kuan[f] collection of dramatic texts. (This collection was originally in the possession of

ᵃ 彩旗兒   ᵇ 眞人   ᶜ 時眞人四聖鎖白猿   ᵈ 施存   ᵉ 業緣   ᶠ 脈望館

some signs of being itself modelled on the same lines. The Taoist protector plays a similar role in opening the action with a warning and finally resolving it by exorcising the white ape and delivering a stolen wife from its possession. The ape introduces itself with the claim to be no less redoubtable than 'the aged Pai-shen-kung[a] of Yü-ling[b]'.[1] The afflicted husband Shen Pi[c], finding himself confronted with the ape who has possessed his wife, exclaims:

Heavens! This means another 'search for a wife on Yü-ling'.[2]

Similarly, traces of the story's influence have been pointed out in the work of Ch'ü Yu[d] (1341–1427), whose literary tale *Shen-yang tung chi*[e] in the collection *Chien-teng hsin-hua*[f][3] again takes up the theme of the predatory ape-demon; and in one of the vernacular tales by Ling Meng-ch'u[g] (d. 1643).[4] But in these cases the motifs of the story as we know it have been subordinated to the techniques and preoccupations of individual authors, and the results happen to throw little light on the question that concerns us here.

As it emerges from Ōta Tatsuo's analysis, the question is—how does the white ape, in traditional legend and more particularly in popular versions of the *Ch'en hsün-chien* story, relate to the character Sun Hsing-che of the early *Hsi-yu chi* tradition? Are we to see the two as closely identified—Sun Hsing-che perhaps even gaining most of his substance from this long-established legendary figure from south China? Sun Hsing-che would in this case have been basically an abductor of women, governed by carnal lusts which he transcended only under the fastidious hands of the sixteenth-century novelist. Ōta argues more specifically that the very name *Wu-k'ung*[h], 'aware of emptiness', may belong originally in this particular context: it would derive its significance from the famous paradoxical identification of *k'ung*[i], 'emptiness', and *se*[j], 'form' so vigorously stated in the Buddhist *Heart Sūtra*, but with the

---

Chao Ch'i-mei[k] (1563–1624), later catalogued in the *Yeh-shih-yüan shu-mu* of Ch'ien Tseng. It is reprinted *in toto* in *Ku-pen hsi-ch'ü ts'ung-k'an*, Fourth Series.) Cf. Fu Hsi-hua (1958), pp. 252–3.

[1] In the introductory *hsieh-tzu*[l] [2*b*] (page numbers not marked).

[2] See first *che* [4*b*].

[3] *Chien-teng hsin-hua* (author's preface dated 1378), pp. 69–72. Cf. Liu Yeh-ch'iu, pp. 52–4.

[4] *Ch'u-k'e P'ai-an ching-ch'i*, ch. 24: cf. Liu, pp. 54–5.

[a] 白申公   [b] 庚嶺   [c] 沈璧   [d] 瞿佑   [e] 申陽洞記   [f] 剪燈新話
[g] 凌濛初   [h] 悟空   [i] 空   [j] 色   [k] 趙琦美   [l] 楔子

debased, sexual, overtones in the term *se* which are in fact found in the prose story of *Ch'en hsün-chien*.[1]

Ingenious as this argument is, there are several features in the material discussed above which now make it seem dubious.

1. The only *Hsi-yu chi* source in which Sun Wu-k'ung is explicitly represented as an abductor is the *tsa-chü* sequence; but it has been argued in chapter 5 above that this version is likely to be unreliable as a reflection of tradition, by reason of liberties taken with the material in the cause of dramatic expediency. Sun Wu-k'ung is cast in a stereotyped acting role of which coarseness and bawdry are integral features. Moreover the abduction motif provides the dramatist with one more stock heroine to sing in his ninth scene.

2. The Kōzanji version, earliest and, in its own way, most genuine of the sources, shows no trace of any such characterization in its monkey-hero. Ōta brushes this aside as paradoxical, or at least too early to be of great relevance: (1959), p. 12; but when the 'Tripitaka' cycle was in its earliest stages the White Ape legend had some centuries of tradition behind it and had already been cast in literary form. That the 'Tripitaka' monkey was here even so quite distinct from the ape-abductor is a fact that should be acknowledged.

3. The Buddhist preoccupations of the white ape appear in any significant sense only in the vernacular story, which almost certainly represents a version no earlier than the late fourteenth century. The fragments of southern drama suggest a plot in which the ape was brought to justice directly by a Taoist saint: there would seem to be no part left for a Buddhist to play. The Buddhist theme may easily have been a relatively late development, perhaps even a characteristic peculiar to the Ming vernacular story.

4. The name Ch'i-t'ien Ta-sheng and the family of monkey-demons are common to only the later versions of each tradition: the vernacular *Ch'en hsün-chien* story and the *tsa-chü Hsi-yu chi* (which however singles out the name T'ung-t'ien Ta-sheng to apply to Sun Wu-k'ung). The *Hsi-yu chi* described by Ch'oe Se-chin does feature the name Ch'i-t'ien Ta-sheng, as does also the sixteenth-century novel, but does not include an abduction among the monkey's crimes.

---

[1] In the story (p. 131) the abbot quotes the scriptural maxim 'Form is emptiness, emptiness is form' (from the *Heart Sūtra*, T. VIII, p. 848 c) in reply to the monkey Shen-yang-kung's confession of uncontrollable lust. Cf. Ōta Tatsuo (1959), p. 11.

We must provisionally conclude that in terms of origins and basic preoccupations the 'Tripitaka' cycle and the legend of the White Ape remain distinct. The monkey-hero in each case has its own identity—Tripitaka's disciple commits crimes which are mischievous and irreverent, but the white ape is from first to last a monstrous creature which has to be eliminated. The two acquire superficial points of similarity when popular treatments of the respective traditions, in each case of Ming date, coincide in certain details of nomenclature.

These are negative conclusions in the sense that they leave the origins and essential functions of Sun Wu-k'ung still obscure, but the details which have emerged in the discussion will serve a further purpose below.

9

Monkeys in *Tsa-Chü* Literature

The *tsa-chü Erh-lang shen so Ch'i-t'ien Ta-sheng*[a] survives in the Mo-wang-kuan collection of dramatic texts.[1] No *prima facie* evidence announces its authorship or background. Ch'ien Tseng was content to list it under a topic heading ('Gods and Immortals') among the 'Anonymous Plays Old and New' of his *Yeh-shih-yüan* catalogue.[2] We have, then, to rely on internal evidence to define its context. The play's evident bearing on the Sun Wu-k'ung tradition makes it necessary to do so.

The action, in brief, is as follows: An ape-demon, Ch'i-t'ien Ta-sheng, steals Taoist elixir and fairy wine from the Immortal Yüan-shih T'ien-tsun[b] and returns with it to his home Shui-lien tung on Hua-kuo shan. The theft reported, Erh-lang is summoned to capture him. The ape meanwhile feasts with members of his family on Hua-kuo shan. Erh-lang, mustering his traditional followers, advances in company with Chü-ling shen and effects the capture. In the final act he surrenders the prisoner to the Taoist deity Ch'ü-hsieh-yüan-chu[c]. The ape begs for clemency and is finally dismissed with only a firm injunction to reform.

A number of details demand attention:

the name of the ape: Ch'i-t'ien Ta-sheng;

the name of his home: Hua-kuo shan, Shui-lien tung;

the members of his family: 'My elder brother T'ung[d]-t'ien Ta-sheng, myself Ch'i-t'ien Ta-sheng, my elder sister Kuei-shan Shui-mu[e], my younger sister T'ieh-se Mi-hou[f], my younger brother Shua-shua San-lang[g]' (speech in the first act);

the stealing of elixir and wine;

the role of Erh-lang and Chü-ling shen;

---

[1] It is also included in the modern collection *Ku-pen Yüan-Ming tsa-chü*.

[2] *Yeh-shih-yüan shu-mu* 10:15a. Huang P'i-lieh (1763–1825) followed this example in his *Yeh-shih-yüan ts'ang-shu ku-chin tsa-chü mu-lu*, p. 392.

[a] 二郎神鎖齊天大聖　　[b] 元始天尊　　[c] 驅邪院主　　[d] 通
[e] 龜山水母　　　　　　[f] 鐵色獼猴　　[g] 耍耍三郎

the 'iron cudgel'[a] with which the ape defends himself in the third act;
the name Sun Hsing-che claimed by the youngest brother in the same
act;

minor details of the battle—the attendants of Erh-lang, the Taoist
gods—also peripherally related to the *Hsi-yu chi* story.

There is no need to labour the obvious similarities in detail shared
with various sources discussed above, except perhaps to stress that the
name Hua-kuo shan and the religious designation 'Hsing-che' date back
to the earliest traces of the 'Tripitaka' cycle in the thirteenth century.
Before proceeding to immediate conclusions it is worth pausing to consider the play's dating more closely.

Dating, and the related plays

The *Ch'i-t'ien Ta-sheng* play finds its full context only when considered
together with a group of three other *tsa-chü* on similar themes, each
involving the 'Crown Prince' Naṭa, or Erh-lang, or both. They are:
Erh-lang shen tsui she so-mo-ching[b],[1] *Meng-lieh Ne-cha san pien-hua*[c],[2]
Kuan-k'ou Erh-lang chan chien-chiao[d].[3] All except the first are assigned
by Ch'ien Tseng to the same subdivision of the 'Anonymous Plays Old
and New'; the first, which he includes among a group allegedly of
anonymous Yüan authorship, is the subject of a study in Yen Tun-i's
Yüan-chü chen-i (pp. 36–48). Because Yen Tun-i's analysis raises several
relevant issues some space may fairly be given here to a summary and
discussion of his conclusions.

His case falls into two parts. The first advances the double thesis that
tsa-chü playwrights of the Yüan period, and indeed northerners in
general, had little taste for wild and unrealistic tales of battle with
demons; that at this period such legends were as yet strictly localized,
and that of Erh-lang in particular showed no signs of having penetrated
beyond Szechuan (where all its different versions originated) or at least
the adjacent southern provinces, into regions where *tsa-chü* dramatists
were active. A complementary section establishes an internal relation-

---

[1] Preserved in the Mo-wang kuan collection. There are two distinct versions, differing
in the final acts: cf. Fu Hsi-hua (1957), pp. 295–6 and 337; more fully analysed in
Yen Tun-i (1960), p. 36 ff. Composite version reprinted in *Ku-pen Yüan-Ming
tsa-chü*.

[2] In the Mo-wang kuan collection; reprinted in *Ku-pen Yüan-Ming tsa-chü*; cf. Fu
Hsi-hua (1958), p. 253.

[3] As in n. 2; cf. Fu Hsi-hua (1958), p. 254.

[a] 鐵棒   [b] 二郎神醉射鎖魔鏡   [c] 猛烈那吒三變化

[d] 灌口二郎斬健蛟

ship between the plays listed above (including also the *Hsi-yu chi tsa-chü*), and places them firmly in the Ming period, arguing from the rich circumstantial evidence that Ch'ien Tseng's dating of the play *So-mo-ching* was unwarranted.

Of this group of contentions, I am unable to accept that the Erh-lang legend had failed to reach the northern areas where Yüan dramatists were active, although Yen Tun-i's supporting arguments are extended and elaborate.[1] It is a simple and well-attested fact that the Erh-lang cult had already by the early twelfth century spread from its seat in Kuan-k'ou, Szechuan, to the Northern Sung capital at K'ai-feng, and was there pursued with enthusiasm.[2] Yen Tun-i's statistical evidence (pp. 39–40) would seem to imply rather that the earliest generations of *tsa-chü* dramatists were disposed by temperament, not obliged by ignorance, to neglect the wilder fantasies of battle with demons. Under Ming rule, particularly as from an edict of 1389, dramatists were savagely restricted to a few politically innocuous subjects, among them 'Gods and immortals'[a].[3] This must have exerted a real enough incentive for fifteenth-century *tsa-chü* poets to turn for material to the gods of local cult-legend.

Reviewing the group of five plays involved here one can accept more readily that they are indeed related together by a fund of common material and treatment. It falls into three categories:

The Erh-lang legend (version centred around Chao Yü[b], Prefect of Chia-chou[c] under the Sui, later canonised in the Taoist pantheon):[4] a close correspondence in detail links the *So-mo-ching* and *Chan-chien-chiao*, and the *Ch'i-t'ien Ta-sheng* alludes to the same essentials. In all these plays, as also in the *Hsi-yu chi tsa-chü* (with the one exception discussed in an earlier chapter—p. 84), virtually the same group of followers attends Erh-lang into battle (cf. Yen (1960), pp. 44–6).

The demons subject to Naṭa: principally the four female demons subdued in the *Ne-cha san-pien* (third scene), and who reappear as identically named members of his suite in the *So-mo-ching* (first scene). Among the other group of demons likewise subdued appear the names Po-yen chin-ching kuei[d], Pa-chiao shih-t'ou[e] kuei, Wu-pien ta-li[f] kuei,

---

[1] Yen (1960), pp. 40 ff.
[2] Cf. below, p. 147, n. 3.
[3] Cf. the relevant historical material quoted by Wang Hsiao-ch'uan, pp. 12–13.
[4] Cf. Huang Chih-kang, pp. 38 ff.
[a] 神仙   [b] 趙昱   [c] 嘉州   [d] 百眼金睛鬼   [e] 八角獅頭
[f] 無邊大力

T'ieh-t'ou lan-t'ien[a] kuei—common also, with slight graphic variants, to the *So-mo-ching*, where they are again put to the same use. Only the Po-yen-kuei, together with a character Chiu-shou Niu-mo-lo Wang[b], both known to the *Hsi-yu chi* tradition,[1] are extracted from the group to play a more individual role (Yen (1960), p. 46).

The character Ch'ü-hsieh-yüan-chu—cognate with the Warrior of the North[c]: common to the *Chan-chien-chiao*, *Ch'i-t'ien Ta-sheng* and *So-mo-ching*, effectively as a superintendent of the action. His verses of self-introduction are identical in the latter two texts, and that in the *Chan-chien-chiao* also resembles them closely.

The most telling evidence on dating is a line near the close of the *Ne-cha san-pien*:

May the Great Ming enjoy peace and order for thousands upon thousands of years.[2]

Whether or not these loyal sentiments at the end of a play suffice to characterize it as a piece for court entertainment,[3] or a 'Palace text'[d],[4] or merely as belonging to a genre of 'celebratory' Buddhist *tsa-chü*,[5] the line quoted here at least does something to help define the text in terms of time. Similar patriotic eulogy is to be found in the closing lines of the *Chan-chien-chiao* and has been remarked above (p. 79) in the *Hsi-yu chi tsa-chü*. It seems more than ever likely that the whole group of plays shares a common background.

Ch'ien Tseng's dating of the *So-mo-ching* is explained by Yen Tun-i (1960, p. 39) in the light of a remark introducing the *Yang-ch'un-tsou*[e], an anthology of drama now extant only in a fragmentary edition of 1609 containing three works. The contents of the original eight *chüan* are however known,[6] and it appears that the *So-mo-ching* was one of the four plays in *chüan* 5. The general introduction to the collection states:

In this book all are songs of the Yüan, but songs from the Ming are added at the end.[7]

The impression of a Yüan dating thus depends upon how these ambiguous words are understood. Yen Tun-i observes (p. 39):

---

[1] Cf. above, p. 65, n. 7; also *HYC*, ch. 3, p. 31, ch. 59, p. 678 etc., and ch. 62, pp. 714, 717, ch. 63, pp. 720, 722 ff., with a Chiu-t'ou Fu-ma[f].

[2] In the song *Ch'ing-chiang-yin*[g]; *Ku-pen Yüan-Ming tsa-chü* ed., p. 10a. Cf. Yen (1960), p. 47. [3] See *Ku-pen Yüan-Ming tsa-chü, T'i-yao*, p. 50a.

[4] See Yen Tun-i (1954), p. 149.   [5] See Sawada Mizuho (1964), pp. 42–3.

[6] See Lo Chen-yü, *Hsü Hui-k'o shu-mu*[h] (1914), 10[i]:20a–21b.

[7] See reprint in *Ku-pen hsi-ch'ü ts'ung-k'an*, Fourth Series, 6, Fan-li[j], p. 2a.

[a] 鐵頭藍天   [b] 九首牛寬羅王   [c] 北方眞武   [d] 內府本   [e] 陽春奏
[f] 九頭駙馬   [g] 清江引   [h] 續彙刻書目   [i] 癸   [j] 凡例

Under the Ming, then, this play was thought to be by a Yüan author, so, when the *Yeh-shih-yüan* list of *tsa-chü* old and new was compiled, it was classed as an anonymous Yüan work...

Another work included in the same *chüan* of *Yang-ch'un-tsou* was the *Yüan t'ing ching*, a play to be discussed immediately below, which appears to have been composed almost certainly in the fifteenth century or later. Ch'ien Tseng's similar verdict in this case was possibly based on the same reading of the above words.

Concerning the *So-mo-ching* play, however, there is a complementary remark by Ch'i Piao-chia, in his *Yüan-shan-t'ang chü-p'in* (compiled before 1645). Ch'i concerns himself in this catalogue primarily with *tsa-chü* of the Ming period. When he writes of this play:

a conception of this order has very much the tone of the Yüan poets, but in the verse a sense of proud vigour is rather lacking[a]. The rhyming is also uneven,[1]

it appears that he is not inferring a Yüan authorship, but commenting on what he feels to be the work of a dramatist who narrowly fails to achieve an idealized 'Yüan' standard. In the early seventeenth century the *So-mo-ching* was thus by no means unanimously accepted as an authentic Yüan work.

In these respects there is reason enough to accept Yen Tun-i's thesis that the *So-mo-ching* play, and probably also its fellows listed above, including the *Hsi-yu chi* and the *Ch'i-t'ien Ta-sheng*, do not appear to belong to the earlier part of the fourteenth century. Yen in fact suggests the mid-sixteenth century, citing the hundred-chapter *Hsi-yu chi* as their probable inspiration (1960, p. 47). Fuller knowledge of earlier prose versions now makes it unnecessary to force so extreme a conclusion.

What needs to be stressed at this point is rather that the names and characteristics we meet in the *Ch'i-t'ien Ta-sheng* play, particularly those of the ape-hero and his demon family, come to resemble closely the case of the *Ch'en hsün-chien* story discussed immediately above. Both works seem, for various reasons, to date from an unspecified time in the Ming period. Recalling that Hua-kuo shan had been the home of the *Hsi-yu chi* monkey already in the Kōzanji version, and that the title 'Hsing-che' attached to his name there and in all later versions gained its significance specifically from the circumstances of Tripitaka's pious

---

[1] *Yüan-shan-t'ang chü-p'in*, p. 167. Part of this sentence is misleadingly taken out of context by Fu Hsi-hua (1957), pp. 295–6.

[a] 少欠振拔

enterprise, we can conclude with some confidence that this play simply reflects an existing *Hsi-yu chi*.

The wider implications will emerge more plainly after some further material has been introduced and discussed.

YÜAN SUN

About the remoter background to this story more is to be said below (pp. 155 ff.). It survives in two distinct treatments: one an anonymous *tsa-chü* with the title (i.e. *cheng-ming*) *Lung-chi shan yeh-yüan t'ing ching*[a],[1] and the other a story in literary idiom in the collection *Chien-teng yü-hua* by Li Chen, (*tzu* Ch'ang-ch'i[b]) (1376–1452).[2] Each of the works presents a certain amount of secondary material loosely associated with a central narrative. What they hold in common amounts to a simple and coherent story:

A Ch'an master styled Hsiu[c], in his remote mountain retreat, finds an ape coming first to listen to his intonation of the scriptures, then, in secret, to play about in the monastery precincts—fingering the books of scripture, trying on the monks' robes etc. It disappears. Later, a ruined official of the Later T'ang dynasty comes to attach himself as a layman to the monastery. His name is Yüan Sun[d] (an obvious play on two words[e] meaning 'monkey').[3] The superior one day summons him to the lecture hall, where, after an exchange of allusive verses (in the play, a scene of question and answer on Ch'an doctrine) Yüan attains enlightenment and dies as a Buddhist, in the seated position. He is then found to be a monkey.

Li Ch'ang-ch'i's story in *Chien-teng yü-hua* opens with an account of the foundation of the monastery and the naming of Lung-chi shan;[4] it

---

[1] The *t'i-mu*: *Ta-hui t'ang Hsiu-kung she chiang*[f]. Cf. Fu Hsi-hua (1957), p. 295. The title is abbreviated below to *Yüan t'ing ching*. References are to the text included in the early seventeenth-century collection *Yüan-Ming tsa-chü* (photographic facsimile of 1929).

[2] The story *T'ing-ching yüan chi*[g]. References are to the annotated edition by Chou I included in *Chien-teng hsin-hua wai erh-chung*.

[3] The device is one of the similarities which Sawada Mizuho (1964), p. 30, traces between this story and the anecdote 'Sun K'o'[h] in *TPKC* 445:3638–41 (the source is given as *Ch'uan-ch'i*[i], evidently the work of that name by P'ei Hsing[j], ninth century).

[4] Li identifies the 'Lung-chi shan' of his story with a Tung-shan[k] in Chi-shui hsien[l] near his own family home at Lu-ling[m] (=Chi-an[n], in central Kiangsi). A local

a 龍濟山野猿聽經　　b 昌祺　　c 修　　d 袁遜　　e 猿猻
f 大惠堂修公設講　　g 聽經猿記　　h 孫恪　　i 傳奇　　j 裴鉶
k 東山　　　　　　　l 吉水縣　　m 盧陵　　n 吉安

adds, at the end of the principal episode, a sequel in which the ape is reincarnated after two hundred years as a Ch'an master of the Southern Sung. The *tsa-chü* begins with a scene in which the ape anticipates its personal appearance by adopting the guise of a woodcutter, learned in the Confucian classics but resigned to a life without recognition, who encounters the master Hsiu on the mountain. It supplies a final scene in which Yüan Sun is received into paradise by an Arhat.

Several essential features distinguish this story from those in the Chinese traditions discussed in these chapters. Not only is it frankly Buddhist in inspiration, constructed on the lines of a chain of incarnations, but it presents a basically different monkey-figure. Wu-chih-ch'i and the White Ape are traditionally monstrous creatures. Conscience and religious fear appear only as the very latest refinements in popular versions of the White Ape story. This ape has both intelligence and access to religious enlightenment; but it is also unstable, imitative and even facetious:

For all his mental brightness and clever, fluent style Sun was also skittish and disorderly, very much given to childish ways. Sometimes he would sit on his couch in the posture of meditation, his head draped in a sheet, and have the monks come and worship him saying: 'This is a manifestation of the White-robed Kuan-yin'. Another time he would sit with legs out-stretched in a niche, his face daubed with indigo, and cause the kitchen hands to salute him, saying that this was the Great Saint of Hung Shan inspecting the food ... (Li, p. 141).

Upon such a central conception the *tsa-chü* in particular imposes a certain amount of further material which shows an immediate relevance to the *Hsi-yu chi* tradition.

gazetteer, the *Chi-shui hsien chih* of 1873, offers confirmation of the existence of a Lung-chi Monastery on this mountain. Its account of the monastery's foundation is slightly less elaborate than Li's, and the founder, also of the Later T'ang period, is named as Hsiu-shan[a] (see 14:6a). In view of the confusion over this name it seems appropriate to draw attention to a tenth-century Ch'an Master, Shao-hsiu[b] of Fu-chou[c], who was known as 'Master[d] of Lung-chi shan'. A number of his Ch'an *dicta* are recorded in the *Ching-te ch'uan-teng lu* (24:10a–11a). The same source also records that for some time he accompanied the famous master Wen-i[e] (885–958) on pious travels, and himself moved on to Lung-chi shan after Wen-i had settled at Fu-chou (=Lin-ch'uan[f] in central Kiangsi). This happened before 943, since the first ruler of the Southern T'ang, who is reported to have had Wen-i move to Nanking (*Sung kao-seng chuan* 13:788b), died in that year. Any identification with the monk of Li's story must of course remain conjectural. It is worth noting that the 'Later T'ang' dating of the account in both Li's story and the gazetteer appears to be strictly unhistorical: from 892 the Kiangsi area was ruled by the Wu[g] dynasty, until in 937 it was taken over by the Southern T'ang (cf. *Hsin Wu-tai shih* 60:10b).

ᵃ 修山   ᵇ 紹修   ᶜ 撫州   ᵈ 主   ᵉ 文益   ᶠ 臨川   ᵍ 吳

In the second act the ape introduces itself with, as well as the conventional spoken passage, a number of songs. One of them contains the lines:

I—I—I have secretly drunk of the precious wine at the Jade Pool[a].[1]
I—I—I have secretly plucked auspicious herbs on Mount P'eng-lai[b].
I—I—I have caused an uproar in heaven over the peaches.
My spiritual powers are not small,
Because in my belly I have the elixir of immortality to guard me from old age.
Summoning the wind and rain, I flaunt my authority.

(p. 6 a: Liang-chou-ti-ch'i[c])

These are obvious allusions to a group of stories on the 'war with heaven' theme, recalling the 'Tripitaka' monkey but differing slightly in detail from the known extant versions . . .

Pak t'ongsa ŏnhae N vi mentions no drinking of wine at the Jade Pool; but the story is alluded to again in the *Hsi-yu chi tsa-chü* (sc. 9) and treated in full in the hundred-chapter novel (ch. 5); the plucking of herbs on P'eng-lai has no immediate parallel in any known version of the cycle, apart from the episode (*HYC* chs. 24–6) of the stolen 'Ginseng-fruit'[d] from the garden of Wu-chuang Kuan[e], in which Sun Wu-k'ung is obliged to visit the Three Islands—not in any strict sense a parallel; the 'uproar in heaven' over stolen peaches is characteristic more of the incident mentioned in *Pak t'ongsa ŏnhae* than of that in the Kōzanji version; the elixir could, by analogy with the *Pak t'ongsa ŏnhae* and the *tsa-chü Hsi-yu chi*, have been stolen from Lao-chün.

Of the whole group of stories in the *Hsi-yu chi* versions only the stealing of fairy robes is completely absent from the *Yüan t'ing ching* play.

Ch'ien Tseng in his catalogue of early *tsa-chü* assigns this play to the section 'Anonymous works of the Yüan'.[2] If the dating were to prove accurate, the play would provide us with earlier reflections of the 'war with heaven' story cast in this particular form than any other known source. It would become important to reconsider the background of the story in later versions of the *Hsi-yu chi*.

Ch'ien Tseng's dating is here, however, not the last word. Chao Ching-shen has shown beyond any reasonable doubt that the *tsa-chü* version of this story was composed directly upon the model of the literary tale in *Chien-teng yü-hua*: the provenance is betrayed by the fact that the

---

[1] The legendary abode of the Queen of the West.
[2] *Yeh-shih-yüan shu-mu* 10:7 a.
[a] 瑤池   [b] 蓬萊   [c] 梁州第七   [d] 人參果   [e] 五莊觀

two versions share several sections of text in common, all of which fit easily and naturally into their context in the prose story, while they are accommodated in the *tsa-chü* only at the cost of much forcing and inaccuracy.[1] Sawada Mizuho has more recently pointed out some circumstantial historical evidence confirming that the play is unlikely to date back to before the Ming period.[2]

Of the six contemporary prefaces to *Chien-teng yü-hua*, four bear the date 1420, among them one by Li himself pointing out that his collection had won a considerable following in the few months since its first reading by Tseng Ch'i[a] (commemorated in the earliest of the 1420 prefaces). This year must therefore be taken as marking the public appearance of the *Chien-teng yü-hua* stories and consequently represents an early limit for the composition of the *tsa-chü* in its present form.

It has been pointed out in another connection (above, ch. 5) that the non-sung parts of extant *tsa-chü* may not necessarily belong integrally to the plays in their original form. The point should be acknowledged again here; but certainly this play as a whole is even so open to considerable suspicion. Li Ch'ang-ch'i's story was set on the very threshhold of his family home in Lu-ling,[3] and there is reason enough to identify its central figure as the tenth-century Kiangsi Ch'an master Shao-hsiu. The story's context seems confined to a closely circumscribed locality. It is possible that Franke is right in suggesting that it derives from a local tradition;[4] but there is certainly an equal chance that Li Ch'ang-ch'i was here adapting the substance of the story from its original form in some Buddhist scripture.[5] Ch'ü Yu, after whose collection *Chien-teng hsin-hua* Li's own stories were modelled, is credited also with a work (now lost) entitled *Strange Items Gleaned from the Buddhist Canon*[b].[6] Li could well have drawn his theme from such a source and recast it around a Buddhist figure of local fame. The story's general distribution in this form is likely to have begun only with the wider circulation of *Chien-teng yü-hua*.

Recalling the monkey's boasted transgressions against heaven and the other attributes quoted above, we now need only to stress that they

[1] Chao Ching-shen (1937), pp. 24–7.
[2] Sawada Mizuho (1964), p. 30.   [3] Cf. Chao (1937), p. 27.
[4] H. Franke, 'Zur Novellistik der frühen Ming-zeit: Das Chien-teng yü-hua des Li Ch'ang-ch'i', *Zeitschrift der Deutschen Morgenländischen Gesellschaft*, N.S. 34 (1959), p. 360.
[5] Cf. the examples cited below in ch. 11.
[6] See *Ch'i-hsiu lei-kao* 33 : 503.

[a] 曾棨   [b] 大藏搜奇

appear just in the lines of a single song and perform no essential function in the action as a whole. This, together with the fact of their absence from Li Ch'ang-ch'i's story, suggests that they derive from some other source, alien to the basic story of Yüan Sun. In the knowledge that this song and its play date from the fifteenth century or even later, we almost certainly see here a further reflection of the Sun Wu-k'ung who, as the early *Hsi-yu chi* sources testify, had long been a famous delinquent and by the end of the fifteenth century was committing virtually the same misdeeds that Yüan Sun here arrogates to himself.

10

Wu-chih-ch'i

For many centuries Chinese scholars have shown interest in this ape-
legend localized at Kuei-shan[a] on the River Huai[b]. What has been
generally regarded as a standard exposition of the legend's growth and
the siting of the cult is provided by Huang Chih-kang, in chapter 15
of *Chung-kuo ti shui-shen*.

Acknowledging the initiative of Chou Yü-ts'ai[c], who had first cited
this tradition in connection with the *Hsi-yu chi* monkey, Hu Shih took up
the idea rather tentatively.[1] Lu Hsün did so more emphatically,[2] and
since his time not only Huang Chih-kang,[3] but more recently Wolfram
Eberhard,[4] Wu Hsiao-ling[5] and Ishida Eiichirō[6] have lent their support
to the theory that the figure Sun Wu-k'ung and his special relationship
with the pilgrim Tripitaka owed a significant debt, perhaps even their
derivation, to the legendary Wu-chih-ch'i.

In summarizing the early history of the legend it will not be necessary
to add more than a number of bibliographical details to the work of
Huang Chih-kang; but his arguments, and those of others, on the relationship with the *Hsi-yu chi* will have to be reconsidered more fully.

Two distinct branches of the legend are recorded.

(1) *The story of Ta Yü*[d]

The earliest sources date from the first quarter of the ninth century.
Li Chao[e], author of *Kuo-shih pu*[f], points out in his preface that the work
covers a period from the K'ai-yüan[g] down to the Ch'ang-ch'ing[h] reigns
(inclusively: AD 713–824): it was presumably written towards the end
of this period.[7] He records:

[1] Hu Shih (1923), pp. 368–70. [2] Lu Hsün (1924), p. 19.
[3] Huang Chih-kang, p. 178. [4] Eberhard (1948), p. 127.
[5] Wu Hsiao-ling, p. 169. [6] Ishida Eiichirō, pp. 125–6.
[7] For Li Chao and the dating of the *Kuo-shih pu*, see *SKCSTM* 79:3b–4a and
140:6b–7b.
[a] 龜山 [b] 淮 [c] 周豫才 [d] 大禹 [e] 李肇 [f] 國史補 [g] 開元
[h] 長慶

There was a fisherman at Ch'u-chou[a] who unexpectedly hooked an ancient iron chain in the Huai, but could not pull it clear. He reported this to the local governor Li Yang[b], who summoned a large number of men to draw it out. At the end of the chain was a black monkey[c]: it jumped out of the water, then plunged back and vanished. Later this was verified in the *Shan-hai ching*, from the words—'A river-beast persistently wrought destruction. Yü chained it below Chün-shan[d]. Its name was Wu-chih-ch'i[e].[1]

Present texts of the *Shan-hai ching* lack this final passage. Its authority cannot be tested. The reference to Chün-shan is obscure unless the character *chün* is ultimately a corruption of *kuei*[f].[2]

The fuller and more famous account of what seems to be the same episode is found in *T'ai-p'ing kuang-chi* (467:3845–6) under the title *Li T'ang*[g] (a name which seems graphically related to the Li Yang to whom Li Chao refers). The source is given as *Jung-mu hsien-t'an*[h], the title of a collection of anecdotes by Wei Hsüan[i]:[3] his preface is dated 831.[4]

In the Yung-t'ai[j] reign (AD 765) a fisherman hooks an iron chain at the foot of Kuei-shan. Li T'ang, then governor of Ch'u-chou, has the chain dragged up. At the end of it an ape-like monster emerges from the water, glares about itself, then returns. Some years later (in 814) Li Kung-tso[k][5] finds part of an ancient text entitled *Yüeh-tu ching*[l] and

---

[1] *Kuo-shih pu* (HCTY) 1:10b. Cf. Huang Chih-kang, p. 168.

[2] Ch'u-chou was on the lower reaches of the Huai, east of the present Hung-tse Lake[m]. Kuei-shan, the site of the legend in all other sources, lies only a few miles to the south-west, whereas Chün-shan is some hundreds of miles to the south in the heart of present-day Kiangsi.

[3] Listed in the *Hsin T'ang shu* 59:12a, which notes that Wei rose to high military rank in the Hsien-t'ung[n] reign (860–73).

[4] Some extracts from this book, including the author's preface but not the 'Li T'ang' passage, are preserved in T'ao Tsung-i's compilation *Shuo-fu*[o], of which a reconstruction in 100 *chüan* was published in 1927 by Chang Tsung-hsiang[p] (Commercial Press, Shanghai), based on MS fragments of Ming date. For the preface, cf. *chüan* 7:14a. In it Wei Hsüan describes his book as recording the conversation of Tsan-huang Kung[q] during a campaign in Shu. Chiao Hung (1541–1620), in *Kuo-shih ching-chi chih* 4 (*hsia*):10a, identifies this raconteur as Li Te-yü[r] (787–849), a native of Tsan-huang whose grandfather Ch'i-yün[s] had been granted the title Tsan-huang Kung (*Hsin T'ang shu* 146:2b). Li Te-yü, who directed a campaign in Shu in 830, had had personal experience of the Huai region, in particular Szu-chou, in 825–6 while Civil Governor of Che-hsi[t] (*Hsin T'ang shu* 180:1a–3a). (A translation of the passage relevant to Szu-chou will be found in C. K. Yang, *Religion in Chinese Society* (Berkeley and Los Angeles, 1961), pp. 200–1.) The story in question would thus seem to have been collected *circa* 825.

[5] Author of several famous pieces of prose fiction, Li seems to have lived from the late eighth to the mid-ninth centuries (cf. Wang P'i-chiang, p. 91).

a 楚州	b 李陽	c 青彌猴	d 軍山	e 無支奇	f 龜
g 李湯	h 戎幕閑談	i 韋絢	j 永泰	k 李公佐	l 岳瀆經
m 洪澤湖	n 咸通	o 說郛	p 張宗祥	q 贊皇公	r 李德裕
s 栖筠	t 浙西				

deciphers it with the help of a Taoist, Chou Chiao-chün[a]. It describes
the storms encountered by Ta Yü when attempting to govern the rivers
around T'ung-pai shan[b] and goes on:

He captured a god of the rivers Huai and Kuo[c] named Wu-chih-ch'i[d]. It
answered readily when spoken to, explaining which were the deep and which
the shallow parts of the Yangtze and the Huai, and how far the marshlands
extended. In shape it was like a monkey, with flattened nose and high brow,
its body black and head white, eyes metallic and teeth like snow. Its neck
stretched out to a length of a hundred feet, its strength exceeded that of nine
elephants. In attack it moved nimbly and swiftly: it was lithe and impetuous,
and one could not keep it in sight or hearing for long. Yü...put it in the
charge of Keng-ch'en[e], who was able to keep it under control...He fastened
its neck with a great cable, pierced its nose (and hung there) a golden bell.
He moved it to the foot of Kuei-shan in Huai-yin[f], with the result that the
Huai thenceforth flowed peacefully into the sea.

Both passages are taken up by later writers.[1]

Nothing of course ensures that the *Yüeh-tu ching* was anything more
than a fiction by Li Kung-tso or some other. Apart from the unconfirmed
quotation from the *Shan-hai ching* there is no clear sign of the legend
before the early ninth century.[2] But at this stage, at least, its characteristics were very clearly defined: in particular the creature's name, its
role as a river demon, the mode of its imprisonment, its association
with the Huai region.

T'ung-pai shan is the name of the range in modern Honan where
the Huai takes its source. Kuei-shan is considerably further downstream
at a point in the north-east corner of modern Anhwei.[3] The names
mentioned in this and later accounts—Szu-chou, Hsü-i[g], Huai-yin—
all belong to the region in which the present-day Huai enters the Hung-
tse Lake. Alterations in the course of rivers and in the contours of the
lake itself have changed the topography significantly in recent centuries.

[1] E.g. T'ao Tsung-i, in *Cho-keng lu*, 29:16ab, and Juan K'uei-sheng (1727–89), in
Ch'a-yü k'o hua, 22:717. Cf. below, p. 143.
[2] Huang Chih-kang, pp. 171–2, suggests a precedent in the pseudo-historical work
Wu Yüeh ch'un-ch'iu[h] (traditionally attributed to Chao Yeh[i] of the first century AD,
although the text as we know it contains a generous proportion of fictional elements
and folk tradition, and may be later in date: cf. *SKCSTM*, 66:1b–3a and Ch'en
Chung-fan, pp. 19–21). A demon of the Huai river seizes the horse of an emissary
from Ch'i[j], and is defeated by him in a protracted underwater battle: cf. *Wu Yüeh
ch'un-ch'iu* (*SPTK*), shang (4):27b–28a. Other near-contemporary versions of this
same story are cited by Ishida Eiichirō, pp. 19–20.
[3] In modern Anhwei there are two mountains named Kuei-shan, distinguished as
Upper and Lower[k]. This, the more northerly of the two, is Lower Kuei-shan.

[a] 周焦君   [b] 桐栢山   [c] 渦   [d] 無支祁   [e] 庚辰   [f] 淮陰
[g] 盱眙   [h] 吳越春秋   [i] 趙曄   [j] 齊   [k] 上下

The most dramatic loss is the disappearance of the former Szu-chou itself in the waters of the Hung-tse Lake, after a series of flood disasters in the sixteenth and seventeenth centuries.[1]

(2) *The role of Saṅgha*

The Buddhist monk Saṅgha[a] came to China from the small state known as Ho-kuo[b], in Russian Turkestan, in the early 660s. The centre of his activities was Szu-chou, where he founded a monastery named P'u-kuang-wang szu[c]. This, with Saṅgha himself, rapidly became a resort of pilgrimage. Saṅgha found favour with the emperor Chung-tsung[d], who wrote the inscription for his monastery, and, particularly after his death in April 710, he came to be a figure celebrated throughout the land.[2]

Tracing his fortunes at the hands of later pious biographers, we receive vivid impressions of his progressive popular canonization. According to the accounts summarized in the *T'ai-p'ing kuang-chi*,[3] he could exude fragrance from a hole in the top of his head, his dead body in Ch'ang-an caused a foul smell to spread through the city which cleared only when the Emperor gave consent for it to be returned to Szu-chou, and the monk Wan-hui[e] identified him for the Emperor as an incarnation of the bodhisattva Kuan-yin. Tsan-ning, in the *Sung kao-seng chuan*, represents him in addition as a protective deity of Szu-chou.[4] Since at least the eleventh century the canonized Saṅgha seems to have assumed the specific character of a protector against flood (from the beginning his cult had been centred in one of the most severely flood-prone parts of China), and he served also as a patron saint of all who worked or travelled on water.[5]

It was no doubt in such a capacity that he became associated with the Wu-chih-ch'i legend and himself credited with the defeat of the river-ape.

---

[1] Cf. *Ming shih* 87:2 *a*–3 *b*; Huang Chih-kang, p. 168.

[2] The earliest account of his life is the *P'u-kuang-wang szu pei*[f] by Li Yung[g] (673–742), in *Wen-yüan ying-hua* 858:1 *a*–3 *b*. Among subsequent literary references are the 'Seng-ch'ieh ko'[h] by Li Po[i] (701–62) (*CTS*, vol. 3, pp. 1720–1) and 'Sung seng Ch'eng-kuan'[j] by Han Yü (768–824) (*CTS*, vol. 5, pp. 3830–1). Other material is cited by Makita Tairyō (*q.v.*) p. 270, n. 3.

[3] *TPKC*, 96:638–9.

[4] *Sung kao-seng chuan*, 18:822–3.

[5] Throughout the above I have been indebted to the thorough study of the popular Saṅgha cult by Makita Tairyō, who cites much important supplementary material.

a 僧伽	b 何國	c 普光王寺	d 中宗	e 萬廻	f 碑
g 李邕	h 僧伽歌	i 李白	j 送僧澄觀		

Chu Hsi[a] (1130–1200), in a gloss from the *T'ien-wen*[b] section of his *Ch'u-tz'u pien-cheng* (*q.v.*), observes:

These words are no more than a popular tradition of the Warring States period, of the same type as the popular (tales) current nowadays about Saṅgha defeating Wu-chih-ch'i[c] and Hsü Sun[d] beheading the serpent-demon...[1]

His contemporary Lo Pi[e] has a brief study of the legend in his *Lu shih*[f],[2] first introducing the theme of Ta Yü ordering the waters and quoting the *Yüeh-tu ching*, then adding:

But Buddhists hold that this was the 'River-mother'[g] defeated by Saṅgha of Szu-chou...

Such an adapted form of the legend must therefore have been common knowledge in southern parts of China already in the twelfth century. Chu Hsi and Lo Pi both challenge its authenticity; and later T'ao Tsung-i opens his paragraph on the subject in *Cho-keng lu* (29:16a) with a similar refutation:

Below the pagoda of Szu-chou is traditionally the place where Szu-chou Ta-sheng[h] chained the 'River-mother'. This is wrong...[3]

He proceeds to quote material on the legend of Ta Yü and Kuei-shan. Szu-chou Ta-sheng was of course Saṅgha: the words Ta-sheng were associated with his name already in the *Sung kao-seng chuan* (823a); his monastery had come eventually to be known as the Ta-sheng szu[i], and it was this building, or sequence of buildings, that formed the centre of Saṅgha's legendary activities from the beginning.[4] Elsewhere in the *Cho-keng lu* (25:16a) T'ao Tsung-i includes in his list of *yüan-pen* the title *Shui-mu*[j]. It may well have presented the legend in the popularized form, with Saṅgha as hero, which T'ao Tsung-i here feels necessary to refute by appealing to more respectable literary authorities.

It seems nevertheless that varieties of the Saṅgha version became standard in popular literature: a title *Mu-ch'a hsing-che so Shui-mu*[k] is credited to the (? thirteenth century) *tsa-chü* playwright Kao Wen-

---

[1] *Ch'u-tz'u pien-cheng* 2 (*hsia*):2a. Cf. Hu Shih (1923), pp. 368–9. For the legend of Hsü Sun, see Huang Chih-kang pp. 58 ff.

[2] Completed in 1170 (cf. *SKCSTM*, 50:17b–18a). For the passage in question, see *Lu shih* (*SPPY*), *Yü-lun*[l] 9:4b–5b.

[3] Cf. Huang Chih-kang, p. 174.

[4] Cf. *Sung kao-seng chuan* (822c); Huang Chih-kang, p. 176.

[a] 朱熹	[b] 天問	[c] 無之祈	[d] 許遜	[e] 羅泌	[f] 路史
[g] 水母	[h] 大聖	[i] 寺	[j] 水母	[k] 木叉行者鎮水母	[l] 餘論

hsiu[a];[1] a similar title, *Szu-chou ta-sheng hsiang*[b] *Shui-mu*, appears in the '*Yüeh-fu*' section of *Pao-wen t'ang shu-mu* (p. 145); and another again (...*yen*[c] *Shui-mu*) in the *Lu-kuei pu hsü-pien* (p. 283), in this case attributed to Hsü Tzu-shou[d].[2]

From these further sources two general characteristics emerge:

1. The Saṅgha legend was a popular tradition. Chu Hsi dismisses it emphatically as 'vulgar'[e]. Lo Pi ascribes it, with some contempt, to Buddhist influence. The material assembled by Makita Tairyō clearly documents the background to their pronouncements.

2. The river-demon, at least in this popular form, is a female creature —*Shui-mu* or *Sheng*[f]-*mu*—and described as 'chained up', 'defeated' or, in the case of Hsü Tzu-shou's play, 'drowned'[g] (perhaps in the sense of 'suppressed under water').

Relevance to the 'Hsi-yu chi' tradition

We can now recall a number of allusions in the *tsa-chü Hsi-yu chi*:

In sc. 9, describing his family, Sun Hsing-che names his second sister as Wu-chih-ch'i Sheng-mu (p. 37). In sc. 10 (p. 45) the song *K'u-huang-t'ien* ends with the lines:

> He is the brother of Li-shan Lao-mu,
> Wu-chih-ch'i is his sister.

In sc. 17 the Queen of the Land of Women sings (p. 77, *Chi-sheng-ts'ao*[h]):

> On your robe, smears of rouge,
> On your cassock the scent of powder.

---

[1] *Lu-kuei pu*, p. 106. The version from the T'ien-i ko library adds in full the *t'i-mu* and *cheng-ming*:

> Moksha the novice monk defeats a demon,
> Ta-sheng of Szu-chou chains up the 'River-mother'

(introducing minor inconsistencies and graphic errors): cf. *Lu-kuei pu*, p. 158, n. 205. Kao Wen-hsiu is listed as one of the 'older generation now dead...' (cf. above, p. 56 etc.). See also Sun K'ai-ti (1958), pp. 171–2. In *T'ai-ho cheng-yin p'u* (p. 29) a title *So Shui-mu* is listed under Kao Wen-hsiu. Moksha appears as one of Saṅgha's prominent disciples whose lives are sketched in at the close of his biography in *Sung kao-seng chuan* (p. 823a,b). The others are Hui-yen[i] and Hui-an[j]. Popular literature later featured both Moksha and Hui-an, often apparently fused into one person, as Kuan-yin's chief disciple: cf. *PTS*, p. 293 (N vi); *tsa-chü Hsi-yu chi*, sc. 7, pp. 31 ff.; *HYC*, ch. 6, p. 59, ch. 12, p. 134, ch. 17, p. 199 etc.

[2] Cf. Yen Tun-i (1954), p. 151; (1960), pp. 40–1 and 47, n. 3; Fu Hsi-hua (1957), pp. 124–5; (1958), p. 32.

[a] 高文秀　[b] 降　[c] 潒　[d] 須子壽　[e] 俗　[f] 聖　[g] 潒＝淹
[h] 寄生草　[i] 慧儼　[j] 岸

Like the Mataṅgī seizing Ānanda on Yin-shan,
Like Kuei-tzu-mu hemming in the Buddha upon Ling-shan,
Or Wu-chih-ch'i capturing Chang the monk[a] on Kuei-shan . . .

The story of Ānanda and the temptress Mataṅgī, in its varying forms, has a well-attested place in traditional Buddhist mythology.[1] Kuei-tzu-mu and Wu-chih-ch'i, cited here as legendary seductresses, appear in an unfamiliar light,[2] but the association of the latter with Kuei-shan is unmistakable.

The argument by analogy, which has appealed to several commentators on this material, is summed up in the following passage by Huang Chih-kang, concerning both the references above and the scene of Sun Hsing-che's capture, in which Kuan-yin orders his life to be spared and has him sealed beneath Hua-kuo shan:

Kuan-yin's suppression of Sun Hsing-che beneath a mountain in this play is an act exactly like Saṅgha's chaining the river-demon in a well or under a pagoda . . . Li[b]-shan Lao-mu here seems to resemble the evil dragon beneath Li-tui[c]. Wu-chih-ch'i is a thing in the Kuei-shan well. They are Sun Hsing-che's sisters, and also his prototypes. The Devarāja Li seems to be Li Ping[d], because he has the Crown Prince Naṭa and Mei-shan Ta-sheng. Sun Hsing-che is an evil dragon and is thus also Wu-chih-ch'i.[3]

Three distinct inferences are implied here, and they represent the essence of the theory under discussion. We shall consider them in this order:

(1) The given relationship with Li-shan Lao-mu and Wu-chih-ch'i, both here regarded as river-demons, is taken to suggest that Sun Hsing-che was also such a demon. First, however, it should be admitted that Huang's interpretation of the figure Li-shan Lao-mu is completely unorthodox. He cites a form of the name as it appears in the dialogue of sc. 9 (p. 37), and it is the graph *li*[b] which suggests to him (author of *China's River-Gods*) the Li-tui river-demon.[4] But in the song *K'u-huang-t'ien* (sc. 10, p. 45) it is replaced by the more familiar graph[e], which at once calls to mind a long attested legendary figure dwelling upon the mountain of her name, in Shensi. Her early Taoist associations

---

[1] For references to its several appearances in the Buddhist *Tripiṭaka* see Ting Nai-t'ung, 'The Holy Man and the Snake-Woman', *Fabula* 8,3 (1966), p. 157, n. 58.
[2] For Kuei-tzu-mu, see above pp. 16 ff.
[3] Huang Chih-kang, pp. 177-8.
[4] Li-tui was the Szechuan site of one of the traditional Erh-lang legends. Cf. Huang, ch. 4.

[a] 張僧   [b] 離   [c] 離堆   [d] 李冰   [e] 驪

show in a passage preserved in *TPKC*, 63:394–6.[1] An oral tale about her was current in the thirteenth century,[2] and her name often appeared in later fiction.[3] In no source is she represented as a river-demon. Her cult at Li-shan has been maintained down to recent times, but a connection with water remains unproven.[4] Nor is there precedent in any other *Hsi-yu chi* source for this family relationship with Sun Hsing-che. Wu-chih-ch'i was indeed a river-demon, but she shared with Sun Hsing-che a fully distinct characteristic: both were monkeys. This in itself is sufficient to account for their association in a family relationship.

(2) The Devarāja Li, identified as Li Ping (a Szechuan hero originally of the Warring States period who since the twelfth century was associated with the god Erh-lang), is involved in the campaign to capture Sun Hsing-che. The early cult-legends of Erh-lang in Szechuan were built around battles with river-demons. Sun Hsing-che must therefore, it is inferred, have been one himself. Again, it is necessary to question the identification: the familiar Devarāja Li is nowhere cognate with Li Ping. In the (admittedly late) sources which elaborate upon his name the Devarāja gains his surname from Li Ching[a] of the seventh century[5] and his Crown Prince Naṭa by extension from the Vaiśravaṇa legend.[6] It has been argued above (chapter 5) that the Seven Sages (*ch'i sheng*) of Mei-shan, the name which appears in sc. 9, p. 42, belong integrally to the complex of Erh-lang legends and remain in this scene apparently only as a result of the dramatist's imperfect adjustment of his plot. Huang Chih-kang's implied point would in this case be more reliably documented by those other *Hsi-yu chi* versions in which Erh-lang was

---

1 'Li-shan mu'[b]: source quoted as *Chi-hsien chuan*[c]. No authentic text of this anonymous work remains (*SKCSTM*, 147:24b–25a). The story is of Li Ch'üan[d] discovering the Taoist classic *Yin-fu ching*[e] and learning its meaning from the Old Woman on Li-shan. The *Hsin T'ang-shu* (59:5a) records a work in one *chüan* ('Li Ch'üan: Li-shan Lao-mu ch'uan Yin-fu hsüan-i'[f]) with a note resuming the same story.

2 *Tsui-weng t'an-lu* I, p. 4.

3 E.g., *SHC*, ch. 53, p. 880, characterizing her as an old woman; *HYC*, ch. 16, p. 180, ch. 23, p. 266, ch. 73, p. 839; *Tung-yu chi*, ch. 41, p. 39. Graphic variants will be found among these references also; cf. also Li Shih-yü, p. 167. The story of Li-shan Lao-mu told in a *pao-chüan* quoted by Huang Yü-p'ien is summarized by Chao Wei-pang, p. 109.

4 Eberhard (1942), pt. I, pp. 360–1, adding material and speculations concerning the ancient tribal background of the cult.

5 Cf. above, p. 34; also *HYC*, ch. 83, p. 946; *Feng shen yen-i*, ch. 14, p. 136.

6 The affiliation of Naṭa to Vaiśravaṇa in Chinese popular legend is clearly brought out in the ninth-century *K'ai T'ien ch'uan-hsin chi*[g] by Cheng Ch'i[h] (d. 899) (*PCHH*, i[i]-chi):9b. Cf. *Sung kao-seng chuan*, 14:791a; *Lei-shuo*, 6:33a; *TPKC*, 92:610.

a 靖   b 姥   c 集仙傳   d 李筌   e 陰符經
f 傳陰符玄義   g 開天傳信記   h 鄭棨   i 乙

indeed the captor of Sun Hsing-che: that described in the *Pak t'ongsa ŏnhae* notes, and the hundred-chapter version. But a serious objection remains in the shape of the Kōzanji version, earliest and most authentic of all the older *Hsi-yu chi* sources. There Hou Hsing-che was disciplined by the Queen of the West for stealing peaches: there is nothing to suggest that he was conceived as a river-demon, nor is there any mention of Erh-lang. Similarly, there is complete silence on the subject of Sangha, Moksha his disciple, or Kuan-yin, with whom Sangha was frequently identified and who shared his disciple Moksha/Hui-an.[1] And this although, as we have seen, the Sangha version of the Wu-chih-ch'i legend was current in twelfth-century China, appears to have been represented among the *yüan-pen* of the early thirteenth century, and was certainly known to late thirteenth-century *tsa-chü* drama. The Erh-lang cult also, whatever the true nature of its origins in Szechuan,[2] had spread to north China by the twelfth century,[3] was known to the popular stage of the twelfth and thirteenth centuries,[4] and appeared by allusion in the prose *p'ing-hua* of the 1320s.[5] That the Kōzanji version of the 'Tripitaka' cycle could in spite of the popularity of these contemporary cult-legends still introduce its monkey without any allusion to them suggests some measure of independence.

In short, we have come to question two of Huang Chih-kang's inferences largely on the grounds that their evidence is drawn entirely

---

[1] Cf. above, p. 144, n. 1. It was on the basis of this analogy that Hu Shih (1923, p. 369) sought to relate Wu-chih-ch'i with Sun Hsing-che.

[2] For the controversial complications of this question, see Li Szu-ch'un, pp. 63–74 and the appended critique by Liu Te-hsing[a] (*ibid.* pp. 75–8).

[3] The *Tung-ching meng hua lu* (8:2a–3a) describes birthday festivities at the Erh-lang temple in Pien-liang on the 24th of the sixth month. Hung Mai (1123–1202), in *I-chien chih* (*ping*[b] collection, 9:2b), reports a transference of a temple from Kuan-k'ou, Szechuan seat of the Erh-lang cult, to K'ai-feng, accompanied by a burst of popular enthusiasm; the date is given as 1117. A corrupt and abbreviated version of this incident reappears in the composite *Hsüan-ho i-shih* (1:14b); (the reign title Hsüan-ho[c] in this passage appears to be a mistake for Cheng[d]-ho). The *Meng-liang lu* 15:9a) records an Erh-lang temple near Hangchow, the Southern Sung Lin-an.

[4] The element 'erh-lang' appears in several titles of early stage entertainments listed in Chou Mi's *Wu-lin chiu-shih* (10:2b, 4b) and T'ao Tsung-i's *Cho-keng lu* (25:16a): cf. the comparative table drawn up by Hu Chi, pp. 190–1.

[5] *Ch'i-kuo ch'un-ch'iu p'ing-hua* 3 (p. 149), with the double simile:
   Just like a murderous Ta-li kuei-wang[e] thrown into a mountain torrent, or the Most Holy Erh-lang fallen in the midst of an armed force...
The figure Ta-li kuei appears also in the episode of Sun Hsing-che's war with Heaven as described in *Pak t'ongsa ŏnhae*: he is sent with Moksha to beg the assistance of Erh-lang (*PTS*, 293 N vi). Cf. also *HYC*, ch. 6, p. 60, ch. 7, p. 69, ch. 55, p. 634. The *Wu-tai shih p'ing-hua* refers to an Erh-lang temple (p. 163).

[a] 劉德馨   [b] 丙   [c] 宣和   [d] 政   [e] 大力鬼王

from the body of relatively late *Hsi-yu chi* sources, among which the *tsa-chü* in particular is of questionable value in a discussion of this kind. The third inference offers a similar case.

(3) The motif of imprisonment beneath a mountain is common to both Wu-chih-ch'i, chained at the foot of Kuei-shan, and Sun Hsing-che, in all versions confined to (sometimes beneath) Hua-kuo shan. To many this has seemed conclusive evidence of their identity. But again the Kōzanji version offers virtually no support: Hou Hsing-che describes himself as 'banished[a] to Tzu-yün tung on Hua-kuo shan'. Not only is there no mention of Kuei-shan, no suggestion of the monkey being chained in place, but even the later motifs of confinement in a rock-crevasse[1] or imprisonment in a stone casket[2] are all absent. There is no evidence to indicate that such a confinement of the monkey had become standard in the *Hsi-yu chi* tradition before the fifteenth, or possibly the fourteenth, century.

Ishida Eiichirō, after an impressive exposition of the Wu-chih-ch'i story's full folkloric context, also suggests a 'prototype' theory on the above lines, and expands it by adding:

since Sung (*sic*) Wu-k'ung, a stone monkey come to life, is said to have dived into the water and explored the grotto Shui-lien-tung in the mountain Hua-kuo-shan, and making himself king of the monkeys, spent his mornings on Hua-kuo-shan and his evenings in Shui-lien-tung, passing in this way 300 years, we can say that he himself has a close relationship with water.[3]

His case rests upon those very episodes at the opening of the hundred-chapter version which are not vouched for in any earlier source. It is vulnerable to exactly the same objections as we have detailed above: no suggestion of a 'prototype', unless in some carefully qualified sense, is acceptable without clear confirmation from the source we know as the earliest. Summing up, then, we find that the 'Wu-chih-ch'i' legend casts no light on the monkey-figure known to us in that basic source. It follows that the 'derivation' theory in its strict form should be suspended.

Whether the legend contributed significantly to later forms of a progressively standardized *Hsi-yu chi* tradition is another question, which must now be discussed in its own right.

---

[1] *PTS*, p. 294 (N vi).   [2] *HYC*, ch. 14, p. 153.
[3] Ishida Eiichirō, pp. 125–6.
[a] 配

The cleaving of Mount Hua

We may regard Moksha, who appears in *Pak t'ongsa ŏnhae*, *tsa-chü* and the hundred-chapter version, as a figure genuinely derived from the Sangha legend, although he appears only as the disciple of Kuan-yin. He is not, however, concerned with the confinement of Sun Hsing-che, and there is reason to look elsewhere for parallels to this theme in the *Hsi-yu chi* tradition.

The *Pak t'ongsa ŏnhae* describes this stage of the story in a reported speech which has in another connection been discussed at length above (pp. 70–2). Kuan-yin proposes:

Let Chü-ling shen be ordered to hold him in custody and take him to the world below. On Hua-kuo shan let the lower half of his body be put in a crevasse in the rock, which should be sealed by drawing the mark of Tathāgata Buddha. Let the mountain spirits and local gods keep guard over him; when hungry let him eat iron pellets, when thirsty drink molten bronze, and thus wait...(cf. above, p. 109).

Chü-ling shen, singled out here as the one who has physically to seal the monkey beneath his mountain, has escaped attention in previous studies of *Hsi-yu chi* tradition.[1] In Chinese legend he was credited with having split apart Mount Hua[a] (in modern Shensi) into its three famous peaks and directed the Yellow River through them on its eastward course. There is an allusion to the story as early as the first century BC,[2] and several more, specifying the name Chü-ling (shen), follow in the subsequent centuries,[3] until in the prose and poetry of the T'ang period such allusions are seen to be a commonplace.[4] Chü-ling is sometimes cited together with Ta Yü as a primeval marshaller of the rivers. He was

---

[1] With the exception of Ōta and Torii (1960, p. 358), who however identify him with the dwarf in the *Han-Wu ku-shih* (*TPYL*, 378:4*b*). The two figures seem related by no more than a joking allusion.

[2] Yang Hsiung[b] (53 BC–AD 18), *Ho-tung fu*[c], quoted in *Han-shu*, 87 (*shang*):15*a*.

[3] E.g. Chang Heng[d] (78–139), *Hsi-ching fu*[e], in *Liu-ch'en chu Wen-hsüan*, 2:3*a*; *Shan-hai ching*, 2:1*ab*; *Shui-ching chu*, 4:11*a*; hymn[f] composed in the year 276 by Tso Kuei-p'ing[g], concubine of Chin Wu-ti[h], quoted in *Chin-shu*, 31:9*a*.

[4] E.g. Chao Yen-chao[i] (seventh to early eighth centuries), 'Feng-ho Sheng-chih teng Li-shan kao-ting yü-mu ying-chih'[j] (*CTS*, 103:1088); Wang Wei[k] (699–759), 'Hua-yüeh' (*CTS*, 125:1246); Tu-ku Chi[l] (725–77), preface to 'Hsien-chang ming'[m] (*CTW*, 389:17*a*–18*a*); Ma Tai[n] (ninth century), 'Hua hsia feng Yang Shih-yü'[o] (*CTS*, 556:6453); Hsüeh Neng[p] (d. 880), 'Hua-yüeh' (*CTS*, 558:6479).

[a] 華嶽   [b] 揚雄   [c] 河東賦   [d] 張衡   [e] 西京賦   [f] 頌
[g] 左貴嬪   [h] 晉武帝   [i] 趙彥昭   [j] 奉和聖製登驪山高頂寓目應制
[k] 王維   [l] 獨孤及   [m] 仙掌銘   [n] 馬戴
[o] 華下逢楊侍御   [p] 薛能

a hero in the puppet theatre of thirteenth-century Lin-an,[1] and the subject of at least one *tsa-chü*, possibly of the late thirteenth century.[2] Later popular fiction recurrently referred to him.[3] His outstanding characteristic was the cleaving of Hua-yüeh with an axe, and this remained with him as a personal weapon even when he eventually became detached from the old legend and served simply as a celestial warrior.[4]

Simultaneously with this tradition developed the popular legend of Prince Ch'en-hsiang[a], offspring of the free union between a mortal, Liu Hsiang[b], and the Goddess of Mount Hua[c]. The story as it survives in popular versions of recent centuries[5] tells how the brother of the goddess (identified in name with the god Erh-lang) indignantly pinned her below Mount Hua, where she remained until her twelve-year-old son, after many tribulations, freed her by cleaving open the mountain with the stroke of an axe.[6] No old treatments of this story, which again is likely to derive from a local cult-legend, are preserved;[7] but the titles of certain *tsa-chü* possibly of the thirteenth century have come down to us, and they closely match those concerned with the Chü-ling shen legend.[8]

It would be idle to broach here another line of unsupported conjecture on possible derivations. The facts tell us this much: a legend in which a goddess was confined for her misdemeanours beneath Mount Hua and which has meanwhile shown itself to be perennially popular as a story of the 'filial son' type was known in thirteenth- and fourteenth-century *tsa-*

[1] *Meng-liang lu*, 20:13 a.

[2] Cf. *LKP*, p. 113: *Chü-ling p'i[d] Hua-yüeh* ('Chü-ling splits open Mount Hua') by Li Hao-ku[e], also one of the 'older generation now dead...' (cf. above, p. 56 etc.). Variants of the title (*Chü-ling shen[f]* etc.) in other versions of the text are listed in the critical edition (*LKP*, p. 189, n. 481). Cf. *T'ai-ho cheng-yin p'u*, p. 36.

[3] E.g., *Ch'in ping liu-kuo p'ing-hua* 3 (p. 257): 'Chü-ling shen before T'ai[g]-Hua shan— one stroke[h] and the three peaks part asunder.' Also *SHC*, ch. 13, p. 192, ch. 80, p. 1318; *tsa-chü Hsi-yu chi*, sc. 20, p. 88; *HYC*, ch. 4, p. 41, ch. 34, p. 394.

[4] *HYC*, ch. 4, p. 42, ch. 61, p. 705, ch. 83, p. 948.

[5] The observations that follow are based on the texts collected in *Tung Yung Ch'en-hsiang ho-chi*, pp. 167 ff.

[6] E.g., *ibid.* p. 180.

[7] Some precedents for certain parts of the story are cited by Tu Ying-t'ao, *ibid.* preface, p. 7, but more about this question needs to be found out.

[8] *LKP*, p. 113: *Ch'en-hsiang T'ai-tzu p'i Hua-shan*, by Chang Shih-ch'i[i], one of the 'former generation now dead . . .'. This item appears only in Ts'ao Yin's version of the catalogue (*LKP*, p. 187, n. 463). A further title—*P'i Hua-shan Shen-hsiang chiu mu*[j] ('Splitting open Hua-shan, Shen-hsiang saves his mother')—appears in the *Pao-wen t'ang shu-mu* (p. 143) and the *Yeh-shih-yüan shu-mu* (10:5 a), in the latter attributed to Li Hao-ku. Hsü Wei includes the title of a southern dramatic version— *Liu Hsi[k] Ch'en-hsiang T'ai-tzu*—among the 'old pieces from the Sung and Yüan' in his *Nan-tz'u hsü-lu* (p. 251).

a 沉香太子   b 劉向   c 華嶽娘娘   d 劈   e 李好古   f 神
g 太   h 擘   i 張時起   j 神香救母   k 劉錫

chü literature. The ancient legend of Chü-ling shen, which apparently enjoyed general popularity from at least the thirteenth century on, centred for the purposes of vernacular literature upon the motif of Mount Hua cloven asunder with an axe, and this motif is exactly that which is and was used at the climax of the Ch'en-hsiang story. The *Hsi-yu chi* monkey, according to a tradition which has not effectively been run to earth, was deported to a mountain, incidentally named Hua-kuo shan. By the fourteenth or fifteenth centuries there was at least one prose version in which he too was specifically confined within the rock of his mountain, and in this same version it was Chü-ling shen, the legendary opener of Hua-shan, who installed him there. There is a possibility, which we are not in a position to assess, that yet other particulars of this confinement[1] had found their way into the *Hsi-yu chi* story in parallel with the Ch'en-hsiang legend.[2]

It is sufficient here to make a simple point: that the capture and confinement of Sun Hsing-che in those known versions which treated the subject were not overshadowed solely by figures from the Sangha/Wu-chih-ch'i legend, nor indeed by any single group of mythological heroes. There are traces of several independent traditions, none of which appears to lie at all close to the roots of the *Hsi-yu chi* story as such. The Kōzanji version is innocent of them all: they emerge only in the later and very different versions reflected in the *Pak t'ongsa ŏnhae* and the *tsa-chü* sequence. Moreover, each of the heroes, although perhaps linked by some tenuously shared motif to Sun Hsing-che's traditional story, loses much of his individuality in the transfer. Moksha appears as Kuan-yin's disciple, but fails to repeat his triumph against the 'River-mother'; Erh-lang appears as a renowned killer of demons, but his opponent is no longer an evil dragon and, in the *tsa-chü*, he parts company with the Seven Sages of Mei-shan; Chü-ling shen is summoned when the delinquent monkey is to be pinned beneath a mountain, but his most

---

[1] Such an example might be the inscribed seal which is placed on the mountain in *PTS* (N vi), *tsa-chü* (sc. 9, p. 42), *HYC* (ch. 7, pp. 76–7), but also in the Ch'en-hsiang story (*Tung Yung Ch'en-hsiang ho-chi*, p. 174).

[2] This is the point at which to acknowledge an early central Indian tradition cited by Uchida Michio (pp. 36–8). Two slightly differing accounts are preserved—in the Buddhist compendium *Fa-yüan chu-lin* 9:8*b*–9*b*, and the *Tz'u-en chuan* 4:240*b*. Basically the story is of a man who strays into a cave of Asuras and fails to escape because, having eaten a magic peach, he finds his body grown too large for any part but his head to emerge from the cave. Only guesswork relates this to the *Hsi-yu chi* story: I have nothing to add to Professor Uchida's suggestion, except a reminder that the sixteenth-century novel is the earliest known source to specify the motif of Sun Wu-k'ung's protruding head (*HYC*, ch. 7, p. 76, ch. 14, p. 153).

famous legendary exploit no longer serves any purpose; the Devarāja Li and the Crown Prince Naṭa shed the protective benevolence that still characterized Vaiśravaṇa/Mahābrahmā of the Kōzanji version, to become little more than celestial warriors.

On this evidence it seems more realistic to infer, not a fundamental derivation or even modification of the monkey-figure Sun Wu-k'ung, but rather the existence of an effectively universal repertoire of supernatural heroes. By the fifteenth century many old and originally strongly localized legends had long been familiar throughout most of China and had individually attracted the attention of artists in the *tsa-chü* medium, probably also of those who published vernacular fiction. Each of the old cult-figures had his own root associations and attributes, but these came to lose their original distinctness. Indiscriminate borrowing and adaptation into new literary contexts—such as the heterogeneous punitive army of the *Hsi-yu chi* story—may have been encouraged by this levelling process, and may in turn have helped it on. The versions known to us through the *Pak t'ongsa ŏnhae* and the *tsa-chü* seem to illuminate rather this period and this literary scene, than the traditional hero of their story.

The hundred-chapter novel shows signs of the levelling process in its most advanced stages. Chü-ling shen, for example, loses even his connection with the mountain confinement[1] and becomes a warrior whose only distinctive feature is his axe. The author, detached from the original cult-legends which once gave life to these several individual gods, must create effects in terms of his own medium. He has recourse again and again to a form of witty allusion—creating sophisticated situations in which characters long divorced from their original identity joke at one another about the very stories in which they had traditionally been involved. One example has already been noted (above, p. 38, n. 1). There are comparable allusions even to the figures discussed in the present section. Sun Wu-k'ung in chapter 66 (*HYC*, pp. 754 ff.) goes for help to Saṅgha of Szu-chou (under the title Ta-sheng Kuo-shih wang p'u-sa[a]) who 'in years gone by defeated the Mistress Shui-mu[b]', and they have a brief exchange about the problems of the Huai river floods. Again, in chapter 6 (*HYC*, p. 63) Sun Wu-k'ung taunts Erh-lang with

---

[1] Here the 'confinement' story takes a different form: the monkey is suppressed beneath a Wu-hsing shan composed of the Buddha's five fingers. The 'five-finger' motif has ancient Buddhist antecedents—cf. Chavannes, vol. 2, p. 115, vol. 4, p. 161.

[a] 大聖國師王菩薩   [b] 水母娘娘

a modified version of the Ch'en-hsiang legend, in which now Erh-lang himself is characterized as the child who releases his mother by cleaving open a T'ao[a]-shan.[1] This easy trifling bears the stamp of an urbane, detached author at home in his relaxed narrative medium.

Concluding remarks

The last three chapters leave us with a single conclusion. In the search for clear information on the origin and essential function of the *Hsi-yu chi* monkey, each group of material considered has shown negative results. This is principally because vernacular literary sources upon which some previous theories depended have been found to date from a time in which origins as such had long been a thing of the past. Features which in thirteenth-century texts would have justified some speculation were in fact shared by works no earlier than the late fourteenth century. To recall one conspicuous example, the monkey's family of demons, including a Ch'i-t'ien Ta-sheng, a Wu-chih-ch'i and with slight variants in its other members, was common to the prose story *Ch'en hsün-chien...* the *Hsi-yu chi tsa-chü* sequence and the play *Ch'i-t'ien Ta-sheng*, each of which for individual reasons appears to date from some undefined point in the Ming period. This kind of evidence need indicate no more than a mannerism which found favour at some particular time in a certain literary environment. Further inferences about the environment have been drawn immediately above.

A more general lesson to emerge from this whole examination is the importance of distinguishing between the relatively accessible world of written popular literature and the more primitive, to us less tangible, world of folklore and popular religious tradition which lies beyond it.

---

[1] More about this version of the story emerges from a work cited in Hu Shih (1931). It is entitled *Ch'ing-yüan miao-tao hsien-sheng chen-chün Erh-lang pao-chüan*[b], printed in 1555. In Hu Shih's words (p. 6), 'it says that [Sun] Hsing-che went to a party and suppressed Erh-lang's mother Yün-hua[c] beneath T'ai[d]-shan. When Erh-lang had rescued his mother,
> Mother and son reunited,
> Sat in the Precious Lotus Palace[e].
> Recalling the Monkey of the Mind's[f] intentions
> They determined to catch Sun Wu-k'ung...
In due course they succeed in pinning him beneath the mountain, from which he is rescued only by Tripitaka, in a scene vividly recalling the hundred-chapter novel (Hu Shih, p. 7, *HYC*, ch. 14, pp. 153 ff.). Several traditional stories thus appear to contribute to this mid-sixteenth-century version, which has not been independently reprinted.

[a] 桃   [b] 清源妙道顯聖眞君二郎寶卷   [c] 雲花   [d] 太   [e] 寶蓮宮
[f] 心猿

In the case of a large proportion of written stories and plays available to us now it is meaningful to talk about dating and even to think in terms of single authors. As products of a certain kind of literary scene they can be studied, with some measure of confidence, in the hope of learning more about that literary scene. We run our greatest danger, however, in seeking to argue back from the evidence of relatively finished written work to the basic traditions from which its subject-matter was derived. The oral medium has its own laws. With enough first-hand material we might indeed be able to trace the movement of themes and motifs between different oral stories in a given environment; in more general terms we might trace the spread of mythologies from one civilization to another. But we should be working in terms quite distinct from those appropriate to written fiction: dating would be of less importance, possibly even irrelevant; the essential elements of particular stories would appear in a more simple and generalized form which might often show up distortions of balance or significance in later written versions.

All this is to say that, with the written play- and story-texts which form the bulk of our present *Hsi-yu chi* material—and indeed of our evidence on parallel legends—we may not expect to conduct an effective search for the origins of a figure like Sun Wu-k'ung. Certainly no derivation theory can be asserted which does not take due and careful account of the evidence of the Kōzanji version: for this, although by no means representing an oral cycle in its pristine condition, at least stands clearly apart from the standardized group of later sources as closer to the popular environment of the twelfth and thirteenth centuries. It was at this period, or even before, that the *Hsi-yu chi* story acquired its monkey-hero: attempts to show how and why this came about should be documented accordingly.

11

Further Theories

Several chapters have now been given to a discussion which, whatever other results it may have yielded, has left the problem of Sun Wu-k'ung's origin and first affiliation to the *Hsi-yu chi* story unsolved. The question nevertheless remains an absorbing one, and I am reluctant to dismiss it without some appraisal of other, possibly more far-reaching theories than those considered above. These do not depend for their authority exclusively upon Chinese vernacular literary sources and for this reason are distinct from the above. The basic question still remains the same: how far do they take us towards an authentic solution?

The theme of progress through incarnations

According to an interpretation recently advanced by Uchida Michio,[1] the *Hsi-yu chi* story spans the sequence of past, present and future. The monkey-hero's career is seen as governed by this underlying pattern. He begins as a lawless delinquent, passes through a purgative period of discipline as Tripitaka's escort and in the final canonization scene attains his deliverance from the chain of rebirth. If the story is constructed on the lines of such an orthodox Buddhist conception one can fairly look for precedents in canonical literature. And indeed Professor Uchida is able to illustrate his point with a short sūtra held to date from the fourth or fifth century AD—*Shih-tzu-yüeh fo pen-sheng ching*[a].[2]

The story is set in the city of Rājagṛha, where the Buddha is at the head of a host of bhiksus and bodhisattvas. One of them, named Vasu-mitra, roams around in the bamboo grove playing like an ape. A crowd gathers to watch him. With an ape-like cry from the top of a tree he then summons 84,000 golden monkeys and performs transformations for the pleasure of his assembled audience. The question is raised as to what precedent in a former existence was responsible for this unseemly

---

[1] Uchida Michio, pp. 39 ff. [2] T. III, no. 176, pp. 443–6.
[a] 師子月佛本生經

display. The Buddha then tells of a monkey who in a past age came to the abode of an Arhat...

It saw him sitting in meditation, fully composed. It then took up a mat belonging to the Arhat and put it on as a *kaṣāya*, leaving the right shoulder bare in the manner of the śramaṇas; it paraded round the bhikṣu with a censer in its hand. Just then the bhikṣu awoke from his meditative trance and saw that the monkey had been moved to piety. At once he snapped his fingers and spoke to the monkey: 'Child of Dharma, the mind that seeks enlightenment has awoken within you'...(p. 444).

The monkey receives instruction and accepts the Five Precepts. Finally:

When the monkey had formed its resolve, it made its way up the high mountain prancing with delight. Climbing the trees and dancing about, it fell to the ground and died.[1] Thanks to having received the Five Precepts from the Arhat its animal *karma* was broken. Now that its life was at an end it was reborn in the Tuṣita Heaven. (*ibid.*)

This ends an 84,000-kalpa period of penance for the sins of an anterior life. The offender has passed through all the great hells and lived through a number of existences in different animal forms.

The self-appointed monkey-disciple who in a later incarnation ascends to the dignity of a Buddhist saint appears again in the Life of Aśoka[a],[2] in a section entitled *Avadāna of Upagupta*[b].[3] The theme is the work of conversion practised by Upagupta. The relevant passage begins:

In the past there were five hundred Pratyeka-Buddhas dwelling on one side of Mount Urumuṇḍa. Five hundred ascetics dwelt on another side, and five hundred monkeys on yet another. At that time the leader[4] of the monkeys went to the abode of the Pratyeka-Buddhas, delight awakened in its heart, and it plucked flowers and picked fruit to give to the Pratyeka-Buddhas. The Pratyeka-Buddhas were then sitting in the posture of meditation and had entered into dhyāna composure. The monkey joined its palms and in a position below them imitated the sitting posture of the Pratyeka-Buddhas. Subsequently the Pratyeka-Buddhas entered *nirvāṇa*. When the monkey passed the flowers and fruit across to them, they showed no sign of accepting. The monkey tugged at their clothing and pushed them, but even this did not shake them. Knowing that they had departed into *nirvāṇa* (the monkey) felt morose...(p. 111c).

---

[1] Cf. a brief story cited in the *Ching-lü i-hsiang* (T. LIII, p. 252c).
[2] T. L, no. 2042, pp. 99–131: translated by An Fa-ch'in[c], third–fourth centuries AD.
[3] *Chüan* 3:111. I am indebted to Dr H. C. Chang for drawing my attention to this passage.
[4] Preferring the variant *chih chu*[d] to *ts'ung chu*[e]. Although these actions could have been performed by the five hundred monkeys at once, the point of this story is to single out the one who is an early incarnation of Upagupta. It seems more convincing that he should be introduced as the leader.

[a] 阿育王傳   [b] 優波毱多因緣   [c] 安法欽   [d] 之主   [e] 從住

The story continues to tell how the monkey then sought out the five hundred ascetics, played havoc with the different forms of self-mortification they were practising and by way of demonstration sat before them in the posture of meditation . . .

The five hundred ascetics spoke thus: 'A monkey has reproved us for what we were doing: let us try to imitate what the monkey is doing.' They then sat in the meditation posture, reflected with fixed attention and were enlightened without (the help of) a master.

The conversion of the ascetics was in this way wrought by Upagupta in a previous existence.

With an effective sense of paradox both these stories elect to make a monkey in its most playful, even objectionable manifestations a vehicle for conversion and enlightenment. In both cases a sequence of incarnations leads to the monkey's glorification—whether as Upagupta, prominent disciple of the Buddha, or through rebirth in heaven.

Professor Uchida points out (pp. 41–2) that Chinese literature was to feature unambiguous reflections of this canonical theme in the story of Yüan Sun, discussed above. Whether these reflections were derived indirectly through popular tradition, or taken deliberately from a scriptural source remains a doubtful issue.[1] But few will dispute that the Yüan Sun story bears little resemblance, aside from certain allusions in the *tsa-chü* version, to the monkey Sun Hsing-che and his role in the 'Tripitaka' cycle. The force of Professor Uchida's suggestion depends upon the reader's willingness to accept his analysis of the cycle as fundamentally a fable of progressive incarnation. Such a reading of the story remains in the end a matter of the reader's own judgement. The suggestion is not of a nature to be refuted in clear-cut terms.

It is worth remarking, however, that no version of the *Hsi-yu chi* story allows for previous incarnations of the monkey-hero. Unlike his colleagues Chu Pa-chieh and Sha Ho-shang, whose place in the traditional story was not of equally long standing, his animal identity had nothing to do with the misdeeds of an earlier existence. He committed crimes and suffered their consequence within the context of a single protracted life. His final transfiguration, in the later versions, was secondary to the triumph of Tripitaka—shared glory; and it was a device not yet clearly developed in the Kōzanji version, whose cryptic closing line elevates Hou Hsing-che to a rank with no overt Buddhist associations.

In these respects it is again the Kōzanji version that is least satis-

[1] Cf. above, p. 137.

factorily accommodated, and the case for tracing the monkey's origins back to scriptural fables on the above lines must suffer accordingly. That the monkey-king of the Kōzanji version inherited several characteristics from Buddhist tradition has been acknowledged in detail above (chapter 2); that his background resembled that of the monkey Yüan Sun is still far from established.

The Fukien cult of Ch'i-t'ien Ta-sheng

Eberhard notes two seventeenth-century references to a cult of Ch'i-t'ien Ta-sheng in Fukien, concedes that there is no evidence of it prior to the hundred-chapter novel, but claims that the cult gives an 'aboriginal' impression ('macht...einen urtümlichen Eindruck') which makes it seem unlikely to have derived from the novel.[1]

To judge from the literary references, the cult in its various branches celebrated a monkey, or an anthropomorphic deity with monkey's head, which bore certain names and attributes associated with the Sun Wu-k'ung of the 'middle' sources—*Pak t'ongsa* and *tsa-chü*—and the sixteenth-century novel. According to Yu T'ung[a] (1618–1704) the citizens of Foochow worshipped Sun Hsing-che (*sic*) as a household god and built temples to the monkey-god Ch'i-t'ien Ta-sheng.[2] T'ung Shih-szu[b] (1651–92) describes the monkey-headed god of Fukien as bearing a metal circlet about his forehead, brandishing an iron cudgel, wearing a tiger-skin and known as Sun Ta-sheng[c]. Traditionally he had appeared in the clouds to beat back an attack from Japanese pirates.[3] P'u Sung-ling (?1640–1715) records a story concerning this same anthropomorphic god, worshipped under the name Ch'i-t'ien Ta-sheng, Sun Wu-k'ung.[4]

A number of further observations bear on this small but interesting group of references. In the first place, there is nothing inherently improbable in suggesting that popular Sun Wu-k'ung cults existed before the appearance of the famous sixteenth-century novel. Not only is there abundant evidence, detailed above, that the monkey's characteristic adventures had already made a mark on the popular literary imagination,

---

[1] Eberhard (1948), p. 125.
[2] *Ken-chai tsa-shuo*,[d] quoted in *Chien-hu chi*[e], *Yü-chi*[f], by Ch'u Chia-hsüan[g] (*PCHSTK* ed., 2:6a).
[3] *Erh-shu*[h] (*Liao-hai*[i] *ts'ung-shu*, eighth collection), p. 10b.
[4] *Liao-chai chih-i*, pp. 1459 ff.

[a] 尤侗   [b] 佟世思   [c] 孫大聖   [d] 艮齋雜說   [e] 堅瓠集   [f] 餘集
[g] 褚稼軒   [h] 耳書   [i] 遼海

but certain passages in the novel itself can be seen as reflecting, not without satirical overtones, existing cultic observances.[1]

On the other hand it is also well possible that 'aboriginal' monkey cults had long before this led their own existence, independent of any gloss from the 'Tripitaka' cycle. Something of the sort seems to emerge from an account in Hung Mai's *I-chien chih*[2] of a Monkey King[a] cult located precisely within the bounds of Foochow prefecture. Here, a wounded monkey used locally as a cult object exerts a malignant influence which spreads terror throughout the region, and, after all attempts at exorcism fail, a Buddhist, Tsung-yen, is alone able to discipline the animal's resentful spirit. Certainly much more remains to be added to this single early reference, but it sufficiently confirms that as early as the twelfth century the folk of Foochow cultivated a form of monkey-worship which anticipated the Ch'i-t'ien Ta-sheng cults described above. The sickness-terror motif in particular brings to mind P'u Sung-ling's story.

The dangers lie only in attempting to look here for an 'original', in any sense, of Sun Wu-k'ung himself. Hou Hsing-che, of the Kōzanji version, lacks any sign of the attributes described in the seventeenth-century references. The monkey-headed figure on the west pagoda at Zayton approaches them only in its ornamental head-band. Nothing relates the Monkey King described by Hung Mai to the *Hsi-yu chi*. There is no evidence at all that the cult had anything in common with the early Hou Hsing-che. Nor was it *a priori* impossible for cults to grow up around fictional heroes. The canonization of the *San-kuo* hero Kuan Yü[b], attributed by Cheng Chen-to to the influence of developing popular story versions,[3] provides a conspicuous example of just this process.

We are left with no grounds for inferring that the *Hsi-yu chi* monkey derived from a Fukien deity or even came under its influence. Conversely, an 'aboriginal' cult such as Hung Mai describes could well have come to acquire superficial characteristics from the Sun Wu-k'ung who

[1] In *HYC*, ch. 44 (p. 510), heavenly messengers appear in the dreams of five hundred suffering Buddhists, bearing news of a Messianic Ch'i-t'ien Ta-sheng who will assuredly bring retribution for injustice. This passage recalls parts of the invocations quoted by Elliott, p. 170. In ch. 87 (p. 997) shrines are built in honour of the pilgrims, in chs. 63 (p. 729) and 95 (p. 1079) their portraits are painted to serve as images. In ch. 93 (p. 1050) they become objects of public worship.

[2] *Chia*[c]-*chih*, 6:2b–3b, '*Tsung-yen ch'ü hou-yao*'[d].

[3] Cheng Chen-to (1929), pp. 168–9.

[a] 猴王   [b] 關羽   [c] 甲   [d] 宗演去猴妖

seems, on the evidence of the above chapters, to have become a household word even before the circulation of the long novel.

The influence of the ' *Rāmāyaṇa*' story

It was through the advocacy of Hu Shih[1] that this theory came into favour, and it now, in spite of individual objections,[2] still commands wide support.[3]

The *Rāmāyaṇa*, an epic in seven books traditionally attributed to the poet Vālmīki (? fourth–third centuries BC), came to serve as the voice of Hindu society's finest ideals. It won fame throughout India, in every milieu and with every social class; its personalities and episodes were celebrated both in the classical Sanskrit drama and universally in vernacular dramatic traditions of India down to recent times. In Indian tradition its leading heroes have for centuries been cult-figures and demigods.[4] Many stories and themes from the epic are known to have spread in popular versions to alien and remote parts of Asia.[5]

An important part of the classical epic is devoted to the story of Rāma, the disinherited royal prince dwelling in the forests, seeking his chaste and beautiful wife Sītā, who has been abducted to the island Laṅkā far in the south by the monster Rāvaṇa. The whole episode of this search and the recovery of the lost wife is dominated by the figure of the wise monkey Hanumat, brother of the Monkey King Sugrīva with whom Rāma concludes a firm pact of friendship and mutual assistance. It is Hanumat's role as companion to a questing human hero, his resourcefulness, boldness and versatility that have suggested the parallel with Sun Wu-k'ung. The claim is, quite simply, that Sun Wu-k'ung derives ultimately from Hanumat.

Particular arguments have taken the following forms: (1) Hanumat and some of his adventures recall the monkey-hero of the *Hsi-yu chi*; India and China were for centuries linked by religious and mercantile traffic; therefore the universally popular *Rāmāyaṇa* story must have spread to China, and the monkey-hero by some metamorphosis attached himself to the pilgrim Tripitaka (Hu Shih (1923), p. 372). (2) Versions

---

[1] Hu Shih (1923), pp. 370–2, with an acknowledgement to Baron A. von Staël-Holstein. Cf. Cheng Chen-to (1933), pp. 291–3.
[2] Lu Hsün (1924), p. 19; later supported and documented by Wu Hsiao-ling (*q.v.*).
[3] Cf. Ōta and Torii (1960), pp. 356–7; R. A. Stein, p. 528.
[4] Cf. M. Winternitz, *History of Indian Literature* (Calcutta, 1927), vol. I, pp. 475–9 and 517.
[5] J. K. Balbir, pp. 9 and 65–7.

of the *Rāmāyaṇa* are known to have found their way, in the form of Tibetan and Khotanese manuscripts, to the cave-library at Tun-huang which also housed the *pien-wen* manuscripts representing the earliest Chinese popular literary texts known to us. Historically, China before *circa* AD 900 had many links with the West, in particular with Khotan. The Kōzanji version of the early 'Tripitaka' story carries echoes of folklore from similar sources. These various points, general and particular, add up to a body of circumstantial evidence suggesting that *Rāmāyaṇa* stories, with their characteristic monkey-hero, could have spread to China from inner Asia at a popular level, perhaps in the form of oral narrative cycles (Ōta and Torii, pp. 356–7).

Readers of the novel *Hsi-yu chi* and the classical *Rāmāyaṇa* will have no difficulty in recognizing ostensible similarities between the two monkey-heroes. They are most apparent in the fifth book of the epic (*Sundara-Kāṇḍa*), in which Hanumat flies an immense distance through the air to the island Laṅkā,[1] exploits his ability to adopt different sizes and forms in order to enter a forbidden place secretly,[2] delivers covert reassurance to a captive princess,[3] enters the belly of an enemy to attack him,[4] destroys a sacred grove of trees,[5] wields an iron bar,[6] holds at bay an army of demons and is finally captured.[7] Scattered motifs elsewhere in the *Rāmāyaṇa* suggest further parallels: two identical monkeys fight together indistinguishably;[8] the ṛṣi Agastya speaks of Hanumat's disorderly youth;[9] the tribe of monkeys discover and enter a cave.[10]

By using this simple method of pairing off motifs one rapidly assembles an impressive quantity of matching material on the two sides. But it is more important to recognize that this represents no advance towards understanding the nature and circumstances of any derivation. Nearly all the illustrations cited here are drawn from the sixteenth-century novel. To begin there and cast back directly to the classical *Rāmāyaṇa* is to employ a dangerous and almost certainly fallacious form of argument.

[1] *Ramayana*, vol. 2, pp. 327 ff. Cf. this important accomplishment of Sun Wu-k'ung: *HYC*, ch. 2, p. 20, and *passim*.
[2] *Ramayana*, vol. 2, pp. 256 and 341; cf. above, p. 65; *HYC*, *passim*.
[3] *Ramayana*, vol. 2, pp. 411 ff.; cf. *HYC*, ch. 70, pp. 802–3.
[4] *Ramayana*, vol. 2, pp. 335–7; cf. above, p. 36.
[5] *Ramayana*, vol. 2, p. 436; cf. *HYC*, ch. 25, p. 282: Sun Wu-k'ung destroys the tree which bears Ginseng-fruit.
[6] *Ramayana*, vol. 2, pp. 439 and 463; cf. above, pp. 38–9.
[7] *Ramayana*, vol. 2, pp. 438–53; cf. Sun Wu-k'ung's war with heaven.
[8] *Ramayana*, vol. 2, p. 197; cf. *HYC*, ch. 58, pp. 665 ff.
[9] *Ramayana*, vol. 3, p. 496; cf. early episodes of the *Hsi-yu chi* monkey's career.
[10] *Ramayana*, vol. 2, pp. 297–300; cf. *HYC*, ch. 1, p. 4.

This remains so even when the Kōzanji version is used as the basis of comparison, and there the parallels are in any case much less spectacular. Hou Hsing-che's sovereignty over a large tribe of monkeys and his supernatural powers vaguely recall the kingship of Sugrīva and paramountcy of Hanumat; the mountain Hua-kuo shan with its evocation of an earthly paradise may recall the beautiful natural home of the *Rāmāyaṇa* monkeys;[1] the youthful liberties of Hanumat seem faintly echoed in Hou Hsing-che's past offence of the stolen peaches. These few generalized and tenuous points of similarity offer less promising ground for any theory of derivation.

Both Hu Shih and, in a more extreme degree, Lin P'ei-chih (*q.v.*)[2] effectively started from their conclusion—identifying two figures from alien traditions—and simply assumed intervening stages not attested in any but the most circumstantial or generalized forms of evidence. Before the *Rāmāyaṇa* theory can be of any substantial assistance there must be clear signs, not simply that some form of the story was current in a popular Chinese environment before, say, the twelfth or thirteenth centuries, but that the monkey-hero as such, in a form identifiable with the Hou Hsing-che of the Kōzanji version, was known to Chinese audiences. The quantities of merely circumstantial evidence serve only, unless they supply this central link, to beg the question—why should no clear trace of the *Rāmāyaṇa* monkey remain in Chinese sources?

Wu Hsiao-ling (*q.v.*) has shown with admirable thoroughness that the Buddhist canon, which represents China's greatest single import from India, carries no more than fragmentary and modified traces of the *Rāmāyaṇa* story and its leading figures, whether in rapid summaries or in passing allusions. These give no grounds for an assumption that the story was generally current in China, and in any case do not feature the monkey-hero at all significantly.[3]

---

[1] *Ramayana*, vol. 2, pp. 155 and 163 ff.

[2] Lin was concerned to show a relationship between the *Rāmāyaṇa* and the White Ape legend, and to this end was prepared to sacrifice even the beneficence and morality of Hanumat in assuming his eventual assimilation with the abductor-villain Rāvaṇa; Cheng Chen-to (1933), pp. 292–3 did the same.

[3] The nearest approach to an account of Hanumat's adventures is found in the *Liu-tu chi-ching* (T. III, no. 152) 5:27*ab*. This was first pointed out and translated by E. Huber in 'Le *Rāmāyaṇa* et les Jātakas', *Bulletin de l'École Française d'Extrême-Orient* 4 (1904), 698–701. See also Chavannes, vol. 1, pp. 173–7, and Raghu Vira, 'Rāmāyaṇa in China' in *Sarasvati-Vihara Series* 8 (Nagpur, 1955). Cf. Wu Hsiao-ling, pp. 166–7. The account introduces an unnamed Monkey King (Sugrīva)—'un grand singe qui se livrait à des manifestations de désespoir' (Chavannes, p. 175). He and his tribe agree to search for the missing wife and find that a nāga has abducted

The manuscript fragments from Turkestan are more explicit. But certainly the Khotanese version takes us no nearer the figure of Hou Hsing-che. In it the brothers Rriṣma and Rāma find a huge and aged monkey, later see two identical monkeys fighting and, having helped the monkey Naṇḍa to victory, entrust their mission to him; the whereabouts of Sītā is discovered by a female monkey and eventually revealed to Rāma and his brother; the monkey-army sweeps toward Laṅkā, is checked by the ocean, and proceeds at once to build the famous bridge described in the sixth book of the classical epic.[1] Hanumat's characteristic expedition of reconnaissance is omitted. No other monkey-hero appears.

The Tibetan versions[2] treat Hanumat's episode more thoroughly. He volunteers to leap across the ocean to Laṅkāpura, where he enters the fortress and finds the Queen Sītā to deliver his message. She warns him of the danger:

Mais Hanumanta sans se presser, allant dans les bosquets du *rākṣasa*, commença à renverser tous les arbres et inventa maintes fantasmagories. 'Un singe indésirable est arrivé.' Disant ainsi [les *rākṣasa*] racontèrent [les méfaits] en s'approchant de Daçakraba qui envoya beaucoup de chasseurs, [mais] le singe tua tous les chasseurs. Daçagriba, le coeur malade, lança, après l'avoir consacré, un lacet des rayons solaires possédant la *siddhi*. Quand il agrandissait la boucle du lacet, le singe devenait petit, et n'était pas pris. Quand il rapetissait la boucle du lacet, le singe devenait grand, et n'était pas pris . . .[3]

Hanumat eventually pleads to die by having his tail ignited and proceeds to set alight the citadel of Laṅkāpura.

This description comes closer than any other source to representing a Hanumat-story on Chinese soil. It also recalls, however remotely, the versatility and resourcefulness of the fourteenth-, fifteenth- and sixteenth-century Sun Wu-k'ung. But F. W. Thomas's assessment of these Tibetan texts affords little further promise of pinning down any relationship. The language is 'what we are accustomed to in inscriptions, edicts, letters, the writings of Mi-la-ras-pa and so forth' (*op. cit.* p. 196); although the documents are held to testify to the 'early currency of popular Rāma narratives following the general lines and scale of the

her. The expedition of Hanumat to Laṅkā is omitted and the narrative continues with the monkey-tribe's preparations to bridge the sea-channel. This broaches already an episode of the sixth book of the epic.

[1] Cf. H. W. Bailey ('Rāma II'), pp. 565–7.
[2] Six distinct documents remain, shared between the India Office Library, London and the Bibliothèque Nationale, Paris. Cf. F. W. Thomas; M. Lalou, 'L'histoire de Rāma en Tibétain', *Journal Asiatique* 229 (1936), pp. 560–2; J. K. Balbir, pp. 9–10.
[3] J. K. Balbir, pp. 62, 34–6; cf. F. W. Thomas, p. 204.

Mahā-Bhārata and departing freely from the classical version of Vālmīki'
(*ibid.*), the present text seems derived from some non-Chinese source
(on the grounds of the general correctness of proper names: p. 195);
'an original in one of the indigenous monosyllabic languages of Chinese
Turkestan is not out of the question' (*ibid.*), or even (p. 196) a Nepalese
source. There is here no positive indication of popular currency in
China proper.

The Tun-huang fragments tempt to speculation, but they simultaneously emphasize that known sources on early Chinese popular
tradition lack any comparable sign of *Rāmāyaṇa* stories, in dramatic or
narrative form. In their absence we can attach no more than a general
folkloric significance to the fund of shared motifs. The Hanumat analogy is a fascinating, perhaps beguiling, subject for conjecture. It by no
means illuminates or defines the origins of the *Hsi-yu chi* monkey.

Towards a positive approach

This book is now near its end, and thus far it finds the problem of Sun
Wu-kung's origin and significance still without apparent prospect of
solution. The unrelieved scepticism of our discussion has sprung chiefly
from one recurrent concern: to affirm the primary importance of the
Kōzanji version as our most significant access to the 'Tripitaka' cycle
in anything approaching its early form. If we are to progress in understanding the provenance of this strangely essential monkey figure, the
first need is to shape our thinking around the source which brings us
closest to the early cycle's true milieu.

In the Kōzanji version we find reflections of popular, sub-Buddhist
cults, traces of scriptural fable and pious legend, but also motifs shared
with the epic literature of Central Asia, as well as with the world
of popular entertainment in China of the thirteenth century and
before. It is towards an environment which encompasses these
elements that any search for the roots of the *Hsi-yu chi* monkey must be
directed.

We face here a new task, and one which none of the theories discussed
above has recognized. It is a task which is frankly excluded from
the scope of this study. But it seems right, in concluding, at least to
discuss briefly one example which illustrates what its possible implications could be.

The following passage is taken from J. J. M. de Groot's account of the
Avalambana celebrations observed in nineteenth century Amoi:

Il arrive souvent que l'on y transforme, pour le plaisir des spectateurs, la légende de Maudgalyāyana en une farce des plus grossières, où deux individus déguisés, l'un en cochon, l'autre en singe ou en chien, suivent partout le saint et font par leurs lazzi les délectations de l'audience. On prétend en effet qu'en se rendant en enfer Maudgalyāyana rencontra deux de ces animaux, qui, touchés de son respect pour la chair de leurs congénères, le suivirent dès lors partout comme ses apôtres. On nomme *poan kâo-hì* [a] 'jouer la comédie des singes', ou *p'ah* [b] *kâo-hì* 'frapper la comédie des singes', la représentation de ce genre de farces. Elle n'a d'ordinaire lieu que pour les gens trop pauvres pour se payer la production sur la scène de comédies ou de tragédies sérieuses.[1]

Similarities in content and environment between the early 'Mu-lien' and 'Tripitaka' cycles have been noted independently above (chapter 2). It was suggested that the two cycles were comparable precisely in their debt to the traditions of monkish folklore and in their intimate relationship with the world of popular entertainment. Whether Mu-lien was attended by similar farcical animal-disciples during the seven-day-long performances of twelfth-century K'ai-feng we are at present not in a position to know. What we have in this passage from de Groot is one brief glimpse of the mystery of Mu-lien's quest as it was enacted for the humblest elements in a pre-modern urban population. It is only of passing interest to note that the appearance of animal 'apostles' in this performance may well owe its inspiration to the 'Tripitaka' tradition: there are precedents for such borrowings, if we choose to regard them as such.[2] But historical considerations are secondary here. The animal disciples seen by de Groot, characteristic of the least sophisticated renderings of the legend, fulfilled a function which was not apparently that of allusion. For the poor of Amoi they somehow made sense as appendages of the folk-hero Mu-lien.

We may have here a remote insight into the manner of Sun Wu-k'ung's first attachment to Tripitaka, and indeed of that of his fellow-disciples, although for the present it remains a matter for conjecture.

---

[1] J. J. M. de Groot, *Les fêtes annuellement célébrées à Émoui* (tr. C. G. Chavannes: *Annales du Musée Guimet* 12, Paris, 1886), pp. 418–19. He adds a footnote observing that monks would often perform comic items at funeral ceremonies.

[2] Cf. the sixteenth-century *hsi-wen* treatment by Cheng Chih-chen: beginning with a scene entitled 'Generals are dispatched to capture an ape' [c] (vol. 2 [d], 58*b*–60*b*), a 'white ape' appears in the course of Mu-lien's long journey westward to see the Buddha. The ape is defeated under the direction of Kuan-yin and recruited as Mu-lien's attendant. There are other features shared with *Hsi-yu chi* versions early and late: the magic peaches of the Queen of the West (p. 58*b*), the somersault (p. 60*a*), the metal band encircling the monkey's head (p. 60*a*). Later episodes also recall the *Hsi-yu chi*: e.g. Sha Ho-shang (pp. 88*b* ff.).

[a] 班猴戲   [b] 撲   [c] 遣將擒猿   [d] 中

But now, certainly, in the case of Mu-lien as of Tripitaka, the same question emerges: we ask, not whether some known legend provides a monkey which can somehow be related to either figure, but rather why a popular religious folk-hero should acquire bizarre animal-attendants, and why the monkey should claim a pre-eminent place among them. Framed in these terms the problems reveal themselves as truly folkloric in nature. Their solution will require a more wide-ranging study of comparable themes in other folk-cultures, in particular the use of comic elements in religious drama, and the function of the monkey as a figure in heroic tradition. At the same time it will be essential to reconcile any findings with what we know of Chinese society and its entertainments during the period of the legend's formation.

In this task we can draw help from the example, perhaps even the substance, of R. A. Stein's study of similar features in the *Gesar* epic, whose tradition lives in an environment to which many elements and influences from Lamaism, Indian Buddhism and Asian folklore have contributed. In one episode of the epic the hero Gesar adopts the guise of three travelling entertainers, each attended by a monkey and an ass. Stein identifies the monkeys as 'des animaux de bateleurs de foires ou de cirques ambulants'.[1] In his analysis of the episode he eventually discerns a reflection of two contrasting but essential facets of the hero's identity: 'Les singes jouent un rôle précis: ils remplacent les lions qui supportent normalement le trône. Ceux-ci représentent l'aspect glorieux et majestueux, les singes le côté ridicule.'[2] Gesar the universal king appears first as comic mischief-maker before his true stature is revealed.[3]

If the parallel is indeed relevant to a study of the 'Tripitaka' monkey, we in turn can expect to find that ultimately the search is not for the monkey so much as for the identity of Tripitaka himself, as he appeared to the popular imagination during the dim centuries which led up to the appearance of the Kōzanji version.

[1] Stein, p. 362. They have been cited above (p. 33) in connection with the 'magic air journey' motif.
[2] Stein, p. 387.
[3] For the full exposition of this question, see Stein, pp. 534–68.

Some Allegorical Devices

Reaction against the excesses of editorial interpretation in the seventeenth to nineteenth centuries has moved some modern scholars to brush aside the question of allegory in the *Hsi-yu chi*.[1] Yet allegorical values of some kind were present in the minds of those—including perhaps the author—responsible for the text of the novel in its earliest extant form: they should be considered in their due place. The question falls within the scope of this study to the extent that certain of the novel's specifically allegorical terms have an independent history of some antiquity, and their assembly and significance in the period immediately before the novel's appearance can be traced in other, less conspicuous sources. It emerges also that the story was being seen in an allegorical light possibly before the hundred-chapter novel was composed.

The symbolic expressions Monkey of the Mind[a] and Horse of the Will[b] recur together throughout the hundred-chapter novel as part of its system of allusive and allegorical verses in chapter-headings and at large in the text. Metaphors relating the monkey to the mind appear at least three times in the actual prose narrative.[2] From the chapter-headings in particular it appears that the two terms expressly represent the monkey Sun Wu-k'ung and the White Horse recruited into Tripitaka's party in the fifteenth chapter. Chapter 7, for instance, which ends with the imprisonment of Sun Wu-k'ung beneath Wu-hsing shan, is headed:

The Great Sage[c] escapes from the Eight Trigrams Furnace,
The Monkey of the Mind is held firm beneath Wu-hsing shan. (*HYC*, p. 69.)

and chapter 15:

On She-p'an Mountain[d] the spirits give covert assistance,
By Ying-ch'ou Torrent[e] the Horse of the Will is bridled. (*HYC*, p. 166.)

With their simple metaphorical suggestion the terms are characteristic of the allegorical thread running through the novel's accessory verses. The larger issue of whether this allegory warrants the thoroughgoing treatment it received in the seventeenth century and later[3] belongs in a separate discussion. We are here concerned with the novelist's raw materials.

---

[1] For a consideration of the various allegorical values to be found in the novel as such, see C. T. Hsia, *The Classic Chinese Novel, a Critical Introduction*, pp. 138 ff.
[2] *HYC*, ch. 28, p. 319, ch. 58, p. 672, ch. 59, p. 675. Cf. H. C. Chang, p. 89, n. 2.
[3] Cf. above, p. 105.
[a] 心猿　[b] 意馬　[c] 大聖　[d] 蛇盤山　[e] 鷹愁澗

The metaphor makes its point simply and graphically: the random, uncontrollable movements of the monkey symbolise the waywardness of the native human mind before it achieves a composure which only Buddhist discipline can effect.

THE METAPHOR IN ANCIENT AND LITERARY SOURCES

The earliest Chinese occurrences are in fact to be found in translated Buddhist sūtras. A common Buddhist origin is certainly attested by precedents and parallels in other, more ancient, Buddhist literatures.[1] In the Pali canon, for instance, the *Samyutta-nikāya* (Book of the Kindred Sayings) has this passage:

> Just as a monkey, brethren, faring through the woods, through the great forest catches hold of a bough, letting it go seizes another, even so that which we call thought, mind, consciousness, that arises as one thing, ceases as another both by night and by day.[2]

A later Sanskrit work, the *Śikṣāsamuccaya* (The Sum Total of the Doctrine), has:

> When he is well treated he is thrilled with delight, lacking steadfastness; being ignorant, when ill treated, he cowers; for like an ape, his mind is fickle: such are the faults of one who delights in talk...[3]

In Chinese the first traceable appearances are in the work of Kumārajīva, most distinguished of the early translators, who died AD 413.[4] His version of the *Vimalakīrti sūtra* (Part 10) contains the lines:

> Since the mind of one difficult to convert is like an ape[a], govern his mind by using certain methods[b] and it can then be broken in.[5]

Again, in the *Mahāprajñāpāramitāśāstra*[c]:

> The mind in its manifestation[d] is nimble, wide-ranging, formless; hard to restrain, hard to grasp, it is constantly in a state of motion—like a monkey[e], or like a stroke of lightning...[6]

A century later, in the translation of *Mañjuśriparipṛcchā*[f] by Saṅghabhara[g], who worked between AD 506 and 520:[7]

[1] For the following references to Indian literature I am indebted to Professor H. W. Bailey.

[2] Mrs Rhys Davids, *The Book of the Kindred Sayings*, second ed. (London, 1952), vol. 2, p. 66.

[3] Bendall and Rouse, *Śikshāsamuccaya* (Indian Texts Series, London, 1922), p. 110. The work was translated into Tibetan between 816 and 838 and may originally have been composed as early as the mid-seventh century: cf. Winternitz, vol. 2, p. 366.

[4] Or in 409: cf. *Kao-seng chuan* 2:333a.

[5] T. XIV, no. 475, p. 553a.

[6] T. xxv, no. 1509, p. 400c.

[7] Cf. *Hsü kao-seng chuan*, 1:426.

[a] 獼猴   [b] 法   [c] 大智度論   [d] 心相   [e] 獼猴子
[f] 文殊師利問經   [g] 僧伽婆羅

because the mind clambers about and cannot be governed, it has no place
of abode: like rushing water, or like a monkey, turning and moving about
without cease, impossible to guard.[1]

Tao-ch'o[a] (562–645), author of *An-lo chi*[b], writes:

The minds of common human beings are like wild horses, their con-
ciousness[c] sports like a monkey, races through the sixfold dust, never
pausing.[2]

At the same period, shortly before the opening of the T'ang dynasty, similar
allusion is to be found in lay literature, although still in a Buddhist context.
The Liang emperor Chien-wen Ti[d], in a poem on the theme of Buddhist repentance, casts the allusion in the now familiar personified form. He writes:

The three ways of discipline[e] exorcise the Horse of Desire[f],
The six kinds of recollection[g] still the Monkey of the Mind.[3]

Here already is a confirmed example of monkey and horse together in a
double metaphor. There is radical change of emphasis when the purposeful
and often elaborate simile is resolved into a more suave metaphorical form by
the device of personification; but the content and its religious connotations
remain unaltered. Hereafter, throughout the T'ang, the association of the two
beasts is progressively confirmed, and the now stereotyped form *hsin-yüan
i-ma* becomes an accepted allusion in literature at large, still without departing
from the Buddhist context.[4] A vigorous natural image has evolved into a
stock allusion. The same process of devaluation eventually takes it out of the
specific Buddhist context. Yü Yen[h] (1258–1314), in a commentary on the old
syncretic text *Ts'an-t'ung ch'i*,[5] writes this passage:

Only long, uninterrupted discipline counts as true application, otherwise
the Monkey of the Mind will be unsettled, the Horse of the Will rush in
all directions and the spiritual ether[j] be scattered in disorder outside: if
you wish to concentrate the elixir[k], it will be difficult indeed![6]

[1] T. xiv, no. 468, p. 503 a.   [2] T. xlvii, no. 1958, p. 11 b.
[3] *Kuang hung-ming chi* 30 (*shang*): 15 a, '*Meng yü ch'an-hui shih*'[l].
[4] For random examples, cf. *Tz'u-en chuan* 9:274 a (from a memorial submitted in
657); Wang Po[m] (648–75), '*P'eng-chou Chiu-lung hsien Huai-lung-szu pei*'[n] (*CTW*,
185:14 b); Shen Ch'üan-ch'i[o] (d. 729), '*Hsia-shan-szu Fu*'[p] (dated 708) (*CTW*,
235:10 a); Hsü Hun[q] (*chin-shih* of 832), '*T'i Tu chü-shih*'[r] (*CTS*, 528:6042); Li
Shan-fu[s] (later in the ninth century), '*T'i Tz'u-yün-szu seng-yüan*'[t] (*CTS*, 643:
7372); Wei Chuang[u] (836–910), '*Pu ch'u yüan Ch'u-kung*'[v] (*CTS*, 698:8030).
[5] For the work, entitled *Chou I ts'an-t'ung-ch'i fa-hui*[w], cf. *SKCSTM*, 146:37 b–38 b.
[6] *Ku-wen Ts'an-t'ung-ch'i chi-chieh* 1 (*shang*), *chung-p'ien*: 42 b. It is perhaps association
with the name of the second century *Ts'an-t'ung-ch'i* which has prompted many
works of reference to cite this passage by Yü Yen as a *locus classicus* for the Monkey–
Horse image.

[a] 道綽	[b] 安樂集	[c] 識	[d] 簡文帝	[e] 三修	[f] 愛馬
[g] 六念	[h] 俞琰	[i] 參同契	[j] 神氣	[k] 結丹	[l] 蒙預懺悔詩
[m] 王勃	[n] 彭州九隴縣懷龍寺碑		[o] 沈佺期	[p] 峽山寺賦	
[q] 許渾	[r] 題杜居士	[s] 李山甫	[t] 題慈雲寺僧院		
[u] 韋莊	[v] 不出院楚公		[w] 周易參同契發揮		

Later, these words of Wang Yang-ming[a] (1472–1528) are reported in the *Ch'uan-hsi lu*[b]:

> One day the discourse ran on application in study. The Master said: In teaching others how to study do not insist on one particular aspect. In the first stages of study the Monkey of the Mind and the Horse of the Will cannot be tied firmly down...[1]

In such cases as these it cannot be assumed that the figures were technical terms of the same order as, say, the complex Taoist metaphorical equipment which Yü Yen uses elsewhere throughout his commentary. No such names appear in the formal Taoist hierarchy, and the concepts 'mind' and 'will' are at odds with the more concrete terms of reference in Taoist anatomy: other references to the 'heart'[c] treat it rather as a physical organ comparable to the kidneys.[2] It is more plausible to see the phrase at this advanced stage simply as part of the Chinese literary language and as such available for legitimate use in any context. The trend is more strikingly reflected in popular literature.

THE METAPHOR IN LYRICAL LITERATURE

Although the orthodox metaphor may be found in a popular work as early as the *Vimalakīrti sūtra pien-wen*,[3] it there fails, because of the work's close Buddhist associations (the topic is scriptural and this manuscript was transcribed by a monk), to betray how freely the metaphor may have been used elsewhere in informal literature. It is above all in the lyrical forms of the Yüan, *san-ch'ü*[d] and *tsa-chü*, that it is found to be in general use.

An example with straightforward Buddhist connotations can be found in a *san-t'ao*[e] (song-sequence) by Kuan Han-ch'ing[f] (late thirteenth century):

> The Horse of the Will held in check,
> The Monkey of the Mind suppressed,
> I leap out of the Red Dust and the evil wind and waves.[4]

And simple analogues in songs of resignation from the world recur, for instance, in the work of Yü T'ien-hsi[g],[5] (possibly his contemporary) or in an anonymous *Hsin-shui-ling*[h] sequence of the Yüan.[6] But in the *tsa-chü Hsi-hsiang chi* we abruptly find a thoroughly secular use, in a song of the first *che*:

> Ah, young maid—by you how can a man fail to be stirred till his will is as a horse, his mind as a monkey?[7]

[1] *Wang Wen-ch'eng kung ch'üan-shu*, 1:26a.
[2] The two organs are the subject of constant parallels and antithesis in commentaries on the *Ts'an-t'ung-ch'i*.
[3] At the end of a fragment dated 947: cf. *Tun-huang pien-wen chi*, pp. 617–18.
[4] *Ch'üan Yüan san-ch'ü*, p. 157.
[5] *Ibid.* p. 224.   [6] *Ibid.* p. 1654.
[7] 1498 version, reprinted in *Ku-pen hsi-ch'ü ts'ung-k'an*, First Series, p. 37b.

[a] 王陽明   [b] 傳習錄   [c] 心   [d] 散曲   [e] 散套   [f] 關漢卿
[g] 庚天錫   [h] 新水令

which in part anticipates the eventual fate of the phrase in colloquial usage of the sixteenth century.

Tsa-chü literature came also to the point of realizing the figures dramatically. In the fourteenth century there were at least two plays in which the Monkey and the Horse appeared on the stage in the manner of an allegorical masque. The one—*T'ieh-kuai Li tu Chin-t'ung Yü-nü*[a] attributed to the playwright Chia Chung-ming[b] (1343-1422)[1]—includes in its third *che* a dream scene, in which the Taoist saint Li T'ieh-kuai seeks to induce a conversion in the hero Chin An-shou[c] by having the two animals chase on to the stage before him, in company with the Baby Boy and Little Girl[d]—both symbols in Taoist anatomy.[2] The scene builds up to a nightmarish climax, at which T'ieh-kuai exclaims:

Quick! Baby Boy, Little Girl! Monkey of the Mind, Horse of the Will! Rush up and seize him![3]

This same stage device is paralleled in the play *Ch'ung-mo-tzu tu pu Ta-lo-t'ien*[e] by Chia's younger contemporary Chu Ch'üan.[4] The plot-setting is also analogous: two Taoist immortals are commissioned to secure the conversion of Ch'ung-mo-tzu, and in the second *che* they reinforce their exhortations by producing a Horse and a Monkey...

Ch'ung-mo-tzu:...But the Monkey of the Mind is still unrestrained, the Horse of the Will difficult to bridle. I humbly beseech you, Holy Master, how can I control them?
Leading Actor: That is not difficult, I shall rid you of them. Summon them over here.
[*All rise from their seats.*] [*Minor actors representing the Monkey of the Mind and the Horse of the Will enter; they act wildly.*]
Leading actor sings 'P'u-t'ien-lo'[f]...Monkey, never again set your feet in the Spirit Tower[g]; Horse—never again make your stable in the Yellow Court[h].[5] Never more concern yourselves with (the human values of) right and wrong.[6]

Upon this there appear in turn the Four Vices, the Three Worms,[7] the Baby Boy, Little Girl and the Yellow Crone[i] [8]—and in turn they are dismissed.

[1] Cf. Fu Hsi-hua (1958), pp. 39 and 41.
[2] Although commonly regarded as alchemical terms they could also be used with anatomical reference: cf. Ch'en Kuo-fu, pp. 449, 451, 452.
[3] Printed version in the *Mo-wang-kuan* collection (*Ku-pen hsi-ch'ü ts'ung-k'an*, Fourth Series) (*ts'e* 34), p. 12*b*.   [4] Cf. above, p. 77, n. 7.
[5] *Ling-t'ai:* i.e. the heart. In Taoist anatomy the Yellow Court denotes the centre (for which yellow is the appropriate colour) of the different zones of the body: cf. Ch'en Kuo-fu, pp. 449–50.
[6] MS version in *Mo-wang-kuan* collection (*ts'e* 33), p. 9*ab*.
[7] *San shih,*[j] believed by Taoists to dwell in each of the three zones of the body and progressively to consume it: the source of mortality. See H. Maspéro, *Mélanges posthumes sur les religions et l'histoire de la Chine* (Paris 1950), vol. 2 (*Le Taoïsme*), p. 20.
[8] *Huang-p'o:* Taoist name for the secretion of the spleen. Cf. Ch'en Kuo-fu, p. 452.

[a] 鐵拐李度金童玉女   [b] 賈仲明   [c] 金安壽   [d] 嬰兒姹女
[e] 冲漠子獨步大羅天   [f] 普天樂   [g] 靈臺   [h] 黃庭   [i] 黃婆   [j] 三尸

What these dramatic representations offer is of course no more than an extension of verbal personification: symbols are enlisted from several different sources to serve in a single, vaguely Taoist allegory. We have seen precedents in philosophical writing for such freedom of vocabulary or easy universalism. A more immediate factor here must be the evident dramatic effectiveness of grotesquely mimed figures in plays whose action would otherwise be purely psychological: they present tangible material around which the lyrical drama can shape itself, without distorting its unity by arrogating too much of the action. And as they perform this function it becomes more than ever a matter of indifference whether their background is consistent with itself or technically appropriate to the subject of the play. They are required primarily as figures on the stage.

THE METAPHOR IN RELATION TO THE 'HSI-YU CHI' STORY

We must first observe: that although both monkey and horse featured in a *Hsi-yu chi* work as early as the Kōzanji version (a white horse was given to Tripitaka in the Land of Women),[1] there is no evidence of any use of the metaphor before the *tsa-chü* version: that there, in the closing song of sc. 10 (p. 47), the Mountain Spirit addresses the departing travellers in the words:

> I charge you, the ape—keep the Monkey of the Mind tied up tight and firm,
> And the Dragon Lord in company with the Master—keep the Horse of the Will's coursing under urgent control.

This, unsupported by any other reference in the text, carries hardly more specific allegorical force than the allusions in other works quoted above. Given the inherited characters of the story and the evident mode for the stereotyped phrase *hsin-yüan i-ma*, common to literature formal and informal, the conceit is an obvious one.

It reappears, in a frank reference to Sun Wu-k'ung, in the *Erh-lang pao-chüan* of 1555 (cf. above, p. 153, n. 1). But before this, and more significantly, it is found in a preface which represents the earliest attempt I know to draw up a full allegorical interpretation of the *Hsi-yu chi* story. It stands before the *tsa-chü Tung-t'ien hsüan-chi*[a]. The writer, Yang T'i[b], describes himself as a disciple of the alleged author of the play, Yang Shen[c] (1488–1559).[2] His preface is dated 1542.[3] He writes:

> Some enthusiasts, stirred by the *yüeh-fu*[d] songs, have also collected stories —of faithful ministers and valiant heroes, righteous men and chaste wives, filial sons and obedient grandsons—and made plays[e] of them, clothing them in sound and spectacle to bring delight to ear and eye.

---

[1] B 2:9*a* (1955, p. 43).
[2] For the anomaly of this attribution, see Fu Hsi-hua (1958), p. 88.
[3] See the printed version of *Tung-t'ien hsüan-chi* in the *Mo-wang-kuan* collection (*ts'e* 35), *ch'ien-hsü*[f].

[a] 洞天玄記   [b] 楊悌   [c] 楊慎   [d] 樂府   [e] 戲文   [f] 前序

These, although regarded as diversions and trivial arts, yet have the power of stirring the emotions. With Buddhist overtones, there is also the work *Hsi-yu chi* which tells fantastic things. The wise castigate it as false, the foolish accept it as true. I have often reflected on its interpretation: by Tripitaka of the T'ang it means man's own true nature; by Chu Pa-chieh[a], the 'black pearl',[1] it means the eye; by Sun Hsing-che the monkey-spirit it means the mind; by the White Horse it means the will—whiteness expresses its purity and peace; when it speaks of nine times reaching the River of Flowing Sands and being seven times swallowed by Sha Ho-shang—Sha Ho-shang is the 'vapour'[b] of anger;[2] when it speaks of them frequently enjoying the saving protection of Kuan-shih-yin, Kuan-shih-yin is wisdom; in speaking of the return to the homeland on a puff of fragrant wind it describes the ease with which the True Way may be attained. If men could with their power of sight first see through the affairs of the world, then suppress the Monkey of the Mind and bind the Horse of the Will, and again with wisdom govern their anger and subdue all evil spirits—what difficulty would there be in attaining the Way?...(pp. 1*a*–2*a*).

Yang T'i proceeds to apply his method of interpretation to the play *Tung-t'ien hsüan-chi* and adds:

This book should be handed down side by side with the *Hsi-yu chi*... (p. 2*b*).

Such a bald account of allegory in the story is too strained to be very impressive, and parts of it—e.g. the interpretation of Chu Pa-chieh, justified solely by its pun—seem to bear no relation to any known version. Its references to the plot are too generalized to make clear exactly what work was under consideration; but from the fact that the whole discussion is concerned with drama, and that in it the *Hsi-yu chi* is associated directly with the *tsa-chü Tung-t'ien hsüan-chi*, we can infer that Yang was concerned not with a work of prose fiction but with a play. There is not enough to reveal whether this was a *tsa-chü*, by Wu Ch'ang-ling, Yang Ching-yen or some other, or a *ch'uan-ch'i*—for the sometimes specific term *hsi-wen* (i.e. the southern drama, ancestor of the *ch'uan-ch'i*) which here introduces the discussion on drama by implication includes the *Tung-t'ien hsüan-chi* itself—a *tsa-chü*. Since Yang claims credit for insight into allegorical subtleties which had eluded the general public, it would seem that nothing of the sort was elaborated in the

---

[1] *Hsüan*[c], 'black', because Chu Pa-chieh was characterized as a black creature (cf. *Hsi-yu chi tsa-chü*, sc. 13, p. 72); *chu*[d], 'pearl', is a pun on his surname.

[2] This interpretation is at first sight obscure. But since at least informally anger is associated with the spleen (cf. the phrase *p'i-ch'i*[e]) there may be a connection here with the term *huang-p'o* (i.e. contents of the spleen), which is the Taoist symbol later attached to Sha Ho-shang in the hundred-chapter *Hsi-yu chi*—(cf. *HYC*, ch. 23, p. 256, ch. 40, p. 464). Yellow is the colour characteristic of Sha Ho-shang, because it is the colour of earth and sand.

[a] 界　[b] 氣　[c] 玄　[d] 珠　[e] 脾氣

text itself—unless some features, e.g. the phrase 'black pearl', were suggested in a lost original. Although Yang's reading of the work was not necessarily as creative and new as he suggests in his preface, it demonstrates that at least in the first half of the sixteenth century the attempt was being made to wrest a quasi-religious interpretation from the story. Like the dramatic personifications cited above, it displays no sense of discrimination over the religious origin of its symbols. Once habit had sanctioned the practice of employing these figures rather for their picturesque value than their religious significance, there was clearly no inducement, especially in an era of eclectic philosophies, to restore a pure discipline in the interpretation of a story so rich in potential symbols.

It was to a comparable preface (to the hundred chapter *Hsi-yu chi*) that Ch'en Yüan-chih[a] referred in his own, commissioned by the Nanking printing house Shih-te T'ang[b] for its edition of the hundred chapter work.[1]

> There was an old preface, which I read through...It held that Sun[c] was equivalent to *sun*[d] ('monkey'), the spirit of the mind; the horse was the Horse symbolising the coursing of the will; Chu Pa-chieh, the eight precepts, was taken as the 'wood' of the vapour[e] in the liver; Sha, the Flowing Sands, as the 'water' of the vapour in the spleen;[2] Tripitaka, the Three Stores[f] of spirit, sound and vapour, was taken as the master protecting them; the demons—obstructions created by mouth, ears, nose, tongue, body and will:[3] fears, distortions[g], fantasies...

The indiscriminate jumble of Taoist and Buddhist references is here even more pronounced, and a feature such as Sha Ho-shang's identification with the contents of the spleen harks directly back to the parade of personifications in the *Ch'ung-mo-tzu* play. He is in fact given the symbolic name *Huang-p'o* in some verses of the novel, which also takes up a number of the other Taoist anatomical terms used in the plays.[4]

Aside from the question of detailed relationship between the symbols brought out here and those used explicitly in the hundred-chapter text, this general background surely betrays the spirit in which the Monkey-Mind image became associated with the *Hsi-yu chi*: with a long history behind it of degeneration from its original force, it now finds itself in the midst of personifications drawn from the Taoist cult, their presence in dramatic works

---

[1] The earliest date attached to this preface was 1592. For details and bibliographical references, see Dudbridge (1969), pp. 145 and 187.

[2] Cf. above, p. 173, n. 2. 'Wood' and 'Water' represent further identifications with the Five Elements, although the element associated with the spleen was usually Earth, and Water belonged with the kidney. Cf. Ch'en Kuo-fu, pp. 448–51.

[3] These are the six senses of Buddhism. The first, 'mouth', should strictly be 'eye'. These senses, personified as the Six Bandits[h], are used as characters in the *Tungt'ien hsüan-chi* and also in the hundred-chapter *Hsi-yu chi* (*HYC*, ch. 14, pp. 159–60, ch. 43, p. 494, ch. 56, p. 643): cf. H. C. Chang, pp. 89–90.

[4] Cf. above, pp. 171–3. *Ying-erh* and *Ch'a-nü* are used, for instance, in headings to chs. 40 and 80.

[a] 陳元之   [b] 世德堂   [c] 孫   [d] 猻   [e] 氣   [f] 藏   [g] 顛倒   [h] 六賊

once justified by a simple pictorial utility, now perpetuated by those anxious to invest the novel with some semblance of intellectual respectability. This their intention they leave in no doubt: the express purpose of all the prefaces here discussed, as well as the prolific tradition of *Hsi-yu chi* interpretation from the seventeenth to the nineteenth centuries, was to justify works which educated men could otherwise not acknowledge.

To employ the Monkey and Horse in this project would appear even so to have had its risks. There is a good deal of evidence to show that by this stage of the sixteenth century the words *hsin-yüan i-ma* had already been degraded in general colloquial usage into a transparent euphemism for the stirring of sexual desire (a force which they retain in present-day use). An example at random may be taken from the *Feng-shen yen-i*:

> In the lamplight (Chou Wang[a]) saw Hsi Mei[b] two or three times part her red lips—a little dot of cherry—and breathe a lovely cloud of sweet air; she turned her liquid eyes—two pools of moving water—and gave him all kinds of captivating wanton glances, till Chou Wang could not suppress the Monkey of the Mind, and the Horse of the Will strained at the leash . . .[1]

Or again in the *Shui-hu chuan*: the episode is the appearance of the girl warrior Ch'iung Ying[c] on the battlefield during the T'ien-hu[d] campaign:

> The Short-legged Tiger Wang Ying[e], when he saw that this was a beautiful girl, galloped out from the ranks. Levelling his spear, he raced to seize Ch'iung Ying. The two armies roared battle-cries. Ch'iung Ying whipped on her horse and brandished her lance as she came forward to the combat. When the warriors had fought through more than ten engagements the Short-legged Tiger could no longer restrain the Horse of the Will and Monkey of the Mind, and his spear-play fell into confusion...[2]

The examples, and several others like them,[3] are unambiguous: they suggest a background of common usage which puts into a new perspective the preface-writers' efforts to create or sustain a valid allegorical symbol.

A survey of the *Hsi-yu chi* tradition shows it clearly emerging from a popular, not an intellectual or literary milieu. The moment when it acquired the Monkey-Mind metaphor can almost be pointed out in the Ming dynasty. In its turn, the metaphor was already nearing the final stages of its development as a well-worn literary conceit, virtually devoid of its scriptural force and at the mercy of common speech. The novelist inherited both this and the symbols of Taoist derivation from an existing body of interpretations, not from the story itself.

In the minds of these allegorists the association does not move in the

---

[1] *Feng-shen yen-i*, ch. 26, p. 241.
[2] *SHC*, ch. 98, p. 1542.
[3] E.g. *SHC*, ch. 45, p. 735, ch. 81, p. 1338; *Hsing-shih heng-yen*, pp. 47, 250.

[a] 紂王   [b] 喜媚   [c] 瓊英   [d] 田虎   [e] 王英

natural direction from abstraction to graphic personification, but rather forcibly overlays a common figure of speech upon ready-made fictional characters. The disproportion in importance between monkey and horse in the story is only one example of the strains involved. We shall therefore almost certainly be misled if, on the basis of these metaphors, we try to read the novel *Hsi-yu chi* as a significant allegory. Whatever may be concluded about allegorical elements more truly inherent in this author's telling of the story, the Monkey–Horse metaphor cannot be seen as an urgent or spontaneous force in his work. A similar conception of the monkey's nature is all that relates the traditional Sun Wu-k'ung to the Monkey of the Mind: it is by independent routes that they come to meet in the novel *Hsi-yu chi*.

Translation and Text

1. The *Hsi-yu chi* fragment in *Yung-lo ta-tien*, ch. 13,139. [Page references are to the reprint of 1960.]

[8*b*] *The Dragon of the Ching river beheaded in a dream* (*Hsi-yu chi*). To the south-west of Ch'ang-an city is a river called Ching-ho[a]. In the thirteenth year of Chen-kuan there were by the riverside two fishermen, one named Chang Shao[b], one Li Ting[c]. Chang Shao said to Li Ting: 'Inside the West Gate of Ch'ang-an there is a fortune-teller called Shen-yen-shan-jen[d]. Every day I give him a carp, and he then directs me where to cast my nets. Following his advice I make a catch every time.' Li Ting said: 'I must ask the Master('s advice) tomorrow!'

While these two were speaking they little thought that in the water there was a *yakṣa* patrolling the river who overheard what they said. (He thought): 'I'll report this to the Dragon King!' The Dragon King was called the Dragon of the Ching River, and at this point was just sitting in state in the Crystal Palace[e]. Suddenly the *yakṣa* came up and said: 'There are two humans on the shore—fishermen—who say that within the West Gate is a Master selling fortunes who knows the internal affairs of the River. If things were to go as he [9*a*] forecasts all the river-people will be caught.' Hearing this the Dragon King was furious. He dressed up as a scholar (*hsiu-shih*[f]) in plain clothes and entered the city, where he saw a placard saying 'The Wonderful Physiognomist Yüan Shou-ch'eng[g] Tells Fortunes Here'. Seeing this the Dragon sat down opposite the Master and contrived innumerable points with which to interrogate and confound him. He asked what day it would rain. The Master said: 'Tomorrow, clouds will form at the hour of *ch'en*[h]; thunder will arise at the hour of *wu*[i]; rain will fall at the hour of *wei*[j]; it will be spent by the hour of *shen*[k].' The Dragon asked how much rain would fall. The Master said: 'Three feet three inches and forty-eight drops will fall.' The Dragon laughed and said: 'It will not necessarily go as you say!' The Master said: 'I will gladly pay a fine of fifty taels if tomorrow no rain falls or the time is wrong.' The Dragon said: 'That will do. But we must meet again tomorrow!' He took his leave.

He returned to the Crystal Palace, and in a moment a Yellow-capped Warrior[l] announced: 'The Jade Emperor commands that you, the Dragon of the Ching river, Governor of the Eight Rivers, on the morrow at the hour of *ch'en* form clouds, at the hour of *wu* mount thunder, at the hour of *wei* let

---

^a 涇河　　^b 張稍　　^c 李定　　^d 神言山人　　^e 水晶　　^f 秀士
^g 袁守成　　^h 辰　　ⁱ 午　　^j 未　　^k 申　　^l 力士

rain fall, at the hour of *shen* (declare) the rain sufficient.' The Warrior then departed.

The Dragon said (to himself): 'I had not thought that this would all agree with that Master's lying forecast. I shall put the time out and send down a bit less rain, and then demand the fine from the Master.'

The next day at the hour of *shen* he formed cloud and at the hour of *yu*[a] let fall two feet of rain. The day after that the Dragon once more changed into a scholar and went into Ch'ang-an to the fortune-teller's. He demanded of the Master: 'Your forecast did not work—now out with those fifty taels!' The Master said: 'There was nothing wrong in my original prognostication— it was rather you who altered the decree of Heaven and sent the rain down wrongly. You are in fact no human being, but the Dragon who yesterday sent down the rain! You may deceive others, but not me!'

The Dragon at this was furious and appeared to the Master in his original form. In a trice the Yellow River had burst both banks and the three peaks of Mount Hua[b] were shaken as (the Dragon's) grandeur brought consternation over ten thousand *li* and wind and rain burst into space. All then fled; only Yüan Shou-ch'eng remained, majestically unperturbed. The Dragon was about to advance and attack him when he said: 'I am not afraid to die. You have disobeyed a heavenly decree and cut short the sweet rain. Your life is in the balance—you will be lucky to escape the knife on the Platform for Dragon Execution!' Then the Dragon, terrified, regretted his mistake. He changed back into a scholar, knelt down and pleaded with the Master saying 'If this really is the case, I hope you can tell me clearly all about it.' Shou-ch'eng said: 'Upon the morrow you die! It will be Wei Cheng[c], Under-Minister of the T'ang, who will despatch you tomorrow at the hour of *wu*.' [9*b*] The Dragon said: 'Save me, Master!' Shou-ch'eng said: 'If you want to escape death you may do so only by having an audience with the T'ang sovereign (and asking him) to urge Wei Cheng to save you—then you might be able to avoid disaster.' The Dragon was grateful, took a respectful leave of the Master and returned.

The Jade Emperor commissions Wei Cheng to behead the Dragon. It was already late: the T'ang Emperor in his palace was half asleep, while his spirit left the palace and strolled about in the moonlight. He saw a wreath of dark cloud settle to the ground in the south-west, and a dragon descended and knelt before him. The Emperor said, in terror: 'Why (is this)?' The Dragon said: 'Simply because last night I went wrong in sending down the sweet rain and violated a heavenly decree. I merit death. But you, my Sovereign, are the true Dragon, I am only a false Dragon. A true dragon is surely able to save a false one!' The Emperor said: 'How am I to save you?' The Dragon replied: 'The sentence for my crime is to be carried out by your own Under-Minister Wei Cheng, tomorrow at the hour of *wu*.' The Emperor said: 'If this affair involves Wei Cheng, I will certainly keep you out of trouble.' The Dragon bowed in thanks and left.

The Emperor awoke—it was a dream. The next morning he held court and summoned the Military Commander-in-chief Yü-ch'ih Ching-te[d] to the

---

[a] 酉   [b] 華嶽   [c] 魏徵   [d] 尉遲敬德

Palace. He told him: 'Last night I dreamt that the Dragon of the Ching river came to plead before me, saying that it had sent down rain wrongly, breaking a heavenly decree, and was due to be executed by Under-Minister Wei Cheng. I promised to save it. I want today to summon the Under-Minister to play chess with me all day in the Rear Palace. He must not leave before nightfall. The Dragon can surely thus be saved.' Ching-te said: 'You are right in what you say!' And he called in Wei Cheng.

The Emperor said: 'I have summoned you for no particular business, but I wish to play a day's chess with you.' He was deliberately slow with his moves. As it approached the hour *wu* Minister Wei suddenly closed his eyes and stayed motionless. He awoke when it came to the hour *wei*. The Emperor said: 'Why were you like this?' Wei Cheng said: 'Some obscure fit came over me suddenly. Your Majesty please forgive my lack of respect!' And he resumed his game of chess with the Emperor. Not more than three moves had been made when they heard an unusual commotion among the people in the market-place of Ch'ang-an. The Emperor asked what it was about, and ministers close by reported that at the crossroads to the south of the Gallery of a Thousand Steps a dragon's head had fallen from the clouds. The people were in commotion about this. The Emperor asked Wei Cheng: 'How has this come about?' Wei Cheng said: 'If your Majesty had not asked I would not have presumed to speak. The Dragon of the Ching river committed the crime of disobeying heaven. I was commissioned by the Jade Emperor to behead it. If I had not obeyed, my crime would have been equal with that of the dragon. Just now when I closed my eyes for a short space I beheaded this dragon.'

This indeed is what we call: Wei Cheng in a dream beheading the dragon of the Ching river.

[10*a*] The Emperor said: 'I wanted to save it—I never expected this would happen!' Upon which they stopped their game of chess.

2. References to *Hsi-yu chi* in *Pak t'ongsa ŏnhae*

[The text of *Pak t'ongsa* proper appears in large characters, each followed immediately by phonetic renderings in the Korean alphabet. Large circles punctuate the text in conveniently small units—whether according to the change of speaker in the dialogue, or into natural sentence-units and smaller groups of words. A translation into Korean is inserted after each such division, and this in turn is occasionally followed by glosses of varied length written in literary Chinese and printed in double columns of small characters. These are presumed to be the work of Ch'oe Se-chin. They are in any case distinct from the text of *Pak t'ongsa*.

For the sake of clarity, the relevant parts of the *Pak t'ongsa* dialogues are here translated as a single whole; the later notes in literary language are added separately at the end. In the translation from *Pak t'ongsa* the marking (N) indicates that a note in literary Chinese is inserted at that point. Those notes selected as relevant are further numbered—thus: (N i), (N ii), and translations of them are given later under those numbers.

All page references are to the *Keishōkaku sōsho* reprint].

[264]—Are your images of the Buddha cast yet, Master? (N)
—The Three Venerable Buddhas are cast. (N) I was just about to put on the gilt when burglars came in about the time of the third watch the day before yesterday (N) and stole all my gold and silver ingots and money gained from two or three years of alms! There is nothing for it but for me to go south of the River again and beg for alms. [265] All at once my luck is thoroughly bad: I'm offering prayers to the Buddhas and Bodhisattvas. Once my vow is fulfilled I don't mind if I die!
—There, there, Master! The true reward of virtue will not be destroyed! Don't fall into a slack frame of mind! Apply yourself diligently on the way! Once upon a time, when Master Tripitaka of the T'ang (N i) fetched the scriptures [266] from the Western Paradise (N ii)—a road of 108,000 *li*! Truly, even thin little birds could not fly so far, and sturdy horses would find the going hard. Over such a wide expanse of country, how much wind and rain, heat and cold he passed through, how much [267] scorching and blowing he suffered, how many evil mountains, perilous rivers and difficult roads he traversed, how many monsters and demons attacked him, how much trouble he encountered from fierce tigers and venomous snakes, how much ill-treatment from evil beings! (N iii) Truly, a good man meets all the more supernatural obstacles. (N) He travelled for six years, and what [268] countless hardships he suffered, to reach the Western Paradise and fetch scriptures for the deliverance of all living beings and their elevation to Buddhahood. Master—don't be in too much of a hurry. Take your time when you go south of the River and beg from door to door. And when your vow is fulfilled you too will gain spiritual rewards and a Golden Body! (N iv)
[292]—Let's go out[1] and buy books.
—Go and buy what books?
—Buy the *Chao T'ai-tsu fei-lung chi*[a] (N) and *T'ang San-tsang Hsi-yu chi* (N v).
—If you are going to buy something [293] it would be as well to buy the Four Books or Six Classics: having read the writings of the sage Confucius you will surely comprehend the principles of the Duke of Chou[b]. What do you want with that sort of popular tale (*p'ing-hua*[c])?
—The *Hsi-yu chi* is lively. It is good reading when you are feeling gloomy.[2] Tripitaka led Sun Hsing-che [294] (N vi) to Ch'e-ch'ih kuo[d] (N) and they had a contest in magic powers with Po-yen ta-hsien[e]. Do you know (that one)?
—Tell it, and I'll listen.

---

[1] The original phrase[f] is obscure. It may refer to some official building in front of which the public could buy and sell: I have chosen to leave the translation deliberately vague.
[2] This sentence ends with the character *yu*[g]. In the *Nogŏltae chipnam* appended at the end of this work (p. 385) it is stated that *yu* was constantly used as a final particle in colloquial language of Yüan times. For many further examples, see Ts'ai Mei-piao, pp. 20, 29, 44, 48, 76, 101, 104 etc.

[a] 趙太祖飛龍記   [b] 周公   [c] 平話   [d] 車運國   [e] 伯眼大仙
[f] 部前   [g] 有

—When Tripitaka[a] went to fetch scriptures from the Western Paradise he came to a city named Ch'e-ch'ih kuo. [295] The king there was a lover of good works and respected the Buddhist Doctrine. In that land there was a (Taoist) Master called Po-yen, also styled Shao-chin-tzu tao-jen[b]. (N vii) Seeing that the king honoured the Buddhist Doctrine he turned his black heart to the destruction of Buddhism. The moment he saw a monk he had him split apart by dragging between two chariots. He built a great temple to the Three Pure Ones[c] (N); [296] in these ways he persecuted the Three Jewels[d].

One day the Taoists were holding a grand service to the Taoist Heaven (N). Tripitaka and his disciple had just come to the Chih-hai Ch'an Monastery[e] in that city to spend the night. They heard the Taoists sacrificing to the stars. Sun [297] Hsing-che explained to his Master (what he was going to do), and went to hide on the altar-site of the Grand Service to Heaven. He stole and ate the tea and fruit offered in sacrifice to the stars, and also gave Po-yen a blow with his iron cudgel. A junior Taoist came forward to have the lamps lit, and he too received a blow from the iron cudgel. Po-yen said: 'This bald fool is ill-mannered!' And then he lost his temper and went to report it to the King. But before he had done so Tripitaka had also led his disciple to the King's residence, [298] and the King invited Tripitaka into the Palace. He received Ta-hsien and made polite enquiries, and the Taoist likewise returned the courtesy with a bow of the head. The Taoist said to Tripitaka: 'Our grievance is no trifle!' Tripitaka said: 'We poor monks are from the East. We don't know you. What grievance do you have?' Ta-hsien opened wide his eyes and said: 'You had your disciple wreck our Service to Heaven [299] and also hit us twice with an iron cudgel. Isn't that a serious grievance? Let the two of us hold a contest in magic powers before the King. The one that loses shall be compelled to bow to the other as master.' Tripitaka asked: 'How do we set about it?' Po-yen said: 'First, sitting in meditation; second, guessing objects in a chest; third, bathing in boiling oil; fourth, replacing one's own severed head.'

When he had finished speaking a bell was sounded, [300] and each mounted the Ch'an throne to meditate. They were not to move a hairsbreadth: the slightest movement would immediately lose the match. A disciple of Ta-hsien named Deerskin[f] plucked out a hair from his head and changed it into a dog-flea, which bit Tripitaka behind the ear. He was on the point of breaking his meditation. But Sun Hsing-che was a monkey[g]: when he saw the flea he took it away and struck it dead. And he too plucked out a hair from his coat and changed it into a mock Hsing-che to stand beside his master; [301] he himself went to Chin-shui River[h] and took a lump of black mud, which he put inside Ta-hsien's nostrils. Then he turned into a black female scorpion and bit him on the back. Ta-hsien cried out and jumped down from the throne. The King said: 'Tripitaka has won!'

Next they told two palace maidens to bring across a red lacquer chest and put it down in front of them. The two were told to guess what was inside.

[a] 唐僧   [b] 燒金子道人   [c] 三清   [d] 三寶   [e] 智海禪寺   [f] 鹿皮
[g] 胡孫   [h] 金水河

[302] The Queen covertly had a palace maiden go and tell the (Taoist) Master that there was a peach in there. Sun Hsing-che changed into an insect[a],[1] flew into the chest and ate all the flesh of the peach, leaving only the stone, before he came out. He told this to his master. The King said: 'This time Tripitaka guesses first.' Tripitaka said it was a peach-stone. The Queen laughed out loud that he had not guessed right. [303] Ta-hsien said it was a peach. A General was told to open the chest and see—but it was a peach-stone. The Taoist had lost again.

Deerskin said to Ta-hsien: 'Now we shall heat up a cauldron of oil and get in to bathe.' Deerskin undressed first and got into the cauldron. The King applauded. Meanwhile Sun Hsing-che pronounced the syllable *Om*[b], and the mountain spirits and local gods all appeared. Hsing-che told the two spirits Ch'ien-li-yen[c] and Shun- [304] feng-erh[d] (N) to keep watch on both sides of the cauldron of oil, and just as the Taoist was about to emerge to grip him by the shoulders and drop[2] him inside. Deerskin could no longer stand the heat; he had just set foot on the edge of the cauldron ready to climb out when the spirits prevented him from coming out, and he perished in the oil. When the King saw that he didn't emerge for a long time (he asked): 'Mightn't he be dead?' The General was ordered to look. He used a golden [305] hook to fish out a Taoist whose very bones were disintegrating.

Sun Hsing-che said: 'Now I am getting in to have a bath.' He took off his clothes, turned a somersault and jumped into the oil. On the point of taking his bath he disappeared. The King said: 'General, lift him out! Hsing-che must be dead!' The General went to lift him out with the hook. Hsing-che changed into a monkey only five inches or so in size. [306] When (the hook) came to the left-hand side to lift him out he dodged across to the right; when it came to the right he dodged to the left: no device succeeded in fetching him out. The General reported: 'The oil has boiled away all Hsing-che's flesh.' Seeing all this, Tripitaka wept. When Hsing-che heard him he jumped out and cried: 'Great King, do you have any soap for me to wash my head with?' The crowd applauded: 'The Buddhists have won!'

Sun Hsing-che was the first to cut off his own head: [307] the neck stood streaming with blood, and the head fell to the ground. Hsing-che picked it up with his hand and fixed it on his neck as before. Po-yen ta-hsien also cut off his head and was just about to fix it back when Hsing-che called upon the Golden- and Silver-headed *Chieh-ti* Guardians[e] and the *Po-lo-seng*[f] Guardians, and after that (N viii) he changed into a large black dog and dragged away the Taoist's [308] head. The Taoist turned into a tiger and pursued him. Hsing-che dragged it right in front of the king and dropped it. The dog disappeared, and the tiger disappeared too. Only a tiger's head fell down. The King said: 'So it was a tiger demon! If it were not for you, Master, how could we have called forth his true form?'

---

[1] In the original the insect is characterized by the phrase 'drying-up shoots', and would thus seem to be some kind of crop-pest.

[2] The graph[g] is a variant form of *tiu*[h]. Cf. *Tan-cha hae, PTS*, p. 404.

[a] 焦苗蟲兒   [b] 唵   [c] 千里眼   [d] 順風耳   [e] 揭地   [f] 波羅僧   [g] 丟   [h] 丟

After saying these words he had an even deeper respect for Buddhists. He presented Tripitaka with three hundred strings of gold cash and one golden almsbowl. [309] To Hsing-che he gave three hundred strings of gold cash; and sent them on their way.

That Sun Hsing-che really was magnificent! Little did Po-yen ta-hsien expect to meet his death at the hands of a monkey! Men of old said that for every ten thousand of the enemy you kill, you lose three thousand of your own.

Notes

[265] (N i) Tripitaka's secular surname was Ch'en[a], his personal name Wei[b]; he was a native of Kou-shih-hsien[c] in Lo-chou[d]. He was styled Hsüan-tsang fa-shih. In the third year of the Chen-kuan reign he received an Imperial command to go to the Western Regions. He collected six hundred rolls of scriptures and returned with them. Again, he was called Master Tripitaka...
[266] (N ii) The *Hsi-yu chi* says: Long ago the Śākyamuni Buddha at the Thunderclap Monastery in the Western Paradise created three baskets[e] of golden scriptures—Sūtra, Vinaya and Śāstra—which had to be delivered to the Eastern Land in order to release and save all those astray. He asked all the Bodhisattvas to go to the East and seek a man to come and fetch the scriptures. But, because from the Western Paradise to the East was a distance of 108,000 *li*, and the way fraught with demons, none of the multitude dared to volunteer lightly. Only the Bodhisattva Kuan-shih-yin of Mount Potalaka[f] in the Southern Sea, riding the clouds and mists, went to the Eastern Land. She saw from afar that a column of auspicious vapour rushed up to Heaven from Ch'ang-an and Ching-chao fu. Kuan-yin changed into an aged monk and entered the city. At the time T'ang T'ai-tsung had mustered all monks and nuns in the Empire and was holding a Grand Assembly. Accordingly the monks had nominated a High Priest to preside and to preach: it was the Master Hsüan-tsang. Seeing the Master, the aged monk said: 'Śākyamuni in the Western Paradise has created three baskets of scriptures and is now waiting for a man to collect them.' The Master said: 'Since there is a way there I must eventually be able to reach the place. Although the Western Paradise is far away, I solemnly vow to go and bring (the scriptures) back.' When they had spoken, the aged monk flew into the air and was gone. The Emperor recognized that this was an incarnation of Kuan-yin and at once commanded the Master to go to the Western Paradise and fetch the scriptures. The Master accepted the mission and left. After six years he returned to the East.
[267] (N iii)...Now when the Master went to the Western Paradise, he first reached the bounds of Shih-t'o kuo and suffered injury from fierce tigers and venomous snakes, then he encountered the Black Bear spirit, the Yellow Wind demon, Madame Ti-yung, the Spider demons, the Lion demon, the Many-eyed demon, the Red Boy demon; he barely escaped with his life. Again, he passed through the Cavern of Thorns and Barbs[g], the Fiery Mountain, the Po-shih Cavern, the Land of Women, and demons and afflictions on every evil

[a] 陳   [b] 偉   [c] 緱氏縣   [d] 洛州   [e] 藏   [f] 落迦山   [g] 釣＝鈎

mountain and perilous river—I know not how many disasters and sufferings. This is what is meant by 'ill-treatment'. See the *Hsi-yu chi*.

[268] (N iv)...What is termed 'spiritual reward' is such a thing as the Master Tripitaka, when he had returned to the East after collecting the scriptures, becoming the Candana Buddha Tathāgata. See below.

[292] (N v) *Hsi-yu chi*: The Master Tripitaka went to the Western Regions, collected six hundred rolls of scriptures and returned. The whole story of his journey there and back was set down in a book entitled *Hsi-yu chi*. See above.

[293] (N vi)...According to the *Hsi-yu chi*, there was in the Western Regions a Mountain of Flowers and Fruit; below the mountain was a Water-curtain Cave; before the cave was a bridge of sheets of iron, beneath the bridge was a torrent ten thousand *chang* deep, beside the torrent were ten thousand small caves, and in the caves a multitude of monkeys. There was a monkey-spirit of mighty spiritual powers, styled Ch'i-t'ien Ta-sheng, who entered the orchard of magic peaches in Heaven and stole the fruit. He likewise stole Lao-chün's holy elixir and made off with the Queen (of the West's) embroidered robes from her own palace. He held a party in celebration of the robes. Lao-chün and the Queen both appealed to the Jade Emperor, who summoned the Devarāja Li to lead 100,000 heavenly warriors and all the spirit-commanders against the Mountain of Flowers and Fruit and engage Ta-sheng in combat. But they lost their advantage, and a Strong Spirit who patrolled the hills reported to the Heavenly King that if they raised the spirit of Kuan-k'ou near Kuan-chou called Erh-lang the Small Saint, the capture could be effected. The Heavenly King sent the Crown Prince Moksha and the Strong [294] Spirit to go and ask the spirit Erh-lang to lead his celestial army and surround the Mountain of Flowers and Fruit. The monkeys all came out to fight, but were defeated, and Ta-sheng was captured. He was about to die when Kuan-yin submitted a request to the Jade Emperor to spare his life: 'Let Chü-ling shen be ordered to hold him in custody and take him to the world below; on the Mountain of Flowers and Fruit let the lower half of his body be put in a crevasse in the rock, which should be sealed by drawing the mark of the Tathāgata Buddha; let the mountain spirits and local gods keep guard over him; when hungry let him eat iron pellets, when thirsty drink molten bronze, and so wait for me to go to the East in search of a man to fetch scriptures; when I pass this mountain I shall see whether Ta-sheng is willing to go with him to the West, and, if so, he can then be released.' Subsequently T'ang T'ai-tsung commissioned the Master Hsüan-tsang to go to the West and fetch the scriptures. The route ran past this mountain, and he saw the monkey-spirit confined in the rock-crevasse, removed the seal of the Buddha and brought him out. He made him a disciple, gave him the religious name Wu-k'ung[a], changed his style[b] to Sun Hsing-che, and set off together with him and Sha Ho-shang and a black pig spirit called Chu Pa-chieh. On the way it was wholly through the agency of Sun Hsing-che's spiritual powers that demons were defeated and the Master saved from difficult situations. When the Master reached the Western Paradise he received the Three Baskets of

^a 吾空   ^b 號

Scriptures and returned to the East. The Master reaped his spiritual reward by becoming the Candana Buddha Tathāgata, Sun Hsing-che by becoming the Strong King Bodhisattva, Chu Pa-chieh the cleanser of altars at the Assembly of Incense and Flowers.

[295] (N vii) The *Hsi-yu chi* says: There was a (Taoist) Master who came to Ch'e-ch'ih kuo. With one breath he could turn bricks and tiles into gold. This amazed the King of the land, who honoured him as a *kuo-shih*. He was styled Po-yen ta-hsien.

[307] (N viii) The *Hsi-yu chi* says: When the Śākyamuni Buddha at the Thunderclap Monastery on Mount Ling expounded the doctrine of the Three Vehicles[a], there were in attendance at his side Ānanda, Kāśyapa, the Bodhisattvas, holy monks, Arhats, Eight Vajras[b], Four *Chieh-ti* Guardians, Ten Kings of Hell, Immortals of Heaven and Earth. (. . .)

[353] (N ix: after the words 'Erh-lang yeh-yeh[c]') . . . According to the *Hsi-yu chi*, there was a monkey spirit of unfathomable spiritual powers called Ch'i-t'ien Ta-sheng in a cave on the Mountain of Flowers and Fruit in the Western Regions. He created an uproar in Heaven, and the Jade Emperor commanded the Devarāja Li to lead spirit-troops to arrest him. They lost their advantage in the fighting; but at the mouth of Kuan-chiang near Kuan-chou there was a temple whose god was called Erh-lang the Small Saint, or Erh-lang hsien-sheng[d]. The Devarāja asked Erh-lang to capture Ta-sheng . . .

[The original text of the *Pak t'ongsa* material translated above (pp. 180–5) is appended here. It is redivided as indicated in the translation.]

[a] 三乘   [b] 金剛   [c] 二郎爺爺   [d] 賢聖

264　長老的佛像鑄了麼。鑄了三尊佛。我待要上金來。前日三更前後賊入來。把我二三
　　年布施來的金銀鈔錠。都偷將去了。沒計奈何。我如今又往江南地面裡布施去。／

265　一來是十分命不快。告諸佛菩薩。願滿之日死時也不愁。罷罷師傅善因不減。你休

266　生怠慢心。沿路上用心好去着。往常唐三藏師傅。西天取／經去時節。十萬八千里
　　途程。正是瘦禽也飛不到。壯馬也實勞蹄。這般遠田地裡。經多少風寒暑濕。受多

267　少日／炙風吹。過多少惡山險水難路。見多少怪物妖精侵他。撞多少猛虎毒虫定害

268　。逢多少惡物刁蹶。正是好人魔障多。行六年受多少／千辛萬苦。到西天取將經來
　　。度脫衆生各得成佛。師傅你也休忙。慢慢的到江南沿門布施。願滿成就着。久後
　　你也得證果金身。

292　我兩箇部前買文書去來。買甚麼文書去。買趙太祖飛龍記。唐三藏西遊記去。買／

293　時買四書六經也好。旣讀孔聖之書。必達周公之理。要怎麼那一等平話。西遊記熱

294　鬧。悶時節好看有。唐三藏引孫行者／到車遲國。和伯眼大仙。鬥聖的你知道麼。

295　你說我聽。唐僧往西天取經去時節。到一箇城子。喚做車遲國／。那國王好善。恭
　　敬佛法。國中有一箇先生。喚伯眼。外名喚燒金子道人。見國王敬佛法。便使黑心

296　。要減佛教。但見和尙。便拿着曳車解鋸。起蓋三淸大殿。／如此定害三寶。一日
　　先生們。做羅天大醮。唐僧師徒二人。正到城裏智海禪寺投宿。聽的道人們祭星。

297　孫／行者。師傅上說知。到羅天大醮壇場上藏身。奪喫了祭星茶果。卻把伯眼打了
　　一鐵棒。小先生到前面教點燈。又打了一鐵棒。伯眼道。這禿廝好沒道理。便焦懆

298　起來。到國王前面告未畢。唐僧也引徒弟去到王所／。王請唐僧上殿。見大仙打罷
　　問訊。先生也稽首廻禮。先生對唐僧道。咱兩箇寃讎不小可裏。三藏道。貧僧是東
　　土人。不曾認的。你有何寃讎。大仙睜開雙眼道。你敎徒弟。壞了我羅天大醮。／

299　更打了我兩鐵棒。這的不是大讎。咱兩箇對君王面前鬥聖。那一箇輸了時。强的上
　　拜爲師傅。唐僧道。那般着。伯眼道。起頭坐靜。第二櫃中猜物。第三滾油洗澡。

300　第四割頭再接。說罷。打一聲鐘響。／各上禪床坐定。分毫不動。但動的便算輸。
　　大仙徒弟名鹿皮。拔下一根頭髮。變做狗蚤。唐僧耳門後咬。要動禪。孫行者是箇
　　胡孫。見那狗蚤。便拿下來磕死了。他卻拔下一根毛衣。變作假行者。靠師傅立／

301 的。他走到金水河裏。和將一塊青泥來。大仙鼻凹裏放了。變做青母蝎。脊背上咬
一口。大仙叫一聲。跳下床來了。王道唐僧得勝了。又叫兩箇宮娥。檯過一箇紅漆

302 横子來。前面放下。着兩箇猜裏面有什麼。／皇后暗使一箇宮娥。說與先生横中有
一棵桃。孫行者變做箇焦苗蟲兒。飛入横中。把桃肉都喫了。只留下桃核出來。說

303 與師傅。王說今番着唐僧先猜。三藏說是一箇桃核。皇后大笑猜不着了。／大仙說
是一顆桃。着將軍開横看。卻是桃核。先生又輸了。鹿皮對大仙說。咱如今燒起油
鍋。入去洗澡。鹿皮先脫下衣服。入鍋裏。王喝保的其間。孫行者念一聲唵字。山

304 神土地神鬼都來了。行者敎千里眼順／風耳等兩箇鬼。油鍋兩邊看着。先生待要出
來。拿着肩膀颺在裏面。鹿皮熱當不的。腳踏鍋邊待要出來。被鬼們當住出不來。

305 就油裏死了。王見多時不出時。莫不死了麼。敎將軍看。將軍使金／鈎子。搭出箇
爛骨頭的先生。孫行者說。我如今入去洗澡。脫了衣裳。打一箇跟阧。跳入油中。
纔待洗澡。卻早不見了。王說將軍你搭去。行者敢死了也。將軍用鈎子搭去。行者

306 變做五寸來大的胡孫。／左邊搭右邊趯。右邊搭左邊去。百般搭不着。將軍奏道。
行者油煎的肉都沒了。唐僧見了啼哭。行者聽了跳出來。叫大王有肥皂麼。與我洗

307 頭。衆人喝保佛家贏了也。孫行者把他的頭。先割下來。／血瀝瀝的腔子立地。頭
落在地上。行者用手把頭提起。接在頸項上依舊了。伯眼大仙也割下頭來。待要接

308 。行者念金頭揭地銀頭揭地波羅僧揭地之後。變做大黑狗。把先生的／頭拖將去。
先生變做老虎趕。行者直拖的王前面颺了。不見了狗。也不見了虎。只落下一箇虎
頭。國王道。元來是一箇虎精。不是師傅。怎生拿出他本像。說罷。越敬佛門。賜

309 唐僧金錢三百貫金鉢盂一箇／。賜行者金錢三百貫打發了。這孫行者正是了的。那
伯眼大仙。那裏想胡孫手裏死了。古人道。殺人一萬。自損三千。

265 三藏俗姓陳名偉洛州緱氏縣人也號玄奘法師貞觀三年奉勑往西域取經六百卷而來仍
呼爲三藏法師（下畧）

266 西遊記云昔釋迦牟尼佛在西天靈山雷音寺撰成經律論三藏金經須送東土解度群迷問
諸菩薩往東土尋取經人來乃以西天去東土十萬八千里之程妖怪又多諸衆不敢輕諾唯

南海落迦山觀世音菩薩騰雲駕霧往東土去遙見長安京兆府一道瑞氣衝天觀音化作老
僧入城此時唐太宗聚天下僧尼設無遮大會因衆僧舉一高僧爲壇主說法即玄奘法師也
老僧見法師曰西天釋伽造經三藏以待取經之人法師曰既有程途須有到時西天雖遠我
發大願當往取來老僧言訖騰空而去帝知觀音化身即勅法師往西天取經法師奉勅行×
年東還。

267　音義云刁難也蹶顛仆而不能行也今按法師往西天時初到師陀國界遇猛虎毒蛇之害×
　　　遇黑熊精黃風怪地湧夫人蜘蛛精獅子怪多目怪紅孩兒怪幾死僅免又過棘鉤洞火炎山
　　　薄屎洞女人國及諸惡山險水怪害患苦不知其幾此所謂刁蹶也詳見西遊記

268　……謂證果者如三藏法師取經東還化爲栴檀佛如來詳見下

292　西遊記三藏法師往西域取經六百卷而來記其往來始末爲書名曰西遊記詳見上

293　……西遊記云西域有花菓山山下有水簾洞洞前有鐵板橋橋下有萬丈澗澗邊有萬箇小
　　　洞洞裏多猴有老猴精號齊天大聖神通廣大入天宮仙桃園偷蟠桃又偷老君靈丹藥又去
　　　王母宮偷王母綉仙衣一套來設慶仙衣會老君王母具奏于玉帝傳宣李天王引領天兵十
　　　萬及諸神將至花菓山與大聖相戰失利巡山大力鬼上告天王舉灌州灌江口神曰小聖二

294　郎可使拿獲天王遣太子木叉與大力／鬼往請二郎神領神兵圍花菓山衆猴出戰皆敗大
　　　聖被執當死觀音上請于玉帝免死令巨靈神押大聖前往下方去乃於花果山石縫內納其
　　　下截畫如來押字封着使山神土地神鎮守飢食鐵丸渴飲銅汁待我往東土尋取經之人經
　　　過此山觀大聖肯隨往西天則此時可放其後唐太宗勅玄奘法師往西天取經路經此山見
　　　此猴精壓在石縫去其佛押出之以爲徒弟賜法名吾空改號爲孫行者與沙和尚及黑豬精
　　　朱八戒偕往在路降妖去怪救師脫難皆是孫行者神通之力也法師到西天受經三藏東還
　　　法師證果栴檀佛如來孫行者證果大力王菩薩朱八戒證果香華會上淨壇使者

295　西遊記云有一先生到車遲國吹口氣以磚瓦皆化爲金驚動國王拜爲國師號伯眼大仙

307　西遊記云釋迦牟尼佛在靈山雷音寺演說三乘教法傍有侍奉阿難伽舍諸菩薩聖僧羅漢
　　　八金鋼四揭地十代明王天仙地仙觀此則揭地神名然未詳何神

353　按西遊記西域花果山洞有老猴精號齊天大聖神變無測鬧亂天宮玉帝命李天王領神兵
　　　往捕相戰失利灌州灌江口立廟有神曰小聖二郎又號二郎賢聖天王請二郎捕獲大聖

Synopses

Chüan 1

[Section 1: missing.]

Section 2: 'On their journey they meet the Monkey Novice-Monk'.

The band of six pilgrims sets out and encounters the *hsiu-ts'ai* scholar in plain clothes, strangely informed about Tripitaka's expeditions in previous lives, who turns out to be the Monkey King. He is initiated as a disciple under the name Hou Hsing-che. The pilgrims continue their journey.

Section 3: 'They enter the Palace of Mahābrahmā Devarāja'.

In the course of conversation about his great age, the Monkey reveals that a feast is about to take place in the Crystal Palace, abode of Mahābrahmā Devarāja, and proceeds to transport Tripitaka there. A great assembly of Buddhist saints is gathered in splendid surroundings. Tripitaka is invited to preach to them, but fails to mount the Crystal Throne. Later, his exposition of the *Lotus Sūtra* is warmly received. The Devarāja gives them magic objects as safeguards on the journey and promises to appear in response to any cry for help.

Section 4: 'They enter the Hsiang-shan monastery[a]'.

On a mountain with pious associations the pilgrims find a derelict monastery, guarded by frightening Vajra figures. They proceed through the Land of Snakes, but these, although of monstrous proportions and besetting them on all sides, do them no harm, but open up a way for them to pass. The Monkey gives warning of the next hazards.

Section 5: 'They pass through the Forest of Lions and the Land of the Tree-men'.

Lions and unicorns meet them with flowers and escort them onwards.

The Land of Tree-men is found to be full of fantastic rocks and ancient trees. They pass a deserted monastery in wonderful surroundings, and lodge in a small house. In spite of a warning of sorcery, the next morning they send a young novice to buy food. He is transformed into a donkey by a man in the vicinity. But Hou Hsing-che retaliates by changing the man's bride, described

[a] 香山寺

[189]

as peerlessly beautiful, into a bundle of grass in the donkey's mouth. The opponents then agree to restore the victims to their original forms. Hou Hsing-che leaves a warning against any further trifling.

Section 6: 'They pass the Long Pit[a] and the Great Serpent Range[b]'.

They are delivered from the resounding darkness of a great pit by flourishing their gold-ringed staff in an appeal to the Devarāja. They pass the harmless Great Serpents and proceed to the Fiery Hollow[c]. Using their magic alms-bowl they appeal again to the Devarāja to save them from the flames. Warned by Hou Hsing-che, they are later approached by a woman all in white, whom Hou Hsing-che challenges. She turns into a tiger and engages him in battle. He destroys her by the device of attack from within her belly.

Chüan 2

Section 7: 'They enter the Nine-Dragon Pool[d]'.

After another warning from Hou Hsing-che they are confronted by nine evil dragons sweeping towards them through turbulent waves. Using the magic aids, Hou Hsing-che overcomes one dragon, and the rest then submit. He extracts sinews from their backs—'to make a sash for my Master'—and belabours them. The sash endows the wearer with magic powers. (Eventually, we learn, the sash is transfigured in Paradise.) Final words missing.

Section 8: Title and opening sentences missing.

The demon named Shen-sha shen[e] is showing Tripitaka bones he has collected from the monk's expeditions in previous lives. But he at once submits to Tripitaka's threatening rebuke and, amid spectacular natural phenomena, holds out a golden bridge with silver rails for the pilgrims to pass over the hazard of the Deep Sands. They leave him, expressing thanks and promising their intercession in the closing verses.

Section 9: 'They enter the Land of Kuei-tzu-mu[f]'.

The travellers pass across a desolate tract of land, enter a country where the inhabitants give no reply to questions and where the Buddhist monastery is deserted.

Eventually they find themselves amid great numbers of three-year-old children, and receive a warm and devout welcome from the King of the land. He gives them rich gifts and finally reveals to them that this country, 'not far from the Western Paradise', is Kuei-tzu-mu kuo[g]. The pilgrims then know that they have been addressing demons.

Some of the closing verses are put into the mouth of a character named Kuei-tzu-mu.

[a] 長坑   [b] 大蛇嶺   [c] 火類坳   [d] 九龍池   [e] 深沙神
[f] 鬼子母   [g] 國

Section 10: 'They pass through the Land of Women'.

In deserted country the only sign of life is the activity of a few peasants in the fields. In an interim exchange of verses Hou Hsing-che urges his master on. They are held up by a torrential stream, but cross when it is dried up by the Devarāja.

Pressing on, they reach the Land of Women and have audience with the Queen. She explains that the grit which here makes their meal uneatable is there because the food was gathered from ground which otherwise remained barren.

Then she takes them into her own opulent quarters, where beautiful women greet them seductively, with invitations to establish a monastery in the land and to become their own husbands. Tripitaka is unbending, the women tearful. The Queen gives him jewels and a white horse. As the travellers depart, the Queen reveals in her final verse that her true name is 'Mañjuśrī and Samantabhadra'.

Section 11: 'They enter the Pool of the Queen (of the West)'.

As they approach the pool Hou Hsing-che tells of his past experience—at the age of eight hundred. He was punished by the Queen for stealing her magic peaches. Tripitaka also is now moved by a desire to steal some.

In the midst of precipitous cliffs they see the peach-trees growing. As Tripitaka urges his monkey disciple to secure the magic fruit for them, three ripe peaches fall into the lake. In succession three small children then emerge, each claiming a greater supernatural age. Hou Hsing-che takes the third and eldest and invites Tripitaka to eat it. Tripitaka refuses, and the child, through Hou Hsing-che's magic arts, becomes a 'milk date'[a], which he swallows. (It is finally noted that the growth of *ginseng*[b] in Szechuan derives from the seed of this fruit, spat out there on the return journey.)

Section 12: 'They enter the Land of Ch'en-hsiang[c]'.

It is marked by a tablet with the name. There is a vast forest of the *ch'en-hsiang* tree, at which the travellers exclaim.

Section 13: 'They enter Po-lo kuo[d]'.

The inhabitants of this celestial land include beautiful women and children playing 'noisily' and 'gleefully rolling balls'. Wild beasts cry, and the place is marked by auspicious signs. (The closing verses, more extensive than the few sentences of prose, are irregular and perhaps corrupt.)

Chüan 3

Section 14: 'They enter the Land of *utpala*[e] flowers'.

Here they find vast stretches of flowers and trees in bloom and never, according to Hou Hsing-che, disturbed by change of season or climate. In rhythmic lines he goes on to explain that the Buddha's paradise knows none of the effects of passing time. They are almost there.

[a] 乳棗   [b] 人參   [c] 沉香   [d] 波羅國   [e] 優鉢羅

Section 15: 'They enter India[a] and "cross the sea"'.

Hou Hsing-che announces their approach to the Cock's-foot mountain[b]. A tablet over a city-gate announces 'India'[a]: the city within is full of auspicious signs of beauty and prosperity. Proceeding to the Buddhist monastery Fu-hsien szu[c] they partake of celestial food. In conversation with the Superior, Tripitaka learns that the Buddha lives in the heights of Cock's-foot mountain, beyond hopelessly inaccessible obstacles. At Hou Hsing-che's suggestion Tripitaka offers up a ceremonial supplication. The Emperor and people of all China join in it. Darkness falls, and after a period of deafening thunder and light-flashes the scriptures are revealed lying on the prepared prayer-mat. Tripitaka finds there 5,048 *chüan*, and only the '*Heart Sūtra*'[d] is wanting. At once they load up the books and set out on their return journey, sped on by the good wishes of all the local populace.

Section 16: 'They return as far as the Hsiang-lin Monastery,[e] where they receive the *Heart Sūtra*'.

In the country P'an-lü[f] they stay in a town named Hsiang-lin. Tripitaka in a dream hears a voice promising the '*Heart Sūtra*' the following day. Ahead of them in the clouds there gradually takes form the apparition of a youthful monk, who produces the *sūtra* from his sleeve and gives it to Tripitaka, enjoining him solemnly to respect its powers and convey it to the people of China. Naming himself as the Dīpaṃkara Buddha, he adds the instruction that monasteries must be built throughout China; Tripitaka and his party of seven must prepare to return to heaven on the fifteenth of the seventh month. Then he sails away towards the west.

Section 17: 'They reach Shensi[g], where the wife of a householder, Wang[h], kills his son'.

In the city Ho-chung fu[i] there is a householder who has had sons (Ch'ih-na[j] and Chü-na[k]) by two successive wives. While he is absent on business the second wife makes several attempts on the life of her step-son, assisted by a maid, Ch'un-liu[l]. He survives each ordeal by miraculous means, but succumbs when cast into a flooding river. His returning father arranges Buddhist memorial services, and Tripitaka, arriving at this point, demands a large fish. The lost boy is found in the maw of this fish. (In the midst of an exchange of verses, Tripitaka ordains that this be the precedent for the split 'wooden fish' accompanying Buddhist ceremonial.)

As the party draws near the capital the Emperor comes to meet them. Together they return and celebrate the new acquisitions with acts of piety. The appointed time of departure approaches: Tripitaka warns his Sovereign of what must happen on the fifteenth day of the month. The Emperor formally confers the title 'Master Tripitaka'.

a 竺國	b 雞足山	c 福仙寺	d 多心經	e 香林寺	f 盤律
g 陝西	h 王長者	i 河中府	j 癡那	k 居那	
l 春柳					

On the appointed day the promised celestial vehicles appear and convey the pilgrims to heaven. The Emperor and those at court celebrate their memory, and in the very last line an honorary title is conferred on Hou Hsing-che.

2. THE 'TSA-CHÜ' SEQUENCE 'HSI-YU CHI'

Scene 1: Disaster encountered on a journey to office.

The Bodhisattva Kuan-yin introduces the action: a mortal is required to collect scriptures for the benefit of China; for this purpose the Arhat Vairo-cana is to become incarnate as the son of Ch'en Kuang-jui[a] in Hung-nung hsien[b] of Hai-chou[c]. Ch'en Kuang-jui is to suffer an eighteen-year-long 'disaster in water'. The Dragon King has been instructed to protect him.

Ch'en Kuang-jui, on his journey to office, has reached the Inn of a Hundred Flowers; he has restored life to a fish which, when he bought it, blinked at him. Preparing to continue the journey to Hung-chou[d], the servant Wang An[e] looks for a boatman. The singer in this act is Ch'en's wife who, being eight months pregnant, is full of anxieties about the journey. In the event Liu Hung[f], recruited as their boatman, murders first Wang An, then Ch'en himself; he agrees to spare the wife and her unborn child on condition that she accepts him in Ch'en Kuang-jui's place—as her husband and the prefect of Hung-chou. She has him agree in turn to a three-year delay—a gesture of filial piety on the part of her as yet unborn son.

Scene 2: The mother forced, the child cast out.

The Dragon of the Southern Seas explains that in compliance with Kuan-yin's direction and in gratitude for Ch'en Kuang-jui's action in saving his life (in the form of a fish at the Inn of a Hundred Flowers), he is holding the murdered Ch'en secure in his Crystal Palace until the eighteen years are up.

Liu Hung enters and declares his intention of ridding himself of the newly born child who constitutes a threat to his security in office.

The Dragon reappears briefly to ensure protection for the incarnate Vairocana who is to suffer hardship on the river.

The wife—again the singer—completes the scene alone. She has been compelled by Liu Hung to cast her month-old son into the river, and now performs the deed carefully, putting the child into a watertight box, together with two gold clasps and an explanatory note written in her own blood.

Scene 3: Chiang-liu recognizes his mother.

The Dragon orders the Arhat to be transported to the island monastery Chin-shan szu[g].

A fisherman finds the box and takes it off to the Abbot.

The Ch'an Master Tan-hsia[h] receives it, inspects the contents and resolves to raise the child and preserve the letter with all the details of its history.

---

a 陳光蕊   b 弘農縣   c 海州   d 洪州   e 王安   f 劉洪
g 金山寺   h 丹霞禪師

Liu Hung here makes a brief appearance, alluding to his present quiet life and sense of security.

The passage of eighteen years is assumed: the Ch'an Master resumes the career of the abandoned child, whom he has brought up as a novice monk and named Hsüan-tsang. He now sends him on a mission of revenge, first explaining the details of his background.

The mother is discovered in a state of anxiety: again she is the singer. Hsüan-tsang enters, there is an extended recognition scene. They arrange for him to return provisionally to Chin-shan szu.

Scene 4: The bandit is taken, revenge is wrought.

Yü Shih-nan[a] has now, in the year Chen-kuan 21, been appointed Prefect of Hung-chou. His first official case is an appeal delivered by the Abbot Tan-hsia and Hsüan-tsang, calling for action against Liu Hung. Men are sent secretly to arrest him.

The dissipated Liu Hung is giving orders to his wife, who is again the singer. Official guards enter and arrest Liu; he makes a full confession. Yü Shih-nan sentences him to immolation on the shore of the river in expiation of Ch'en's death. As the sacrificial verses are pronounced Ch'en's body is borne out of the water by the Dragon King's attendants. There is a final explanation.

Kuan-yin appears on high:[1] she summons Hsüan-tsang to the capital, first to pray for rain to break a great drought there, and further to fetch 5,048 rolls of Mahāyāna scriptures from the West.

The wife sums up the whole action in her closing songs.

Scene 5: An Imperial send-off for the westward journey.

Yü Shih-nan narrates how he presented Hsüan-tsang at court: the prayers for rain were successful, Hsüan-tsang was honoured with the title Tripitaka and invested with a golden kaṣāya and a nine-ringed Ch'an staff. His parents also received honours.

Now, in official mark of his departure for the West, Ch'in Shu-pao[b] and Fang Hsüan-ling[c] representing officials civil and military, enter to greet him. Hsüan-tsang is ushered on. The official party is headed by the aged Yü-ch'ih Kung[d], the singer in this act. He sustains a dialogue, partly in song, with Hsüan-tsang, leading finally to a request for a Buddhist name. Hsüan-tsang names him Pao-lin[e].[2]

The pine-twig is planted which will point east when Hsüan-tsang returns. Finally, he gives spiritual counsel to members of the crowd.

---

[1] The direction reads: 'on a high erection'[f]. Chao Ching-shen (1935, p. 275) suggests a parallel in modern stage practice.

[2] The detail of this name is at odds with other Yü-ch'ih Kung stories, in which it is a name of his son. (Cf. Chao Ching-shen (1935), p. 274; Sun K'ai-ti (1939), p. 372.)

[a] 虞世南   [b] 秦叔寶   [c] 房玄齡   [d] 尉遲恭   [e] 寶林
[f] 高粱

Scene 6: A village woman tells the tale.

In a village outside Ch'ang-an some local characters return from watching the spectacle of Tripitaka's departure. The singer is a woman nicknamed P'ang-ku-erh[a]. Her songs describe the scene from the crowd's point of view. There is a good deal of observation of various side-shows and theatrical performances.[1]

Scene 7: Moksha sells a horse.

The Fiery Dragon of the Southern Sea is being led to execution for the offence of 'causing insufficient and delayed rainfall'. His appeals succeed in enlisting the help of Kuan-yin, who persuades the Jade Emperor to have him changed into a white horse for the transport of Tripitaka and the scriptures.

Tripitaka is discovered at a wayside halt, troubled by the lack of a horse.

Moksha[b], disciple of Kuan-yin and the singer in this act, comes to offer him the white dragon-horse. His songs extol the horse's qualities. Finally he uncovers the design, reveals the dragon in its original form, and ends the scene with allusions to the coming recruitment of Sun Wu-k'ung on Hua-kuo shan.

Scene 8: Hua-kuang serves as protector.

Kuan-yin first announces a list of ten celestial protectors for Tripitaka on his journey. The Heavenly King Hua-kuang[c], sixth on the list, is the last to sign on: he enters and for the rest of the scene sings on this theme of protection, pausing only to receive Kuan-yin's greeting. In the last song there is a further allusion to Hua-kuo shan.

Scene 9: The Holy Buddha defeats Sun.

Sun Hsing-che now appears: after an initial poem vaunting his celestial birth, his ubiquity and power, he lists out the members of his ape family, alludes to his career of misdeeds and his wife, the abducted Princess of Chin-ting[d] kuo.

Devarāja Li appears, with orders to recover the possessions stolen by Sun from the Queen of the West. He issues orders to his son Naṭa[e], who enters with troops upon orders from the Jade Emperor to capture Sun Hsing-che in his home Tzu-yün-lo-tung[f] on Hua-kuo shan.

The princess-wife now enters (the singer in this act) and tells in song the story of her abduction and the life on this mountain. She is joined by Sun and they prepare to feast.

The celestial troops surround them, Sun's animal guards flee and Sun himself escapes. Devarāja Li 'combs the hills' and meanwhile finds the Princess, who now sings through the remainder of her suite of songs until it is decided to give her escort back to her home.

Sun Hsing-che eludes the forces of Naṭa and is captured only by the intervention of Kuan-yin, who has him imprisoned beneath Hua-kuo shan to await the arrival of Tripitaka, his future master.

---

[1] Chao Ching-shen (1935, p. 273) points out uses elsewhere of this character and this kind of scene.

[a] 胖姑兒   [b] 木叉   [c] 華光天王   [d] 金鼎   [e] 那吒   [f] 紫雲羅洞

Scene 10: Sun is caught, the charm rehearsed.

The singer is a Mountain Spirit guarding Sun beneath Hua-kuo shan: he opens the act with songs about his own permanence and his present duties.

Tripitaka comes seeking hospitality. The Spirit responds with a sung discourse which is interrupted by the shout of Sun Hsing-che eager to be delivered. Tripitaka releases him, and Sun's immediate reaction is to seek to eat him and escape. Kuan-yin intervenes to curb his nature with Buddhist disciplines in the shape of an iron hoop, a cassock and a sword. She gives him the name Sun Hsing-che.

To Tripitaka she teaches the spell that works the binding hoop on Sun's head, and they successfully prove it.

The Spirit adds (in speech) a warning about the demon of Liu-sha River[a] and they again set out.

Scene 11: Hsing-che expels a demon.

The Spirit of Liu-sha ho, characterized as a monk adorned with hanging skulls, announces that he has devoured nine incarnations of Tripitaka (nine skulls represent them), towards the total of a hundred holy men he must eat in order to gain supremacy.

Sun Hsing-che enters and is attacked by this Sha Ho-shang[b]. Sun vanquishes him, and he is recruited for Tripitaka's band of pilgrims.

A new demon named Yin-o chiang-chün[c] enters, inhabitant of the impregnable Huang-feng shan[d]. He has abducted the daughter from a nearby Liu family.

The father Liu is the singer in this act: he explains his plight to Tripitaka and the party of pilgrims. They fight and kill the demon, and restore the girl to her home. As they set out again, Liu gratefully awaits their return from the West.

Scene 12: Kuei-mu is converted.[1]

The pilgrims are now approached by the Red Boy[e] feigning tears. Sun Hsing-che, against his own better judgement, is made to carry the child, cannot sustain the intolerable weight and tosses him into a mountain torrent.

Sha Ho-shang at once reports that the child has borne away their Master. They go off to appeal to Kuan-yin; she in turn takes the case to the Buddha, who now appears in company with the Bodhisattvas Mañjuśrī[f] and Samantabhadra[g]. He explains that this is the son, named Ai-nu-erh[h], of Kuei-tzu-mu[i]. Four guardians have been sent to capture him with the help of the Buddha's own almsbowl. The bowl is now brought in, with the Red Boy confined beneath it. The pilgrims return to rejoin their Master.

The mother Kuei-tzu-mu enters to sing vindictive songs about this action. The Buddha defends himself from her attacks; she attempts to have the

---

[1] Translating the Buddhist term *kuei-i*[j]: 'take refuge'.

[a] 流沙河   [b] 沙和尚   [c] 銀額將軍   [d] 黃鳳山   [e] 紅孩兒
[f] 文殊   [g] 普賢   [h] 愛奴兒   [i] 鬼子母   [j] 皈依

bowl lifted clear; finally she is overcome by Naṭa. Tripitaka is freed and himself offers her alternative sentences: she chooses to embrace Buddhism.

Scene 13: A pig-demon deludes with magic.

Chu Pa-chieh enters, announces his background, past history and present home (Hei-feng tung[a]) and describes a plan by which he means to substitute himself for the young man Chu-lang[b], the bridegroom to whom a young local girl is promised and for whom she waits nightly. (Her father P'ei-kung[c], we learn, is disposed to retract the agreed match for financial reasons.)

The girl, with her attendant, expects a visit from young Chu the same night. She (the singer in this act) goes through the actions of burning incense as she waits for him.[1] Chu Pa-chieh enters, carries on a burlesque lovers' dialogue with her and prevails on her to elope with him.

The pilgrims appear briefly on the stage, preparing to seek lodging near the frontier of Huo-lun[d] Chin-ting kuo.

Scene 14: Hai-t'ang[e] sends on news.

The girl, again the singer, is now in Chu Pa-chieh's mountain home, has discovered the deception and despairs of seeing her home again; she is obliged to entertain the debauched Chu Pa-chieh, who agrees however to let her visit home.

Sun Hsing-che enters, overhears their conversation and at once attacks Chu. He offers to carry a verbal message for the girl. She trusts him with this and warns him that her family and the Chu's are already disputing the case.

Scene 15: They take the daughter back to P'ei.

The heads of the Chu and P'ei families argue out their marriage contract and its alleged violation and are stopped from going to court only by the arrival of Tripitaka and his party. Sun Hsing-che produces the message in the form of a little song.

To determine what demon this abductor is they summon up the local guardian spirit (t'u-ti[f]), who reports that he takes the form of a pig. Sun Hsing-che at once sets out to attack.

The P'ei girl sings a series of heartbroken songs. Sun Hsing-che comes and offers to take her home: she now sings gratitude, against some jeering comment from Sun. They leave.

Tripitaka, with the two family heads, await them and welcome back the daughter. She reveals that Chu fears only the hunting dogs of Erh-lang. The family affairs are now resolved.

Chu Pa-chieh decides to follow her home. Sun Hsing-che arranges to take

---

[1] This part of the scene, and even a particular line in the dialogue, is transparently a borrowing from the tsa-chü Hsi-hsiang chi (Hsi-yu chi, sc. 13, p. 59, compare Hsi-hsiang chi, p. 50a). The line in question—'Maidservant [for "Hung-niang"][g], take the incense-table and put it by the rockery'.

[a] 黑風洞 [b] 朱郎 [c] 裴公 [d] 火輪 [e] 海棠 [f] 土地 [g] 紅娘

her place in the bridal chamber where Chu expects to find her. They fight: Chu escapes, taking with him the Master Tripitaka. Erh-lang must now be called in.

Scene 16: The hunting hounds catch the pig.

Erh-lang, the singer in this act, begins with a series of truculent and threatening songs, then demands Chu's surrender to Buddhism. Chu fights first with Sun Hsing-che, who has entered with Erh-lang; then the dogs are put on him and finally seize him. Tripitaka is released and instantly urges mercy. Chu accepts the Buddhist faith.

Erh-lang's closing song alludes to the coming perils of the Land of Women and Huo-yen shan[a].

Scene 17: The Queen forces a marriage.

The pilgrims arrive in the Land of Women.

The Queen enters alone(she is the singer), describes her situation and her longing for a husband, and declares an intention to detain Tripitaka for this purpose.

The pilgrims again enter, warned of their danger in a recent dream granted by one of their guardians—Wei-t'o tsun-t'ien[b]. The Queen seeks to tempt Tripitaka with wine, then embraces him and finally bears him off to the rear of the Palace. Other women do the same with the three disciples.

The Queen and Tripitaka re-enter, and she continues to sing her entreaties until Wei-t'o tsun-t'ien appears and drives her back. Sun Hsing-che is summoned and Wei-t'o, giving him a brief allocution, retires.

Sun confesses that his own near lapse was forestalled only by the tightening of the hoop upon his brow. He now ends the scene by singing a suggestive ditty to the tune *Chi-sheng-ts'ao*.

Scene 18: They lose the way and ask it of an Immortal.

The pilgrims require guidance.

A Taoist in the mountains sings a set of literary verses on the Four Vices. When the pilgrims come and ask the way of him he at once gives details of the nearby Huo-yen shan and the female demon T'ieh-shan kung-chu[c] whose Iron Fan alone is able to put out the flames on the fiery mountain. With more songs, of a warning nature, the Taoist leaves them.

The pilgrims reach the mountain, Sun Hsing-che undertakes to borrow the fan. From the mountain spirit he ascertains that T'ieh-shan kung-chu is unmarried and accessible to offers of marriage. He resolves to approach her.

Scene 19: The Iron Fan and its evil power.

T'ieh-shan kung-chu (the singer) enters and introduces herself, giving her background, members of her family.

Sun Hsing-che arrives with his request to borrow the fan; she dislikes his

[a] 火焰山   [b] 韋馱尊天   [c] 鐵扇公主

insolence and refuses. They threaten one another, then fight until she waves him off with the fan and Sun Hsing-che somersaults off the stage.

Sun Hsing-che, in the closing remarks of the scene, prepares to retaliate by seeking the assistance of Kuan-yin.

Scene 20: The Water Department quenches the fire.

Kuan-yin enters and decides to employ the masters of Thunder, Lightning, Wind and Rain, with all the attendant spirits of the celestial Water Department, to ensure Tripitaka's safe passage across Huo-yen shan.

These characters now enter and introduce themselves. The singer is Mother-Lightning[a], and her first series of songs is purely descriptive.

Tripitaka enters to offer brief thanks, and the scene ends with more songs as the spirits escort the party of pilgrims over the burning mountain. The last song predicts the imminent end of their pilgrimage.

Scene 21: The Poor Woman conveys intuitive certainty.[1]

The party has arrived in India and prepares to advance to the Vulture Peak— Ling-chiu shan[b]. Sun Hsing-che is sent on ahead to look for food.

The Poor Woman enters and introduces herself as one whose trade is selling cakes and who, without presuming to enter the Buddha's own province, has attained to great spiritual accomplishments. (She is the singer here.)

Sun Hsing-che appears to announce his mission, and they quickly engage in a sophistical dialogue on the term *hsin*[c] in the '*Diamond Sūtra*'. It becomes a burlesque in which Sun is ridiculed. Tripitaka enters and sustains a more competent discussion. He asks some plain questions about the Buddhist paradise, and the Poor Woman then urges them on.

Scene 22: They present themselves before the Buddha and collect the scriptures.

The Mountain Spirit of the Vulture Peak introduces the situation: the pilgrims are about to be received into the Western Paradise; the householder Chi-ku-tu[d] (Sanskrit: Anāthapiṇḍada) is to escort them. He enters, the singer in this act. He introduces Tripitaka to heaven, answers his questions and announces the entry of the Buddha.

The Buddha appears in the form of an image (Buddha leaving the mountains) 'represented'[e] by the monks Han-shan[f] and Shih-te[g]. He decrees that the three animal disciples may not return to the East; four of his own disciples will escort Tripitaka on the return journey. Tripitaka is led off to receive the scriptures.

The character Ta-ch'üan[h] is responsible for their issue. All assist in loading them on to the horse, who alone is to return East with Tripitaka and the disciples of the Buddha.

The three disciples in turn offer their final remarks and yield up their

---

[1] Rendering the Buddhist term *hsin-yin*[i].

[a] 電母   [b] 靈鷲山   [c] 心   [d] 給孤獨   [e] 扮   [f] 寒山   [g] 拾得
[h] 大權   [i] 心印

mortal lives. Tripitaka remembers each of them in a spoken soliloquy before
he sets out on his return journey.

Scene 23: Escorted back to the Eastern Land.

The first of the four Buddhist disciples, Ch'eng-chi[a], is the singer. The
opening of the scene consists solely of his songs on the implications of the
journey; he pauses only to reveal that the trials on the westward journey were
contrived by the Buddha.

In Ch'ang-an the pine-twig has been seen to turn eastward, and a crowd
has come out to welcome Tripitaka's return. Yü-ch'ih Ching-te again appears
to receive him.

Ch'eng-chi's final song gives warning that the scriptures must be presented
the following morning before the Emperor.

Scene 24: Tripitaka appears before the Buddha[b].

The Śākyamuni Buddha enters[1] and gives orders for Tripitaka to be led
back to the Vulture Peak to meet his final spiritual goal.

The Winged Immortal who receives these orders is the singer. He escorts
Tripitaka before the Buddha, whose closing remarks, as well as the Spirit's
last songs, invoke conventional benedictions upon the Imperial house.

[1] The original direction reads: 'The Buddha—(upon) a high erection—and four Vajra
(guardians) enter . . .' Cf. above, note to Scene 4.

[a] 成基   [b] 朝元

List of Works Cited

The works listed here, subdivided into Abbreviations, Primary and Secondary Sources, include the most frequently cited works in Western languages and the great majority of those in Chinese and Japanese. Bibliographical details of all works not included are provided in relevant footnotes throughout the book.

ABBREVIATIONS

Cheng-shih   Hui-tsuan yüan-p'u nan-ch'ü chiu-kung cheng-shih: see p. 123, n. 5.

CTPS   Chin-tai pi-shu 津 逮 祕 書.

CTS   Ch'üan T'ang shih 全 唐 詩. Peking 1960 reprint, 12 vols.

CTW   Ch'in-ting ch'üan T'ang wen 欽 定 全 唐 文. Palace edition, preface dated 1818.

HCTY   Hsüeh-chin t'ao-yüan 學 津 討 源.

HYC   Hsi-yu chi 西 遊 記 (abbreviation reserved for the reprint of the hundred-chapter novel by the Tso-chia ch'u-pan-she, Peking 1954).

LKP   Lu-kuei pu 錄 鬼 簿. By Chung Szu-ch'eng 鍾 嗣 成. Critical edition in *Chung-kuo ku-tien hsi-ch'ü lun-chu chi-ch'eng* 中 國 古 典 戲 曲 論 著 集 成 vol. 2, Peking 1959.

PCHH   Pai-ch'uan hsüeh-hai 百 川 學 海.

PCHSTK   Pi-chi hsiao-shuo ta-kuan 筆 記 小 說 大 觀.

PTS   Pak t'ongsa önhae 朴 通 事 諺 解. See pp. 60–1.

SHC   Shui-hu ch'üan-chuan 水 滸 全 傳. Peking 1954, 3 vols.; reprinted Hong Kong 1958, 4 vols.

SKCSTM   Ch'in-ting szu-k'u ch'üan-shu tsung-mu 欽 定 四 庫 全 書 總 目 (submitted to the throne, 1782): facsimile reprint, Taipei 1964.

SPPY   Szu-pu pei-yao. 四 部 備 要.

SPTK   Szu-pu ts'ung-k'an 四 部 叢 刊.

T.   Taishō Tripiṭaka.

TPKC   T'ai-p'ing kuang-chi 太 平 廣 記. Peking 1961 edition, 10 vols.

TPYL   T'ai-p'ing yü-lan 太 平 御 覽. *SPTK* edition.

Tz'u-en chuan   Ta-T'ang Ta Tz'u-en-szu San-tsang fa-shih chuan 大 唐 大 慈 恩 寺 三 藏 法 師 傳. By Hui-li 慧 立 and Yen-ts'ung 彥 悰. T. L, no. 2053

In the case of all Standard Histories, references are to the *SPTK Po-na* 百 衲 edition.

PRIMARY SOURCES

Ch'a-yü k'o-hua 茶餘客話. By Juan K'uei-sheng 阮葵生 (1727–89). Peking 1957 edition.

Ch'i-hsiu lei-kao 七修類稿. By Lang Ying 郎瑛 (b. 1487). Peking 1959 edition.

Ch'i-kuo ch'un-ch'iu p'ing-hua 七國春秋平話 in *Ch'üan-hsiang p'ing-hua wu-chung* (q.v.).

Chien-teng hsin-hua 剪燈新話. By Ch'ü Yu 瞿佑 (1341–1427) in *Chien-teng hsin-hua wai erh-chung* 外二種. Shanghai 1957.

Chien-teng yü-hua 剪燈餘話. By Li Ch'ang-ch'i 李昌祺 (1376–1452). *Ibid.*

Ch'ien Han-shu p'ing-hua 前漢書平話 in *Ch'üan-hsiang p'ing-hua wu-chung*.

Ch'in ping liu-kuo p'ing-hua 秦併六國平話 in *Ch'üan-hsiang p'ing-hua wu-chung*.

Ching-te ch'uan-teng lu 景德傳燈錄. By Tao-yüan 道原 (fl. early eleventh century). *SPTK* edition.

Cho-keng lu 輟耕錄. By T'ao Tsung-i 陶宗儀 (?1320–?1402). *SPTK* edition.

Chu Wen-kung chiao Ch'ang-li hsien-sheng wen-chi 朱文公校昌黎先生文集. Han Yü 韓愈 (768–824). *SPTK* edition.

Ch'u-k'e P'ai-an ching-ch'i 初刻拍案驚奇. By Ling Meng-ch'u 凌濛初 (d. 1643). Shanghai 1957 edition (ed. by Wang Ku-lu 王古魯).

Ch'u-tz'u pien-cheng 楚辭辨證. By Chu Hsi 朱熹 (1130–1200) in *Ch'u-tz'u chi-chu* 集注. Facsimile reprint, Peking 1953, of 1235 edition.

Chui po-ch'iu 綴白裘. By Wan-hua chu-jen 玩花主人 *et al.* Peking/Shanghai 1955 reprint (ed. Wang Hsieh-ju 汪協如).

Ch'ü-hai tsung-mu t'i-yao 曲海總目提要. By Huang Wen-ch'ang 黃文暘 *et al.* Revised edition, Peking 1959.

Ch'üan-hsiang p'ing-hua wu-chung 全像平話五種. Facsimile reprint, Peking 1956.

Ch'üan Yüan san-ch'ü 全元散曲. Ed. Sui Shu-sen 隋樹森. Shanghai 1964, 2 vols.

Fa-yüan chu-lin 法苑珠林. By Tao-shih 道世 (d. 683). *SPTK* edition.

Feng-shen yen-i 封神演義. Peking 1955 edition.

Hou-ts'un hsien-sheng ta-ch'üan-chi 後村先生大全集. By Liu K'o-chuang 劉克莊 (1187–1269). *SPTK* edition.

Hsi-yu chi tsa-chü (six-part dramatic sequence). Reprint of Shibun kai 斯文會 edition, Tokyo 1928, in *Ku-pen hsi-ch'ü ts'ung-k'an*, First Series (q.v.).

Hsien-ch'un Lin-an chih 咸淳臨安志. Edition by Wang Yüan-sun 汪遠孫 of 1830/31, reprinted Hangchow 1891.

Hsing-shih heng-yen 醒世恆言. Ed. Feng Meng-lung 馮夢龍, *circa* 1628. Peking 1956 edition, reprinted Hong Kong 1958.

Hsü kao-seng chuan 續高僧傳. By Tao-hsüan 道宣 (d. 667). T. L, no. 2060.

Hsüan-ho i-shih 宣和遺事. *SPPY* edition.

I-chien chih 夷堅志. By Hung Mai 洪邁 (1123–1202). Shanghai (Commercial Press) 1927 edition.

Kōzanji seikyō mokuroku 高 山 寺 聖 敎 目 錄. *Shōwa hōbō sōmokuroku* (*q.v.*), vol. 3, no. 67.

'Kōzanji version', see ch. 2, pp. 25–6.

Ku-chin hsiao-shuo 古 今 小 說. Ed. Feng Meng-lung 馮 夢 龍, *circa* 1620. Reprint: Peking 1958, reissued Hong Kong 1961. Facsimile: Shih-chieh shu-chü, Taipei 1958.

Ku-pen hsi-ch'ü ts'ung-k'an 古 本 戲 曲 叢 刊. Compiled by Ku-pen hsi-ch'ü ts'ung-k'an pien-chi wei-yüan-hui 編 輯 委 員 會. First Series (初 集): Shanghai 1954; Second Series (二 集): Shanghai 1955; Third Series (三 集): Peking 1957; Fourth Series (四 集): Shanghai 1958; Ninth Series (九 集): Peking 1964.

Ku-pen Yüan Ming tsa-chü 孤 本 元 明 雜 劇. Ed. Wang Chi-lieh 王 季 烈. Shanghai 1941, reprinted 1958.

Ku-wen Ts'an-t'ung-ch'i chi-chieh 古 文 參 同 契 集 解. Ed. Chiang I-piao 蔣 一 彪. *CTPS* edition.

Kuang hung-ming chi 廣 弘 明 集. By Tao-hsüan 道 宣. *SPTK* edition.

Kuo-shih ching-chi chih 國 史 經 籍 志. By Chiao Hung 焦 竑 (1541–1620). *Yüeh-ya-t'ang ts'ung-shu* 粵 雅 堂 叢 書 edition.

Liao-chai chih i 聊 齋 志 異. By P'u Sung-ling 蒲 松 齡 (?1640–1715). Peking 1962 edition, 3 vols.

Lu-kuei pu hsü-pien 錄 鬼 簿 續 編 in *Chung-kuo ku-tien hsi-ch'ü lun-chu chi-ch'eng*, vol. 2 (see under *LKP*).

Meng-liang lu 夢 梁 錄. By Wu Tzu-mu 吳 自 牧. *HCTY* edition.

Ming shih-lu 明 實 錄. Facsimile reprint (Academia Sinica), Taipei 1965.

Mu-lien chiu mu ch'üan-shan hsi-wen 目 連 救 母 勸 善 戲 文. By Cheng Chih-chen 鄭 之 珍; in *Ku-pen hsi-ch'ü ts'ung-k'an*, First Series (*q.v.*).

Na-shu-ying ch'ü-p'u 納 書 楹 曲 譜. By Yeh T'ang 葉 堂 (eighteenth century). Hsiu-keng-shan-fang 修 綆 山 房 edition, n.d.

Nan-tz'u hsü-lu 南 詞 敍 錄. By Hsü Wei 徐 渭 (1521–93) in *Chung-kuo ku-tien hsi-ch'ü lun-chu chi-ch'eng* (see under *LKP*), vol. 3, Peking 1959.

Nan-yu chi 南 遊 記 in *Szu-yu chi* (*q.v.*).

Ou-yang Wen-chung kung wen-chi 歐 陽 文 忠 公 文 集. By Ou-yang Hsiu 歐 陽 修 (1007–72). *SPTK* edition.

Pao-wen-t'ang shu-mu 寶 文 堂 書 目. By Ch'ao Li 晁 瑮 *et al.*; in *Ch'ao-shih* 晁 氏 *Pao-wen-t'ang shu-mu wai i-chung* 外 一 種, Shanghai 1957.

Pei-yu chi 北 遊 記 in *Szu yu chi* (*q.v.*).

Ramayana. The Ramayana of Valmiki. Trans. Hari Prasad Shastri. London 1953, 1957, 1959, 3 vols.

San-kuo chih p'ing-hua 三 國 志 平 話 in *Ch'üan-hsiang p'ing-hua wu-chung* (*q.v.*).

Shan-hai ching 山 海 經. *SPTK* ed.

Shantung k'uai-shu 'Wu Sung chuan' 山 東 快 書 武 松 傳. Peking 1957.

Shōwa hōbō sōmokuroku 昭 和 法 寶 總 目 錄. Taishō Issaikyō Kankōkai 大 正 一 切 經 刊 行 會. Vols. 1–2, Tokyo 1929, vol. 3, Tokyo 1934.

Sung kao-seng chuan 宋 高 僧 傳. Tsan-ning 贊 寧 *et al.* T. L, no. 2061.

Szu yu chi 四 遊 記. Shanghai 1956 reprint.

Ta-T'ang hsi-yü chi 大唐西域記. By Pien-chi 辯機 (seventh century). T. LI, no. 2087.

T'ai-ho cheng-yin-p'u 太和正音譜. By Chu Chüan 朱權 (d. 1448) in *Chung-kuo ku-tien hsi-ch'ü lun-chu chi-ch'eng* (see under *LKP*), vol. 3, Peking 1959.

Tao-tsang 道藏. Photolithographic reprint of the 1444 and 1607 collections. Commercial Press, Shanghai, 1924–6.

Tsui-weng t'an-lu 醉翁談錄. By Lo Yeh 羅燁. Shanghai 1957 edition.

Tu-ch'eng chi sheng 都城紀勝. By Nai-te-weng 耐得翁 in *Lien-t'ing ts'ang shu shih-erh-chung* 楝亭藏書十二種.

Tun-huang pien-wen chi 敦煌變文集. Ed. Wang Chung-min 王重民 *et al.* Peking 1957.

Tung chieh-yüan Hsi-hsiang chi 董解元西廂記. Ed. Ling Ching-yen 凌景埏. Peking 1962.

Tung-ching meng hua lu 東京夢華錄. By Meng Yüan-lao 孟元老. *CTPS* edition.

Tung Yung Ch'en-hsiang ho-chi 董永沉香合集. Ed. Tu Ying-t'ao 杜穎陶. Shanghai 1957.

Tz'u-nüeh 詞謔. By Li K'ai-hsien 李開先 (1501–68) in *Chung-kuo ku-tien hsi-ch'ü lun-chu chi-ch'eng* (see under *LKP*), vol. 3, Peking 1959.

Wang Wen-ch'eng kung ch'üan-shu 王文成公全書. By Wang Yang-ming 王陽明 (1472–1528). *SPTK* edition.

Wen-yüan ying-hua 文苑英華. Foochow edition of 1567.

Wu-lin chiu-shih 武林舊事. By Chou Mi 周密 (d. 1298). *PCHSTK* edition.

Wu Sung 武松. By Wang Shao-t'ang 王少堂. Ed. Yang-chou p'ing-hua yen-chiu hsiao-tsu 揚州評話研究小組. Nanking 1959.

Wu-tai shih p'ing-hua 五代史平話. (*Hsin-pien* 新編 *Wu-tai shih p'ing-hua.*) Shanghai 1954 reprint.

Wu-wang fa Chou p'ing-hua 武王伐紂平話 in *Ch'üan-hsiang p'ing-hua wu-chung* (*q.v.*).

Yeh-shih-yüan shu-mu 也是園書目. By Ch'ien Tseng 錢曾 (1629–99+). *Yü-chien-chai ts'ung-shu* 玉簡齋叢書 edition.

Yeh-shih-yüan ts'ang-shu ku-chin tsa-chü mu-lu 藏書古今雜劇目錄. By Huang P'i-lieh 黃丕烈 (1763–1825) in *Chung-kuo ku-tien hsi-ch'ü lun-chu chi-ch'eng* (see under *LKP*), vol. 7, Peking 1959.

Yüan-ch'ü hsüan 元曲選. By Tsang Mao-hsün 臧懋循 (first published 1615–16). Peking 1958 edition, 4 vols.

Yüan-shan-t'ang chü-p'in 遠山堂劇品. By Ch'i Piao-chia 祁彪佳 (1602–45) in *Yüan-shan-t'ang Ming ch'ü-p'in chü-p'in chiao-lu* 明曲品劇品校錄. Ed. Huang Shang 黃裳, Shanghai 1955.

Yüan-shan-t'ang ch'ü-p'in 曲品. *Ibid.*

SECONDARY SOURCES

BAILEY, H. W. 'Rāma II', *Bulletin of the School of Oriental and African Studies* 10,3 (1941), 559–98.

BALBIR, J. K. *L'histoire de Rāma en tibétain d'après des manuscrits de Touen-houang*. Paris 1963.

CHANG, H. C. *Allegory and Courtesy in Spenser, a Chinese View*. Edinburgh 1955.

CHANG Wei-ching 張 衞 經. 'Yu-kuan *Hsi-t'ien ch'ü ching* ho *Hsi-yu chi* liang-chung tsa-chü' 有 關 西 天 取 經 和 西 遊 記 兩 種 雜 劇 (article appended to Hatano Tarō 波 多 野 太 郎, 'Saiyuki denki josetu' 西 遊 記 傳 奇 序 說. *Tōhō shūkyō* 東 方 宗 教 20 (1963), 1–17.

CHAO Ching-shen 趙 景 深. 'Wu Ch'ang-ling ti *Hsi-yu chi* tsa-chü' 吳 昌 齡 的 西 遊 記 雜 劇. *Wen-hsüeh* 文 學 (Shanghai) 5,1 (1935), 273–5.

—'*Chien-teng* erh-chung' 剪 燈 二 種. Chapter 3 in *Hsiao-shuo hsien-hua* 小 說 閑 話. Shanghai 1937.

—*Yüan-jen tsa-chü kou-ch'en* 元 人 雜 劇 鈎 沈. Shanghai 1956.

—1959 a. 'Mu-lien chiu mu ti yen-pien' 目 連 救 母 的 演 變 in *Tu-ch'ü hsiao-chi* 讀 曲 小 記, Peking 1959, pp. 74–90.

—1959 b. 'Yüan-ch'ü cha-chi' 元 曲 札 記 in *Tu-ch'ü hsiao-chi*, pp. 11–19.

CHAO Wei-pang 'Secret religious societies in North China in the Ming dynasty'. *Folklore Studies* (Peking), 7 (1948), 95–115.

CHAVANNES, E. *Cinq cents contes et apologues extraits du Tripiṭaka chinois*. Paris 1962 edition, 4 vols.

CH'EN Chung-fan 陳 中 凡. 'Lun *Wu-yüeh ch'un-ch'iu* wei Han Chin chien shuo-pu chi ch'i tsai i-shu shang ti ch'eng-chiu' 論 吳 越 春 秋 爲 漢 晉 間 說 部 及 其 在 藝 術 上 的 成 就. *Wen-hsüeh i-ch'an tseng-k'an* 文 學 遺 產 增 刊, 7 (Peking 1959), 14–34.

CH'EN Ju-heng 陳 汝 衡. *Shuo-shu shih-hua* 說 書 詩 話. Peking 1958.

CH'EN Kuo-fu 陳 國 符. *Tao-tsang yüan-liu k'ao* 道 藏 源 流 考. Second edition, Peking 1963.

CHENG Chen-to 鄭 振 鐸. 1929. '*San-kuo chih yen-i* ti yen-hua' 三 國 志 演 義 的 演 化. Reprinted in *Chung-kuo wen-hsüeh yen-chiu* 中 國 文 學 研 究, (Peking 1957), vol. 1, pp. 166–239.

—1933. '*Hsi-yu chi* ti yen-hua' 西 遊 記 的 演 化. Reprinted *ibid*. pp. 263–99.

—*Chung-kuo su-wen-hsüeh shih* 中 國 俗 文 學 史. Second edition, Peking 1954, 2 vols.

CHENG Ch'ien 鄭 騫. 'Yoshikawa chu *Yüan tsa-chü yen-chiu* Chung-i-pen hsü' 吉 川 著 元 雜 劇 研 究 中 譯 本 序. Reprinted in *Ts'ung shih tao ch'ü* 從 詩 到 曲, Taipei 1961, pp. 205–208.

—*Chiao-ting Yüan-k'an tsa-chü san-shih-chung* 校 訂 元 刊 雜 劇 三 十 種. Taipei 1962.

CH'ENG I-chung 程 毅 中. 'Kuan-yü pien-wen ti chi-tien t'an-so' 關 於 變 文 的 幾 點 探 索. *Wen-hsüeh i-ch'an tseng-k'an* (see under Ch'en Chung-fan) 10 (Peking 1962), 80–101.

CHIANG Jui-tsao 蔣 瑞 藻. *Hsiao-shuo k'ao-cheng* 小 說 考 證. Shanghai 1957.

CH'IEN Chung-shu 錢 鍾 書. *T'an i lu* 談 藝 錄. Hong Kong 1965 reprint.
CH'IEN Nan-yang 錢 南 揚. *Sung Yüan hsi-wen chi-i* 宋 元 戲 文 輯 佚. Shanghai 1956.
DUDBRIDGE, G. 'The *Hsi-yu chi*: a study of antecedents and early versions'. Unpublished doctoral dissertation, University of Cambridge, March 1967.
—'The hundred-chapter *Hsi-yu chi* and its early versions', *Asia Major*, N.S. 14,2 (1969), pp. 141–91.
EBERHARD, W. *Typen chinesischer Volksmärchen*. FF Communications no. 120, Helsinki 1937.
—*Volksmärchen aus Süd-ost-China. Sammlung Ts'ao Sung-yeh.* FF Communications no. 128, Helsinki 1941.
—*Lokalkulturen im alten China.* Part 1: Supplement to *T'oung Pao* vol. 37 (Leiden 1942). Part 2: *Monumenta Serica*, Monograph III (Peking 1942).
—*Die chinesische Novelle des 17.–19. Jahrhunderts.* Supplement IX to *Artibus Asiae* (Ascona, Switzerland, 1948).
FU Hsi-hua 傅 惜 華. *Yüan-tai tsa-chü ch'üan-mu* 元 代 雜 劇 全 目. Peking 1957.
—*Ming-tai* 明 代 *tsa-chü ch'üan-mu.* Peking 1958.
—*Ming-tai ch'uan-ch'i* 明 代 傳 奇 *ch'üan-mu.* Peking 1959.
FU Yün-tzu 傅 芸 子. *Pai-ch'uan chi* 白 川 集. Tokyo 1943.
GETTY, A. *The Gods of Northern Buddhism.* Second edition, Oxford 1928.
HIRANO Kensho 平 野 顯 照. '*Dai Tō Sanzō shu kyō shiwa* no ichi kōsatsu' 大 唐 三 藏 取 經 詩 話 の 一 考 察. *Shina gakuhō* 支 那 學 報 1,1 (1956), 43–7.
Hōbōgirin 法 寶 義 林. Ed. P. Demiéville *et al.* Maison Franco-Japonaise, Tokyo 1929–37.
HRDLIČKOVÁ, V. 'The professional training of Chinese storytellers and the storytellers' guilds'. *Archiv Orientálni* 33 (1965), 225–48.
Hsi-yu chi yen-chiu lun-wen-chi 西 遊 記 研 究 論 文 集. Tso-chia ch'u-pan-she, Peking 1957.
HSIA, C. T. *The Classic Chinese Novel, a Critical Introduction.* New York 1968.
HU Chi 胡 忌. *Sung Chin tsa-chü k'ao* 宋 金 雜 劇 考. Peking 1959.
HU Shih 胡 適. 1923. '*Hsi-yu chi* k'ao-cheng' 西 遊 記 考 證. Reprinted in *Hu Shih wen-ts'un* 胡 適 文 存 (Hong Kong 1962 edition), vol. 2, pp. 354–99.
—'Pa *Hsiao-shih Chen-k'ung pao-chüan*' 跋 銷 釋 眞 空 寶 卷. *Kuo-li Pei-p'ing t'u-shu-kuan kuan-k'an* 國 立 北 平 圖 書 館 館 刊, 5,3 (1931), 1–8.
HUANG Chih-kang 黃 芝 崗. *Chung-kuo ti shui-shen* 中 國 的 水 神. Shanghai 1934.
ISHIDA Eiichirō 石 田 英 一 郎. 'The *Kappa* Legend'. *Folklore Studies* (Peking), 9 (1950), 1–152.
K'UNG Ling-ching 孔 另 境. *Chung-kuo hsiao-shuo shih-liao* 中 國 小 說 史 料. Shanghai 1959.
LÉVY, A. 'Études sur trois recueils anciens de contes chinois' *T'oung Pao* 52 (1965), 97–148.

Li Shih-yü 李世瑜. 'Pao-chüan hsin-yen' 寶卷新研. *Wen-hsüeh i-ch'an tseng-k'an* (see under Ch'en Chung-fan) 4 (Peking 1957), 165–81.

Li Szu-ch'un 李思純. *Chiang-ts'un shih lun* 江村十論. Shanghai 1957.

Lin P'ei-chih 林培志. '*La-ma-yeh-na* yü *Ch'en hsün-chien Mei-ling shih ch'i chi*' 拉馬耶那與陳巡檢梅嶺失妻記. *Wen-hsüeh* (Shanghai) 2,6 (1934), 1142–1153.

Liu Ts'un-yan. *Buddhist and Taoist Influences on Chinese Novels*: Volume I—*The Authorship of the Feng-shen yen-i.* Wiesbaden 1962.

Liu Yeh-ch'iu 劉葉秋. '*Lüeh t'an Pu Chiang Tsung Po-yüan chuan* chi yü-ch'i yu-kuan ti ku-shih' 略談補江總白猿傳及與其有關的故事. Reprinted in *Ku-tien hsiao-shuo lun-ts'ung* 古典小說論叢 (Peking 1959), pp. 47–56.

Lord, A. B. *The Singer of Tales.* Cambridge, Massachusetts, 1960.

Lu Hsün 魯迅 (pseudonym of Chou Shu-jen 周樹人). 1912. *Ku-hsiao-shuo kou-ch'en* 古小說鈎沈. Reprinted in *Lu Hsün ch'üan-chi* 全集 (20 vol. edition, reprinted 1948), vol. 8.

—1923. *Chung-kuo hsiao-shuo shih-lüeh* 中國小說史略. Reprinted *ibid.* vol. 9.

—*Chung-kuo hsiao-shuo ti li-shih ti pien-ch'ien* 中國小說的歷史的變遷. (Lecture course given originally in 1924.) Reprint by Chung-liu ch'u-pan-she 中流出版社. Hong Kong 1957.

—1927. 'Kuan-yü *San-tsang ch'ü ching chi* teng' 關於三藏取經記等. Reprinted in *Lu Hsün ch'üan-chi* vol. 3, pp. 372–7.

—1931. 'Kuan-yü *T'ang San-tsang ch'ü ching shih-hua* ti pan-pen' 關於唐三藏取經詩話的版本. Reprinted *ibid.* vol. 4, pp. 262–4.

Ma Yau-woon 馬幼垣 and Ma Tai-loi 馬泰來. '*Ching-pen t'ung-su hsiao-shuo* ko-p'ien ti nien-tai chi ch'i chen-wei wen-t'i' 京本通俗小說各篇的年代及其眞偽問題. *Ch'ing-hua hsüeh-pao* 清華學報, N.S. 5,1 (1965), 14–29.

Makita Tairyō 牧田諦亮. 'Chūgoku ni okeru minzoku bukkyō seiritsu no ichikatei' 中國に於ける民俗佛教成立の一過程. Silver Jubilee Volume of the Zinbun Kagaku Kenkyūsyo 人文科學研究所. Kyoto 1954, Part 2, pp. 264–86.

Masuda Wataru 增田涉. '"Wahon" to yū koto ni tsuite' 話本ということについて. *Jimbun kenkyū* 人文研究 (Osaka) 16,5 (June 1965), 22–33 (456–67).

Mochizuki Shinkō 望月信亨. *Bukkyō daijiten* 佛教大辭典. Tokyo 1936–7.

Nagasawa Kikuya 長澤規矩也. *Shoshigaku ronkō* 書誌學論考. Tokyo 1937.

—'*Dai Tō Sanzō hōshi shu kyō ki* to *Dai Tō Sanzō shu kyō shiwa*' 大唐三藏法師取經記と大唐三藏取經詩話. *Shoshigaku* 書誌學, 13,6 (1939), 165–9.

Ogawa Kanichi 小川貫弌. '*"Dai Tō Sanzō shu kyō shiwa* no keisei*"* 大唐三藏取經詩話の形成. *Ryūkoku daigaku ronshū* 龍谷大學論集, 362 (1959), 56–78.

Ōta Tatsuo 太田辰夫. *Chūgoku rekidai kōgobun* 中國歷代口語文. Tokyo 1957.

—'*Boku-tō-ji genkai* shoin *Saiyuki* kō' 朴通事諺解所引西遊記考. *Kōbe gaidai ronsō* 神戶外大論叢, 10,2 (1959), 1–22.

—'Kaisetsu' 解說 in *Saiyuki* 西遊記, *Chūgoku koten bungaku zenshū* 中國古典文學全集, vol. 14 (Tokyo 1960), pp. 405–10.

—'*Shōshaku shinkū hōken* ni mieru *Saiyuki* koji' 銷釋眞空寶卷に見える西遊記故事. *Kōbe gaidai ronsō* (see under 1959) 15,6 (1965), 17–30.

—'*Dai Tō Sanzō shu kyō shiwa* kō' 大唐三藏取經詩話考. *Kōbe gaidai ronsō* 17, 1–3 (June 1966), 135–60.

—'*Genjō Sanzō toten yurai engi* to *Saiyuki* no ichi kohon' 玄奘三藏渡天由來緣起と西遊記の一古本. *Kōbe gaidai ronsō* 18,1 (1967), 1–13.

Ōta Tatsuo and Torii Hisayasu 鳥居久靖. 'Kaisetsu' 解說 in *Saiyuki*, *Chūgoku koten bungaku zenshū* (see under Ōta Tatsuo 1960), vol. 13 (Tokyo 1960), pp. 354–68.

P'an Po-ying 潘伯英 and Chou Liang 周良. 'Su-chou p'ing-t'an k'ou-chüeh' 蘇州評彈口訣. *Ch'ü-i* 曲藝, 51 (March 1962), 51–7.

Průšek, J. 'The narrators of Buddhist scriptures and religious tales in the Sung period'. *Archiv Orientální* 10 (1938), 375–89.

—'Researches into the beginnings of the Chinese popular novel. Part I. Story-telling in the Sung period'. *Archiv Orientální* 11 (1939), 91–132.

Sawada Mizuho 澤田瑞穗. *Hōken no kenkyū* 寶卷の研究. Nagoya 1963.

—'Shakkyōgeki joroku' 釋教劇叙錄. *Tenri daigaku gakuhō* 天理大學學報, 44 (June 1964), 21–43.

Schafer, E. H. *The Vermilion Bird, T'ang Images of the South*. California 1967.

Shimura Ryōji 志村良治. '*Dai Tō Sanzō shu kyō shiwa* yakuchū' 大唐三藏取經詩話譯注. Part 1: *Aichi daigaku bungaku ronsō* 愛知大學文學論叢, 19 (1959), 61–90.

—*Idem*. Part 2: *Ibid*. 21 (1961), 71–98.

Stein, M. A. *Serindia*. Oxford 1921.

Stein, R. A. *Recherches sur l'épopée et le barde au Tibet*. Paris 1959.

Sun K'ai-ti 孫楷第. 1939. 'Wu Ch'ang-ling yü tsa-chü *Hsi-yu chi*' 吳昌齡與雜劇西遊記. Reprinted in *Ts'ang-chou chi* 滄州集 (Peking 1965), vol. 2, pp. 366–98.

—1941. 'Shu-hui' 書會. Reprinted *ibid*. pp. 349–55.

—*Yüan-ch'ü chia k'ao-lüeh* 元曲家考略. Shanghai 1953.

—*Su-chiang, shuo-hua yü pai-hua hsiao-shuo* 俗講說話與白話小說. Peking 1956.

—*Chung-kuo t'ung-su hsiao-shuo shu-mu* 中國通俗小說書目. Second edition, Peking 1957.

—'Yüan-ch'ü chia k'ao-lüeh hsü-pien' 元曲家考略續編. *Wen-hsüeh yen-chiu* 文學研究, 2 (June 1958), 171–7.

Szu Su 思蘇. 'Shuo-shu yu-wu chüeh-pen?' 說書有无脚本. *Ch'ü-i* 曲藝, 52 (April 1962), 44–5.

T'AN Cheng-pi 譚正璧. *Chung-kuo hsiao-shuo fa-ta shih* 中國小說發達 史. Shanghai 1935.

—*Hua-pen yü ku-chü* 話本與古劇. Shanghai 1956.

—(Ed.) *Ch'ing-p'ing-shan-t'ang hua-pen* 清平山堂話本. Shanghai 1957.

THOMAS, F. W. 'A Ramayana story in Tibetan from Chinese Turkestan' in *Indian Studies in Honor of Charles Rockwell Lanman*, Cambridge, Massachusetts, 1929, pp. 193–212.

THOMPSON, Stith. *Motif Index of Folk Literature*. Bloomington, Indiana, 1955–8, 6 vols.

TORII Hisayasu 鳥居久靖. 'Saiyuki kenkyū rombun mokuroku' 西遊 記研究論文目錄. *Tenri daigaku gakuhō* (see under Sawada Mizuho, 1964) 33 (1960), 143–54.

TORII Ryūzō 鳥居龍藏. 'Saiyuki zuyō wo chōkokuseru gazōseki' 西遊 記圖樣を彫刻せる畫像石. *Hōun* 寶雲, 11 (Tokyo 1935), 13–21.

TS'AI Mei-piao 蔡美彪. *Yüan-tai pai-hua pei chi-lu* 元代白話碑集錄. Shanghai 1955.

UCHIDA Michio 內田道夫. 'Saiyuki no seiritsu ni tsuite' 西遊記の 成立について. *Bunka* 文化, 27,1 (1963), 23–46.

UCHIYAMA Chinari 內山知也 'Ho Kō Sō hakuenten kō' 補江總白猿 傳考. *Uchino hakushi kanreki kinen tōyōgaku ronshū* 內野博士還曆記 念東洋學論集, Tokyo 1964, pp. 235–60.

WADDELL, L. A. *The Buddhism of Tibet*. Second edition, reprinted Cambridge 1959.

WALEY, A. D. *Catalogue of Paintings recovered from Tun-huang by Sir Aurel Stein*. London 1931.

—*The Real Tripitaka*. London 1952.

—*Ballads and Stories from Tun-huang*. London 1960.

WANG Hsiao-ch'uan 王曉傳. *Yüan Ming Ch'ing san-tai chin-hui hsiao-shuo hsi-ch'ü shih-liao* 元明清三代禁毀小說戲曲史料. Peking 1958.

WANG P'i-chiang 汪辟疆. *T'ang-jen hsiao-shuo* 唐人小說. Revised edition, Shanghai 1955.

WU Hsiao-ling 吳曉鈴. 'Hsi-yu chi yü Lo-mo-yen shu' 西遊記與羅摩 延書. *Wen-hsüeh yen-chiu* 文學研究, 2,1 (Peking 1958), 163–9.

YANG Lien-sheng 楊聯陞. 'Nogöltae Pak t'ongsa li ti yü-fa yü-hui' 老乞 大朴通事裏的語法語彙. *Li-shih yü-yen yen-chiu-so chi-k'an* 歷史 語言研究所集刊, 29 (1957), 197–208.

YEH Te-chün 葉德均. *Sung Yüan Ming chiang-ch'ang wen-hsüeh* 宋元明 講唱文學. Peking 1959.

YEN Tun-i 嚴敦易. 1954. 'Hsi-yu chi ho ku-tien hsi-ch'ü ti kuan-hsi' 西遊記和古典戲曲的關係. Reprinted in *Hsi-yu chi yen-chiu lun-wen-chi* (q.v.), pp. 145–52.

—'Ku-chin hsiao-shuo szu-shih p'ien ti chuan-shu nien-tai' 古今小說四 十篇的撰述年代. Appended to the 7 vol. edition of *Ku-chin hsiao-shuo* by Wen-hsüeh ku-chi k'an-hsing-she, Peking 1955.

—*Shui-hu chuan ti yen-pien* 水滸傳的演變. Peking 1957.

—*Yüan-chü chen i* 元劇斟疑. Peking 1960, 2 vols.

Yü Chia-hsi 余 嘉 錫. *Szu-k'u t'i-yao pien-cheng*. 四 庫 提 要 辨 證. Reprinted as appendix in *SKCSTM* (*q.v.*).

Yüan T'ung-li 袁 同 禮. ''Yung-lo ta-tien* hsien-ts'un chüan-mu piao' 永 樂 大 典 現 存 卷 目 表. Separate issue of *Pei-p'ing t'u-shu-kuan yüeh-k'an* 北 平 圖 書 館 月 刊, 2,3/4 (1929), 215–51.

—''Yung-lo ta-tien* ts'un-mu' 永 樂 大 典 存 目. *Kuo-li Pei-p'ing t'u-shu-kuan kuan-k'an* (see under Hu Shih, 1931), 6,1 (1932), 93–133.

Addenda

p. 7: Professor Wolfram Eberhard in a recent article, 'Notes on Chinese story tellers' (*Fabula* 11 (1970), 1–31), describes the results of research in modern Taipei, where published fiction has made serious encroachments upon the art of the story-teller. Eberhard characterizes this (p. 3) as the final stage before the complete extinction of traditional story-telling.

p. 11: Professor Průšek's current views on the problems described in the foregoing section are given at length in his recent book, *The Origins and the Authors of the 'hua-pen'*, Prague, 1967.

p. 47, n. 1: Iwaki Hideo, 'Sōdai engeki kikan', *Chūgoku bungaku hō* 19 (1963), 102–27.

p. 114, n. 1: A more comprehensive study of the subject is now available in the shape of R. H. van Gulik's *The Gibbon in China* (Leiden, 1967).

pp. 116–117: For a study of a related folk-tale complex, see Ting Nai-t'ung, 'AT Type 301 in China and some countries adjacent to China: a study of a regional group and its significance in world tradition', *Fabula* 11 (1970), 54–125.

p. 121, (1.): The point is in fact made also by Inada Osamu, in 'Sō Gen wahon ruikei kō' (Part 2), *Kagoshima Daigaku bunka hōhoku* 8 (1959), 131–54.

p. 146, n. 2: There is no evidence to confirm or refute the suggestion that this or other items from the same passage were already linked with a *Hsi-yu-chi* cycle: cf. T'an Cheng-pi (1956), pp. 17, 36; Ch'en Ju-heng, pp. 54–5; Ōta and Torii, p. 360a.

General Index

*References in italics indicate that the relevant Chinese characters are
to be found on those pages*

Ai-nu (-erh), cf. Priyaṅkara, *18*, *196*
Alexander, Romance of, 13 n
almsbowl, 17, *18*, 32, 74, 196
Amazons, Kingdom of, 13 n
Amitābha Buddha, 95 n, 99
Amoghavajra (705–74?), *12 n*, 20, 34
Amoi, 164–5
amṛta (kan-lu), *19*, *94 n*
Ānanda, 145, 185
An-t'ien hui, title of play, *87*, 88 n
Ao-kuang, name of Dragon King, *49*
arhat, 32, 40, 135, 156, 185, 193
Asuras, 151 n
Āṭavaka, *21 n*
Avalambana, Buddhist festival, *43*, 164
axe, weapon of Chü-ling shen, 150–2

Bailey, H. W., 163 n, 168
Bakkula, name of arhat, *40*–1
Balbir, J. K., 160 n, 163 n
banishment, 37, *148*
bear-spirit, 73, 183
belly, attack from within, 36, 161, 190
birthday celebrations, 37
black bear demon, *73*, 183
black lion demon, 73
Brahmaloka, 34; —— Palace, *33 n*
bride, substitute for, 87, 197–8
Buddha, 15 n, 17, 32 n, 40, 69, 70, 77,
    86 n, 92–5, 109, 112, 145, 155–6, 165,
    195, 199–200
Buddhism, 36, 41–5, 50, 90, 94, 120, 125,
    134–5, 181
Buddhists, 33 n, 64, 67, 94, 159

Candana (Sandalwood), name of Buddha,
    109, 184
cap of invisibility, 32
Central Asia, 13, 34, 35, 42, 164
Central Pleasure-ground (*Chung wa-tzu*),
    26
Ch'a-yü k'o hua (Juan K'uei-sheng),
    141 n
Chadwick, N. K., 2 n
Ch'ai Chin, *Shui-hu* hero, *32 n*
chair, folding, *33*

Chang, bookseller of Hangchow, 26
Chang the Monk, *145*
Chang Chao (1691–1745), 88
chang-che ('householder'), *39 n*, *192*
Chang Cho (eighth century), *54*
Chang Hsin-chang, 156 n, 167 n, 174 n
Chang Hua (third century), *115 n*
Chang Shao, *177*
Chang Shih-ch'i (? thirteenth century),
    150 n
Chang Wei-ching, 78 n
Ch'ang-an, 53, 71, 95, 142, 177–9, 183, 200
Chao Ch'i-mei (1563–1624), *126 n*
Chao Ching-shen, 43, 81 n, 83 n, 88 n, 136
Chao K'uang-yin (927–76), Sung dynasty
    founder, 27; cf. T'ai-tsu
Chao T'ai-tsu fei-lung chi, title of story,
    63 n, *180*
Chao Wan-li, *56*
Chao Wei-pang, 93 n, 146 n
Chao Yü (sixth–seventh century), *131*
Ch'ao Li (sixteenth century), *118 n*
Ch'ao-yeh ch'ien-tsai (Chang Cho), *54*
Chavannes, Édouard, 14 n, 33 n, 41 n,
    73 n, 152 n, 162 n
Ch'e-ch'ih kuo, fictional country, *63–8*,
    73, 97, 103, 108, *180–3*, 185
Chen-k'ung Lao-tsu, *93 n*
Ch'en Chung-fan, 141 n
Ch'en-hsiang, legendary prince, *150–1*,
    153; Land of, *191*
Ch'en Hsin, *118* ff.
Ch'en hsün-chien Mei-ling shih ch'i chi,
    short story, *118–27*, 133, 153
Ch'en Ju-heng, 3 n, 4 n, 5 n, 6 n, 210
Ch'en Kuang-jui, *67 n*, *193–4*
Ch'en Lung-kuang, 76
Ch'en Yüan-chih (sixteenth century), *174*
Cheng Chen-to, 33 n, 39 n, 44 n, 52 n,
    90 n, 92 n, 103, 105 n, 121 n, 159–60,
    162 n
Cheng Ch'ien, 79 n, 80 n
Cheng Chih-chen, 33 n, 43 n, 165 n
cheng-mo, role in *tsa-chü* drama, *81*
cheng-tan, role in *tsa-chü* drama, *81*
Ch'eng-chi, Buddhist saint, *200*